D0866956

BLACKS IN THE
DUTCH WORLD

Blacks in the Diaspora

Darlene Clark Hine

John McCluskey, Jr.

David Barry Gaspar

General Editors

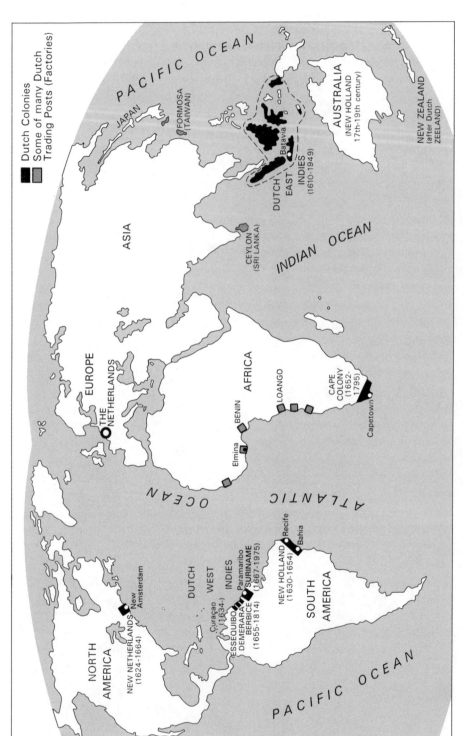

1. The Scope of the Dutch Maritime Empire. Prepared by Georgetta C. Cooper.

Dutch Colonies

Some of many Dutch Trading Posts (Factories)

PACIFIC OCEAN

ASIA

EUROPE

THE NETHERLANDS

JAPAN

FORMOSA (TAIWAN)

DUTCH EAST INDIES (1610-1949)

Batavia

CEYLON (SRI LANKA)

INDIAN OCEAN

AUSTRALIA (NEW HOLLAND 17th-19th century)

NEW ZEALAND (after Dutch ZEELAND)

AFRICA

BENIN

Elmina

LOANGO

CAPE COLONY (1652-1795)

Capetown

ATLANTIC OCEAN

NORTH AMERICA

NEW NETHERLANDS (1624-1664)

New Amsterdam

DUTCH WEST INDIES

Curaçao (1634-)

ESSEQUIBO
DEMERARA
BERBICE (1655-1814)

Paramaribo
SURINAME (1667-1975)

NEW HOLLAND (1630-1654)

Recife

Bahia

SOUTH AMERICA

PACIFIC OCEAN

BLACKS
in the
DUTCH
WORLD

The Evolution of
Racial Imagery in a
Modern Society

Allison Blakely

Indiana University Press
Bloomington and Indianapolis

The paper used in this publication meets the minimum
requirements of American National Standard for Information
Sciences—Permanence of Paper for Printed Library Materials,
ANSI Z39.48-1984.
⊚™
Manufactured in the United States of America

Library of Congress Cataloging-in-Publication Data

Blakely, Allison, date.
Blacks in the Dutch world : the evolution of racial imagery
in a modern society / Allison Blakely.
p.   cm.—(Blacks in the diaspora)
Includes bibliographical references and index.
ISBN 0-253-31191-8 (alk. paper)
1. Blacks—Netherlands—History.   2. Racism—Netherlands.
3. Netherlands—Race relations.   I. Title.   II. Series.
DJ92.B53B57   1993
305.896′0492—dc20
92-43743

1 2 3 4 5   97 96 95 94 93

To
Shirley,
Shantel,
and
Andrei

CONTENTS

Contents

ACKNOWLEDGMENTS

LET ME first beg forgiveness from the many friends in the Netherlands for whom I have spoiled forever the simple pleasures in visiting museums and art collections. Never again will they be able to browse without looking for those often unnoticed black figures they have been helping me catalogue over my decade of research on this project. Meanwhile my interaction with the unimaginable diversity of people and institutions inherent in this research has also permanently, positively, altered my own perspective. In a quest of such broad scope and long duration, there was of course a very large number of people in several countries who guided me along the way. I can only list here a few of the most prominent individuals and organizations. Others are duly acknowledged in the chapter notes; and to those not named I extend my heartfelt thanks.

I owe a special debt of gratitude to three scholars who offered vital and timely encouragement from the time when this project was only an idea and who have continued to inspire me by their example as well as their counsel: Hilda van Neck Yoder, Thomas C. Holt, and Winthrop R. Wright. Other extraordinarily generous contributions were made by Gert Oostindie, Pieter Emmer, and Herman Wekker, who read and critiqued earlier drafts of the manuscript. However, it should be emphasized that responsibility for this final product is entirely my own.

Since this study is about cultures earlier foreign to me, it goes without saying that an especially important role was played by those who facilitated my access. In this regard what must have seemed like an inordinate amount of time and effort was volunteered by Maarten Brands, Frauke Wieringa, Ingrid Koulen, Grace and Wim Dechering, and Helen and Gerard Verkuyl. I must also give special mention to Sytske Schreuder, who provided invaluable research assistance. Among others who provided important guidance to sources were Peter Pott, Stanley Wassenaar, Peter Meel, Felix de Rooy, Claartje Gieben, Philippus Bosscher, Pram Sutikno, J. M. van der Linde, G. M. van der

Meiden, André Köbben, Jan Erik Dubbelman, Daphne van Schendel-Labega, Wilma Labega, Lianne Leonora, Rose Mary Allen, and J. M. Capricorne. For exceptionally gracious hospitality and general assistance I wish also to thank Minke Krings and family, Joanna Wind, Ioanna and Emmanuel Rammos, Georgina and Dale Carr, Alex van Stipriaan, Annet Nugter, Peter Pots, Saskia Schouten, Marita and Dick van Toledo, and the staff of the University of Leiden International Centre.

Of the countless collections I consulted in the Netherlands, I wish especially to thank the staffs of the Koninklijk Instituut voor Taal-, Land- en Volkenkunde in Leiden; Leiden University's Instituut voor Culturele Antropologie, its Instituut voor Nederlandse Lexicologie, and its Departments of History and Art History; the P. J. Meertens Instituut's Folklore and Music departments in Amsterdam, and the University of Amsterdam's Music History Collection; the Atlas van Stolk Collection in Rotterdam; the K. C. Pieters Instituut voor Volkskunde and the Print Room of the Plantin Moretus Museum in Antwerp; and the Archeological-Anthropological Instituut Nederlands Antillen in Curaçao.

The depth in which I explored this topic would not have been possible without the generous support I enjoyed through a Fulbright-Hays Research Fellowship in 1985–1986, which allowed me a year of affiliation with the Centre for the History of European Expansion at the University of Leiden, and a Ford Foundation Post-Doctoral Fellowship, which supported full-time study, writing, and association with the Johns Hopkins University Program on Atlantic History, Culture, and Society during 1987–1988. I gained further valuable insights through participation in a seminar on Emblemata and Seventeenth-century Dutch Art offered by the Folger Shakespeare Library and conducted by Arthur Wheelock of the United States National Gallery of Art. The quality of the actual presentation of this work of course owes much to the Indiana University Press and to the editor of the Blacks in the Diaspora series, Darlene Clarke Hine; their enthusiasm and expertise contributed greatly to strengthening the manuscript.

Finally, the completion of this work owes most of all to my family: to my wife, Shirley Reynolds Blakely, our daughter, Shantel, and our son, Andrei, for allowing this adventure at times to dominate their lives as well.

INTRODUCTION

THE STARTING POINT for this study was the question of how it developed that as the non-European population in the Netherlands has suddenly increased toward the end of the twentieth century a centuries-old reputation and self-image of Dutch society as a haven for those escaping intolerance elsewhere has begun to show cracks. Two relatively minor, but telling, controversies in the 1980s and the beginning of the 1990s can serve as illustrative symptoms. One concerns the Dutch Santa Claus tradition, in which the beloved *Sinterklaas* (short for St. Nicholas) is accompanied on his rounds by a black servant, the beloved but simultaneously feared *Zwarte Piet* (Black Pete) (see fig. 2). By the mid-1980s the seemingly innocent Black Pete became a perennial target of vocal, if not widespread, charges that he is a racist symbol.

The second example is a heated controversy surrounding the book chosen for the 1991 national Children's Book Week celebration. The book, entitled *Het wonder van Frieswijck* (The Miracle of Frieswijck), by Thea Beckman, is set in the fifteenth century and realistically depicts the reaction of the people of the town of Kampen to the arrival of a Negro slave boy, the first black African they had ever seen (see fig. 3). One critic cited numerous examples of what he viewed as negative stereotyping in the book, for example the populace's referring to the black boy variously as "little nigger," "little Moor," "the creature," and "son of a witch." They speculated over whether the boy was a man or beast. A merchant feared that the boy, who was led around by his master on a leather leash attached to his collar, would bite him. When in the course of the story the boy was freed by his master, and his good fortune attributed to a local holy shrine, the book stated: "Danga had become human, to whom special grace was given, even though he was black." Bitter protests surrounding the book award, especially from some black Netherlanders, fueled a widespread discussion in all the media, which in turn generated additional rave reviews from its defenders.[1] A closer look at the historical

2. *St Nicholas' Triumphal Entry in Amsterdam*, from Henriette Van Nierop, *Santa Claus the Dutch Way* (New York: The Netherlands Information Service, 1955).

background of the controversies surrounding Zwarte Piet and Danga reveals that they are just the outward signs of much more serious and deep-seated societal problems.

What makes the Dutch experience with racial attitudes particularly interesting is the Dutch traditional preoccupation with humanism and liberalism, which bear a constant concern with issues growing out of religion and economic, social, and political structures. The perpetual engagement with such issues has left a treasure

Introduction

3. Jan Wesseling, cover of Thea Beckman, *Het wonder van Frieswijck* (Amsterdam: Stichting Collectieve Propaganda voor het Nederlandse Boek, 1991).

house of sources relevant to the history of racial attitudes. These issues also reveal the Netherlands as the modern society *par excellence*. It formally came into existence just in the modern period and has remained a leader in experiencing modern currents. Its history therefore lends itself very well to the consideration of the impact of modernization proposed here. With respect to this role as experimental model, the Netherlands also offers a good example of a society where for centuries there was little actual presence of people of color in the metropole, but which then suddenly has had to contend with their arrival. This unintended consequence of earlier empire affords a useful contrast for comparison in addition to that provided by the differences between home and the colonies and between the various colonies in earlier periods.

The current examples of unrest described above highlight the dilemma of the historian who seeks to study such topics. Does not examination and representation of stereotyping risk lending dignity to it by giving it a pedigree, implying it is more understandable if it has great age, is part of hallowed "tradition"? Black students as well as liberal whites often cringe before examples of stereotyping and at times would prefer not to open up such ugly topics. However, in undertaking this study I have reached the conclusion that racial and color bias must be confronted, must be looked in the face if it is to be resisted. Moreover, its roots must be traced to the earliest origin possible in order best to understand how to combat it. Yes, there is a danger that for some such knowledge can provide reinforcement for prejudice. However, this is a risk worth taking.

Civilized society has evolved to a scale and complexity where it is imperative for the historian of society to formulate ways of understanding its workings in terms comparable to the natural scientist's approach to his or her subject. The task of the student scanning the face of society for the origins and character of such an elusive phenomenon as racial bias resembles that of the geologist reading the earth's history through patterns and layers which are often only subtly announced on its surface. The present study reveals that the existence of color prejudice in a predominantly "white" society does not require the presence of racial conflict or even of a significant "colored" population. Furthermore, it finds that although such bias is irrational by definition, the advent of rationalism and science may serve more to reinforce than to dispel it.

Such flat contradictions suggest that the searches for both the cause and the cure of these attitudes, which in modern societies can have just as harmful effects as a pathological virus, may be proceeding on the basis of false assumptions. At one extreme there has been a tendency to seek explanations in simple, monistic causation, such as religious or economic determinism; at the other there has been the resort to intuitive beliefs about innate racial inequality. Not enough attention has been devoted to the middle ground, where, I contend, the best answers lie. Here what must be sought are not simple answers, but rather identification of intricate combinations of factors which are involved. Many more objective studies need to be carried out in search of these combinations before the discussion about the nature of color bias can move far beyond where it now stands.[2]

The present study joins a growing number of recent works which move in this direction. Inherent in a search for such combinations is an interdisciplinary approach. Hence the present effort combines a broad historical overview with deliberate focusing on folklore, art, literature, and religion, to seek correlations between historical developments, attitudes, and shifts in attitude. As shown by the table of contents, the definition of what is meant here by "the Dutch World" and a tracing of the imagery concerning blacks reflected in these respective disciplinary areas comprise the basic structure of the book's first five chapters. Chapter six then surveys the actual presence of blacks in that world; and chapter seven offers a summary analysis. It can be readily seen how these disciplines could shed light regarding the controversies about Black Pete and *The Miracle of Frieswijck*. In what follows it will become apparent that this type of study inevitably involves many other disciplines, often overlapping, for example, anthropology, sociology, and linguistics. The last is especially important since language of various sorts plays such a key role in the perception, definition, and communication of images.

This study has a twofold purpose. On the one hand it seeks to tell a story that has not been adequately told about the interaction between black history and Dutch history. On the other it seeks to exploit that history to gain understanding about the historical development of racial attitudes related to color. Because Dutch history and culture unfold in the Western modern era, this simultaneously provides an opportunity to give special attention to the process of modernization in considering the evolution of racial attitudes. This in no way distracts from the focus on Dutch culture since, as will become apparent from this study, Dutch consciousness of motifs universal in Western civilization during this epoch played a major role in Dutch attitudes.

Modernization is the broader common experience which has been most distinctive for Western civilization. For present purposes this process may be characterized by the following interrelated features: an unprecedented interest in the empirical world, the present, and the future; increased control over the physical environment through advances in science and technology; a revolutionary rate of economic, social, and political change; growing involvement of the masses in civilization; and increased organization and consolidation of societies to produce wealth, military power, and Western dominance over the rest of the world. This study therefore holds up the evolving image of blacks against the backdrop of such developments as Western exploration and expansion, the agricultural, scientific, and Industrial revolutions, and the advent of modern secular doctrines.[3]

In some respects this might be viewed as a partial response to the classicist Frank M. Snowden, who in his recent study on the ancient view of blacks insists that color prejudice did not exist in the ancient Greek and Roman worlds and remarks that he is uncertain when it first appeared.[4] An underlying hypothesis in the present study is that the psychology of racial bias became all the more pronounced in the modern period because of the rise then and broad appeal of the concept of progress in Western civilization at the very same time that that civilization achieved physical domination over the rest of the world. One result was that the subjugated peoples were defined as "backward," and therefore inferior. The fact that most of these peoples were "colored" encouraged the notion that there was a logical connection between this and their relative status. The obvious physical distinctions also proved an appealing basis of inclusion and exclusion regarding the idea of civilization.

Thus as modernization progressed in the West, blacks became more marginal by definition, figuring prominently from time to time in the histories of Western societies, but never considered really part of them. This general framework of interpretation seems the most plausible explanation for the variety of imagery presented here concerning blacks in the Dutch world. Leaving aside the still highly debatable question of whether color prejudice did exist before the modern period, the present study weighs the proposition that there may be factors unique to the modern period which may account for the trends in such prejudice and attempts to determine what the Dutch experience reveals concerning these.

The emphasis on the modern also carries this study beyond the scope of Winthrop Jordan's related work *White Over Black*, which concentrated on the British and American traditions and stopped with the early nineteenth century, and George M. Fredrickson's *The Black Image in the White Mind*, which focused on the Afro-American experience between 1817 and 1914. Fredrickson's *White Supremacy*, a comparative study of American and South African history, has obviously even more direct bearing. These studies along with many similar ones of course provide helpful insights for mine. However, there has still been relatively little scholarly attention devoted to the subject of color prejudice in Europe. James Walvin's work, beginning with *Black and White: The Negro and English Society 1555–1945*, is the foremost exception. Meanwhile Hans Debrunner, in his more recent *Presence and Prestige: Africans in Europe*, specifically mentions the Netherlands as one neglected area which merits more attention on this subject.[5]

Of all the major European peoples who have been involved in world empire, the Dutch have received the least attention commensurate with their importance. Even Simon Schama's admirable, massive foray into Golden Age Dutch culture, *The Embarrassment of Riches*, fails to make a connection between the global empire and developments at home. There is scant reference, for example, to Africa, Suriname, or even Indonesia. One of the great strengths of that work for present purposes is its impressive demonstration of the use of art and artifacts in interpreting social and cultural history.[6] One reason for the neglect of the Netherlands is that relatively few outsiders have bothered to learn the Dutch language, which is essential for such study. Another is that topics such as imperialism and racism, which are central to a discussion of color prejudice in the modern world, are not ones which Dutch scholars have been comfortable in reconciling with the traditions of their very self-critical society. However, the question of studying such topics has now moved from the realm of choice to that of necessity. With mounting colored populations and rising racial and ethnic tensions throughout Europe it is time to see what history can teach us about this aspect of our present.

BLAKELY, ALLISON.   ORDER NO:
                      ORDER DATE: 11/18/94

BLACKS IN THE DUTCH WORLD : THE EVOLUTION OF   F
RACIAL IMAGERY IN A MODERN SOCIETY.   I
                                                 R
BLACKS IN THE DIASPO   M

INDIANA U PR   1993   1 VOLS O
                              35.00 CLOTH   R
0-253-31191-8 92-43743   D
N2-771054   E
                         QTY ORDERED: 001   R
YNMMC   QTY SHIPPED: 001
VARIED   790905/0018
BLACKWELL NORTH AMERICA

MARYMOUNT MANHATTAN COLLEGE | 2104500021 NMMC

BLACKS IN THE
DUTCH WORLD

4. Prepared by Georgetta C. Cooper.

THE DUTCH WORLD

But coming to the Netherlanders, Hollanders, Zeelander, Friese, etc. What shall we say of them, but that they all excel as seafarers, and might well be called Neptune's brood, Tritonic Sea children (so to speak), the makers of all sorts of ships, who yield to no nation in the world in quick and adroit navigation, skillful, and who carry on massive trade and wage mighty war at sea with very little help, roaming around the world and opening up every corner they have seen so far; and through the Most High's blessing their domain has become like a map of the whole earth, and like a sea into which all rivers of the earth's goods discharge: a land swarming with all kinds of peoples, a Land of Milk and Honey, a widely renowned Tyre, a learned Athens, an inn for the Church of God, a wonder of the world, a scourge to Spain and the Indies, a land which is devoted to God, an Island encircled by water as with arms, so full of convenient harbors, ports and roads, that one might well say:

> If I would seek a paradise on Earth,
> I would go nowhere but the Netherlands. . . .
> If I wanted to garner wisdom and wealth,
> I have a Solomon in the Netherlands.
> Blessed shall he be who in his import and export trade,
>   Observes the Lord's will, with praise.

And where all other Lands, Like Egypt, Libya, Persia, Ethiopia, etc., are heavily plagued by savage animals, crocodiles, Lions, Bears, leopards, tigers, wolves, etc., vipers, serpents, scorpians, etc., our land is free of these. Also in our country it is not too hot, like in Guinea and Sao Tome; nor too cold, like in Novaya Zemlia and Spitsbergen. Our shortest day has just 7.8 hours of sunshine, the longest day 17.17 hours. Where is there a province so blessed, so prosperous?[1]

The Historical Setting

THE NETHERLANDS was created in the late sixteenth and early seventeenth centuries out of intense European religious and political conflicts. As a result the Dutch world from the beginning included an internal dimension concerned with the spiritual as well as an external dimension concerned with political consolidation and commercial prosperity. This is captured well in the excerpt above from the cleric Adam Westermann's seventeenth-century guide for seamen, merchants, and soldiers. He touches upon several characteristic features of the Dutch cultural milieu as well as the physical landscape. Within the physical dimension the eternal battle against the sea to gain and maintain a tenuous hold on the land fostered a constant concern with material well-being and with commerce. The mastery of the sea gained from their struggle at home coupled with this concern led the Dutch in the seventeenth and eighteenth centuries to build one of history's most impressive trading empires. Another motivating influence was the Dutch desire to consolidate their independence from the German Hapsburg dynasty, which ruled Spain and Portugal as well for much of the first century of the United Republic of the Netherlands.

In addressing these challenges the new republic was an international leader in applying modern principles in contributions to the natural and social sciences and the humanities. Their special burning curiosity about and concern with the empirical world and the practical can be seen in the seventeenth century in the work of such scientists as Anton van Leeuwenhoek; the widely acclaimed achievements of the statesman and jurist Hugo Grotius (Huig de Groot); the pioneering South Seas explorations of Abel Tasman; and the rich tradition of Dutch genre paintings. The life all this produced at home has been extensively chronicled by Simon Schama in his compelling interpretative study *The Embarrassment of Riches*. Schama traces in depth the complex of distinctive traits which shape the Dutch identity, an identity which defies simple summarization.[2]

It was the scope of this bold achievement by such a small land which gave rise to Westermann's ringing tribute. The creation of an empire raised the dichotomy between internal and external to yet another level, juxtaposing the homeland to the world abroad. On both levels the internal dimension was considered superior, and more sacred. This also bore an implication that the Dutch people were superior to other peoples, or at least more favored by God.[3] For this reason alone a study of the image of blacks in Dutch history and culture would have to include the empire as well as the homeland. However, the impact of the traits engendered by the trading empire phase of Dutch history is so great that any substantive study of Dutch history and culture should be approached through the broader, global perspective.

The student of Dutch history senses very early the difficulty of generalization, given the complex regional and cultural variety and the changes over time. The Netherlands is so much a land of immigrants that the very definition of "Dutch" is problematical. In the present study the term "Dutch" refers to the European culture so described and to those who are either native to it or become completely assimilated. This study does not attempt to include all regions ever controlled by the Dutch, not even all those containing blacks. Even in Europe the study is limited to the northern seven provinces of the original Netherlands. Inclusion of what was to become Belgium, which undeniably played an equally important role in the origination of Dutch culture, would have made an already ambitious project far more difficult. However, there will be some discussion of Flemish art because of the difficulty of making a clear distinction in this instance.

Of the northern provinces, attention here will center on Holland and Zeeland, which were the two most active in maritime activity during the era of European expansion. Similarly, a selection of areas has been made in the wider "Dutch world." Western New Guinea, for example, an area with distinctly negroid peoples, which came late into the Dutch orbit, is not treated. The study centers on the Netherlands and on six areas which were at some time under Dutch rule and which entailed both extensive contact between the Dutch and peoples of black African descent and significant ties to the Netherlands and other parts of the empire: the Dutch East Indies, Cape Colony, Suriname, the Dutch Caribbean islands (which in the twentieth century would become the Netherlands Antilles), Dutch Brazil, and New Netherlands. The Dutch fortresses and activities along the West African coast are also covered, mainly in connection with the Dutch role in the slave trade and in Christian missionary work.

The Dutch colonial world was radically different from that at home; but it was a deliberate and direct extension of certain aspects of the Netherlands. The colonies were initially founded and governed by the East and West India trading companies, the main instruments through which Dutch commercial might in Asia and the New World was built.[4] The United Provinces States General granted the United East India Company (often abbreviated as VOC, the acronym of the Dutch words), founded in 1602, a subsidy and a monopoly for Dutch trading in the world from the Cape of Good Hope through the Pacific. The United East India Company was governed by a board in the Netherlands called the Heeren XVII (literally, Seventeen Gentlemen, or Council of Seventeen). The West India Company (WIC), founded in 1621, was given the trade monopoly in the Americas and West Africa and a special mission of supporting the war effort against Spain through privateering as well as trade. Its governing board was the Heeren XIX. Both companies had chambers of commerce in major Dutch cities which managed the invested capital from the surrounding areas and which elected the members of the central governing boards, which were proportionally based upon capital invested.

Both companies freely employed non-Dutch officials, soldiers, and clergy: Belgians, Germans, Britons, Frenchmen, Poles, and others. The societies which evolved in Dutch colonies were characteristically multinational, multiracial, multireligious, that is, they were just as cosmopolitan as that of Amsterdam, but with distinctive new mixtures of cultures, and they were guided primarily by the same overriding commercial imperatives that governed in Amsterdam. The chambers in Zeeland and Holland were rivals for control of affairs in both companies' boards. This commercial nexus largely determined the shape and scale of the empire and the character of Dutch life and attitudes in the colonies. It also contributed significantly to developments in the Netherlands.

Of the types of trading in which the Dutch engaged, the African slave trade is most important for present purposes. The Dutch role in this trade contains much of the explanation of Dutch attitudes and practices toward blacks during the slavery era and even beyond. It accounts for important inconsistencies in behavior and stark contrasts between the prevailing values at home and those in the colonies. When Dutch involvement in the slave trade first began in the late sixteenth century, it was contrary to Dutch law. When a Dutch privateer brought a hundred and thirty slaves he had captured on a Portuguese ship to the province of Zeeland in 1596 the burgomaster of Middelburg held that they could not be kept or sold as slaves and so they were freed. Others captured at sea were given control of captured ships or were put ashore on the nearest land.[5]

At the same time, however, in order to consider this issue in its proper historical perspective, it is important to keep in mind that the acceptance of the practice of slavery was not new to any of the Eu-

The Dutch World

ropean societies. Varying degrees of slavery had been practiced in Europe, including the Netherlands, from the period of the Roman Empire until the Middle Ages. In Batavia, as the region of Holland was called during the Roman era, the practice waned after the time of Charlemagne; and from the thirteenth century forward it was possible for slaves to purchase their freedom.[6] Various forms of unfree labor were practiced throughout Europe at the time of its discovery of the Americas. Well into the medieval period Venetian and Genoese merchants played the dominant role in supplying Western Europe with slaves from the Black Sea region.

Thus, what the Dutch were participating in during the early modern period was not entirely new, but rather a resumption of supplying Europe with large numbers of slaves from abroad, except now for use in distant European colonies rather than in the Mediterranean countries of Europe.[7] A major impetus to looking toward somewhere other than Eastern Europe as a source of slaves was that the Moslem empires had gained control of the Mediterranean during the Middle Ages. Meanwhile, the ending of slavery within Europe can be explained largely in terms of the population depletion brought by the bubonic plague and the wars of the fourteenth and fifteenth centuries, by mounting urbanization and expansion of European states, and by a preference for wage laborers as capitalism grew. In this it can be seen that the very process of the modernization of Europe, with its freer subjects and citizens and its increasing wealth and military might, projected, at least to the Europeans, an image of themselves as superior to the peoples of Asia, Africa, and the Americas. At the same time, both the dominant Christian religious doctrines and the increasingly popular humanist secular ideas included some tenets which denounced slavery. As later chapters will show, this denunciation featured considerable vacillation. It was out of this mixed legacy that a well of opposition to slavery existed in the Netherlands, although of undetermined depth.

What was new about the modern slave trade, and what is of greatest significance for the present essay, is that the slaves were all black and nearly all the masters were white. While there was also still a prevalent feeling in Holland that slavery was wrong, the requirements of the competition for colonies abroad began to bring about changes in the earlier moral reservations. At least by 1604 Dutch merchants were accepting orders from Spanish planters on Trinidad for slaves.

These were black market transactions, since only the official *asiento*, the license granted by the Spanish crown for shipment of African slaves to the so-called New World, could legalize the commerce. A Dutch man-of-war sold African slaves in Virginia in 1619. These had probably been captured at sea. Some Indian slaves were used in the American colonies. There was even one reported incident in which Dutchmen in Barbados sold fifty Portuguese captured in Brazil as slaves. The Dutch also used Indonesian slaves extensively in their Eastern empire and some Japanese slaves at their base at Nagasaki, which shows that they had not specifically targeted black peoples initially.[8] This changed dramatically, however, when the West India Company grasped fully the potential for profit in the African slave trade. From that time forward any opposing public conscience there was became subservient to the quest for profits.

For its part, the older, East India Company never mirrored the role of its Western counterpart with respect to African slavery, even though its domain included the Cape Colony in South Africa. As will be seen, that particular African colony was an importer rather than exporter of black slaves, acquiring slaves from West Africa as well as the East Indies. Pragmatic reasons in fact dictated that slaves for each of the various colonies be brought from abroad. In both the East Indies and the Americas enslavement of indigenous peoples was curtailed after initial attempts because it created bad relations with those remaining free and was disruptive of commerce. While it did engage in sporadic shipment of black African slaves to the East, for the most part the East India Company met its needs through indigenous Asian slave systems, such as that in the Celebes.[9] In contrast, the native populations of the Caribbean islands and the Guianas were too small to meet the labor needs of the colonizers.

For the West India Company the lure of profits in the human cargoes which most easily satisfied this need for migrant labor was irresistible. This was true notwithstanding the fact that the company eventually decreased its activity after it turned out that the trade was on the whole actually unprofitable for the Dutch.[10] The company began systematically to challenge the Portuguese on the West African coast for slave stations. In August 1637 Johan Maurits, the company's governor in Northern Brazil, led a fleet of nine ships in the capture of the Portuguese fortress at Elmina on the Gold Coast. Luanda and other Portuguese coastal settlements were soon to experience the same fate. At first the main sources of slaves were Guinea, Angola, and the Congo; the main Dutch market was in Brazil and the Antilles. Through conquest the Dutch soon displaced Portugal on the West African coast, and the trade grew to such proportions that it contributed vital financing for the Dutch empire on both sides of the Atlantic. The Dutch now competed successfully on the coast with English, Swedish, and Danish trading companies. The Dutch Factor at Elmina in the 1690s, Willem Bosman, observed in a letter to his uncle in Holland: "I doubt not but that this trade seems very barbarous to you, but since it is followed by meer [sic] necessity it must go on."[11]

The demand for slaves in the Caribbean had increased with the shift from tobacco to sugar in the plantation economies, while the demand in Brazil remained strong. The Dutch West India Company found that it was able to supply the Spanish and French as well as the Dutch colonists with slaves, as this trade proved a more lucrative contraband activity than the privateering already taking place. With the establishment of Curaçao as a slave depot in 1654 and transformation of the Lesser Antilles into sugar-producing islands, the slave trade became the main occupation of the West India Company for the rest of its existence. By 1668 a warehouse on Curaçao could house 3,000 slaves for immediate delivery. In 1675 the Dutch finally obtained the *asiento* from Spain, through a surrogate, the Portuguese Antonio Garcia, and in the 1680s it came briefly into the hands of the Amsterdam merchant house of Johannes and Balthasar Coymans. Although growing competition between slavers of various nationalities made enforcement of this license impossible, Dutch involvement in the trade would remain sufficiently high for them to account for shipment of some half-million Africans to the Americas before it ended.[12]

Another direct impact of the slave trade on the Netherlands, along with the wealth it produced, was its exacerbation of already existing internal economic and political rivalries. The West India Company was given a monopoly on the slave trade, which it maintained until 1730, after which free trade exceeded that carried on by the company. However, it had constantly to resist attempts by other Dutch interests to remove the restriction. The company was hurt by illicit Dutch competition as well as by the British and other foreign rivals. At home the main friction stemmed from the constant conflict between the chambers of commerce in Zeeland and Holland, with Amsterdam controlling the majority of the seats on both boards.

All this combined to give the issue of the African slave trade many dimensions in the Netherlands from the late seventeenth century until the 1780s when the Dutch slave trade virtually ended after the Netherlands was eclipsed by England and France in this sphere as well as others and the trade was clearly no longer profitable. Slavery itself would be ended in the Dutch empire in 1863. However, one permanent, tangible consequence of the trade and the institution would be an African element in the population. In fact, five of the six Dutch colonies considered here can be described as slave societies; and in three of them the overwhelming majority of the slaves were of black African descent. Not until the late twentieth century did the Netherlands proper experience a large part of its population that looked so conspicuously different. Thus arose the question of how to incorporate these newcomers into Dutch society and culture.

The Netherlands

An attempt at characterization of the Netherlands in the limited scope possible here is thinkable only because the focus is on those aspects of the Dutch experience which relate to attitudes toward blacks. In this regard, one of the most interesting themes is that of pluralism, often noted as one of the most characteristic features of Dutch society. Often paired with the concept of tolerance, this Dutch pluralism has contributed much to the reputation the Netherlands has enjoyed at home and abroad as a haven for religious and political refugees. While the themes of pluralism and toleration by no means encompass all aspects of Dutch culture, they have bearing on so many that a consideration of them may serve as a convenient avenue for gaining an instructive impression of Dutch society. For present purposes it is particularly interesting to relate these to the history of racial and ethnic minorities in the Netherlands.

The presence of newcomers in the population has been a characteristic feature of Dutch society for centuries.[13] Immigration has occurred with a persistence and on a scale which leaves few present Dutch families without at least one ancestor from abroad. A spectacular early example was the arrival in the sixteenth century of approximately 150,000 Flemings and 75,000 Huguenots fleeing religious intolerance in France. The same century also witnessed a stream of Sephardic Jews from Spain and Portugal escaping the Inquisition. In addition, by the end of the seventeenth century 5,000 of Amsterdam's 7,500 Jewish population were Ashkenazi.[14] In the eighteenth and nineteenth centuries the lure for a much smaller European immigration was labor in such industries as agriculture, mining, shipbuilding, and textiles. In the 1920s thousands of German girls moved to the Netherlands to work as domestics; many remained. The largest single wave of immigration came upon the severing of ties between the Netherlands and her former colony in Indonesia in 1949. With many being forced to leave by the new regime, some 300,000 Eurasians, very Dutch in culture and most already bearing Dutch passports, were "repatriated." However, a quite separate part of this group were the South Moluccans, who to the present insist, at times militantly, that the Dutch government owes them assistance in retrieving their lost homelands.

Notwithstanding the increase the newcomers represented for the Dutch labor force, in the 1960s the demand for more, and less expensive, labor once again fueled immigration, this time spurred by vigorous recruitment. Between 1960 and 1974 so-called guestworkers were brought especially from the Mediterranean lands, with the presumption that they would return home after temporary work stints in the Netherlands. Instead, changing conditions have led first to many of their families joining them and then to indefinite residence. In 1987 they numbered around 300,000 men, women, and children: 156,000 from Turkey, 112,000 from Morocco, and 25,000 from Spain. The Turks and Moroccans are particularly conspicuous because of their Islamic faith.

The wave of twentieth-century immigrants that has captured the most attention is that from the Dutch former colonies of Suriname and the Netherlands Antilles. Between 1970 and 1974 some 150,000 came from Suriname and 40,000 from the Antilles. More than 80 percent of the Antilleans have some black African ancestry.[15] The most distinctive feature of these groups, in addition to the suddenness of their influx, is the large proportion of immigrants of black African descent among the Surinamers and Antilleans. Those who are not black represent the other elements of the diverse Suriname society: Hindustani, Javanese, Chinese, Lebanese, and a small number of Europeans.[16]

Like the Indonesians, immigrants from the American colonies too were thoroughly imbued with Dutch culture and carried Dutch passports. It is estimated that in the 1980s there were also more than 25,000 illegal residents in the Netherlands from various places. In addition, Dutch society continues to be a haven for refugees. These number around 20,000, including recent arrivals from Ghana, the Cape Verde Islands, Sri Lanka, New Guinea, Latin America, and the Middle East. The remainder of the national minorities in the Netherlands, mainly workers from member countries of the European Economic Community, qualify as actual foreigners. However, as Common Market citizens they may travel freely in and out of the Netherlands. In 1983 there were 150,000 worker/travelers: 44,000 West Germans, 41,000 Britains, 24,000 Belgians, 21,000 Italians, and 6,000 Frenchmen. Another 13,000 were present from the United States, Canada, and Australia. Altogether the non–Dutch minorities amount to about 7 percent of the current population of about fifteen million. So far there is little sense of common identity uniting the various ethnic minorities, or *allochtonen* groups, as the citizens from abroad are called. There is, however, growing social and political consciousness within some of them regarding the interests of their respective groups.

How does the process of assimilation work in Dutch society? The operative principle in Dutch society concerning minorities has not been that of "the melting pot." The tendency has been to accommodate rather than assimilate. The essence of what is often referred to as tolerance in Dutch society is a consensus that disagreement and diversity need not mean disharmony. For example, a visitor to the Netherlands today can visit numerous places of worship used by minority religions over the centuries, which were tolerated only on condition that they remained inconspicuous. Although the Calvinists were a privileged group until the nineteenth century, Dutch Catholics, who in fact were rarely a numerical minority during the period, and who received religious freedom only in the nineteenth century, unofficially practiced their religion during most of the two and a half centuries when its open practice had been banned.

This attitude has allowed the Netherlands since its beginnings in the sixteenth century to reconcile regional, political, religious, and ethnic differences well enough not only to survive, but to prosper. Arend Lijphart, analyzing the Dutch reconciliation between social and ideological fragmentation and a working democracy, concluded that the Dutch experience is one example where the idea of "separate but equal" has worked.[17] In his view the key has been the way in which the basic divisions in Dutch society, which have centered around religion and class, have been accommodated almost in the manner of international affairs, where the leaders have been wedded to the desirability of preserving the system at all costs.[18]

The evolution of Dutch pluralism over the centuries was, indeed, an outgrowth of practical necessity, although this does not detract from the stature of the Dutch achievement. The interplay of crosscurrents from the Renaissance and the Reformation out of which the United Provinces of the Netherlands emerged in the early seventeenth century left indelible impressions on the society which developed there in the economic and political spheres as well as in the religious. The strength of the challenge to traditional Christendom by humanism, capitalism, and liberal Protestantism in the region in the previous century had ensured the protracted struggle in the society which would ensue. The political structure was a compromise from the beginning, with the United Provinces defined primarily by which territories could be successfully wrested and kept from Spanish control. Meanwhile, those within the confederation, especially Holland and Zeeland, were often as much rivals as allies. The recognition by all the provinces of the main leader of one as primary stadholder was just one more, reluctant bow to practical necessity. Moreover, a particularistic attitude has existed down to the village and neighborhood level throughout Dutch history. Up until the mid-twentieth century the strongest unifying force was a kind of religious nationalism, based on Calvinism, even though the ruling figure was at times Catholic.[19]

Apart from the sense of identity the Dutch acquired from their assertion of political and religious independence from Spain, which found further expression in the global economic rivalry between the Dutch and the Portuguese, local identity in the Netherlands was stronger than any sense of national unity. This would increase only gradually after Dutch economic success attracted strong challenges from other nations, especially the French and the British. Neither the

Batavian Republic created by Napoleonic rule nor the mild monar-
chism which has succeeded it introduced fundamental changes in the
basic structure of Dutch society. That is not to say that there were no
significant changes. Religious freedom was one by-product of the
Napoleonic era for Europe in general. The constitution formulated
for the new Kingdom of the Netherlands in 1815 led to the introduction of parliamentarism for the first time in 1848 and culminated in
the adoption of manhood suffrage in 1918. However, there was no
significant support for return to a republican form of government,
precisely because the monarchy is more consistent with Dutch pluralism, which would prefer a system with counterbalanced ministers
and parliament to one where the leaders of any one party rule.[20]

One of the essential features of the Dutch social structure which
has aided its success is the relative absence of sharp class divisions.
First of all, it is a society which has had only two main classes: the
middle class, which may be further broken down in various segments, and the lower class. As would be expected in a state founded
by merchants, it was the upper middle class which set all standards in
the Netherlands, in sharp contrast to other contemporary European
powers prior to the present century. Class divisions have been further
muted by the fact that historically the various religious and secular
interest blocs have included members of all classes. Thus the current
multiparty political system, in which parties also represent religious
and cultural groupings, still bears some of the imprint of the basic
system of subsocieties, or "pillars," which at least until the 1960s
expressed the pluralism so deeply ingrained in Dutch tradition.

Attempts to integrate the recent, rapid wave of immigration into
the Netherlands have, however, raised issues that the traditional system has not been able to resolve. Increasingly in recent years those
minorities who are non-European in appearance have found themselves subjected to growing prejudice and discrimination by the majority population. Studies have revealed systematic discrimination in
housing, employment, education, law enforcement, and politics. At
the same time, some of the public blames the minority presence for
the unemployment, housing shortage, deficiencies in education, and
other problems such as rising crime rates, including drug trafficking.

These problems evoke no simple solutions, especially since the
late 1970s and early 1980s witnessed a declining economy, rising un-

employment, and further strain on limited space and resources in one of the world's most densely populated countries. The new multiethnic population requires new policies to aid its access to employment, education, health, welfare, politics, and social services. As might be anticipated, the new immigrants often occupy bad housing, often in poorer neighborhoods of the larger cities. They hold mainly menial and factory jobs when employed at all. The fact that the Netherlands enjoys one of the highest living standards and one of the most comprehensive social welfare systems in the world shields the newcomers from the type of privation suffered by their counterparts in countries with less generous policies. However, this simultaneously places more stress on the resources and increases the perception that the new residents are a burden.

Prominent in all of this are the minorities of African descent. Surinamers are clustered especially in Amsterdam, Rotterdam, and The Hague. The Turks and Moroccans originally located mainly near the industries for which they were recruited. While they can be found throughout the country, they live mainly in the most populous region, within the triangle formed by Amsterdam, Rotterdam, and Utrecht. There they form more than 2 percent of the population. About half reside in the large cities, where they in places comprise 4 to 7 percent. Regarding the Surinamers and Antilleans, the government made a conscious, but unsuccessful, attempt to avoid their concentrating in the large cities. Economic realities dictated otherwise, however. One quarter in Amsterdam, the Bijlmermeer, is particularly conspicuous for its high proportion of Surinamers. Although it is by no means segregated, and offers housing of various economic levels, some of the tall apartment buildings in this outlying section with high Surinamer population resemble similar dwellings in "colored" neighborhoods in the United States of America.[21]

Dutch pluralism is being put to a new and severe test. While for most contemporary Dutch citizens the present dilemma might seem produced by an abrupt intrusion from the outside world, the historical perspective reveals a different account. Most of the non-European population now in the Netherlands was in fact already part of the Dutch world, even if rarely seen or thought of in the Dutch homeland. Their belonging now is just one of the consequences of the colonial past, which contributed vitally to Dutch wealth and glory.

The Dutch East Indies

While the activities of the Dutch involving blacks in the East Indies was limited mainly to their employment of several thousand African troops there in their foreign legion in the nineteenth and early twentieth centuries, a characterization of what was called Batavian society is still relevant here because this was the most important Dutch colony of all. This means that it contributed much to the general Dutch outlook about foreign peoples, especially colored peoples. Indeed, the term "black" was at times used to describe some of the peoples of Indonesia. [22] The ancient ancestors of some of the peoples of the region were surely black African, but too remote for practical significance in the present discussion. Another reason for beginning the discussion of Dutch colonies with the East Indies is that the patterns of policies and behavior there reveal in a more fully developed form some of the traits which appear more abbreviated elsewhere and are therefore more difficult to examine.

The Dutch colonies were primarily trading colonies, although in some instances settlement was attempted later. There was only a very limited desire to conquer new territories, as in the Guianas. In Indonesia it was not until the twentieth century that a serious effort was even undertaken to gain control of the entire region. During the period from the seventeenth through the nineteenth centuries the Dutch government was content simply to control the economy through a network of strategically scattered civil servants who supervised exaction of tribute in coffee and other goods by local native magnates. Initially all the Dutch wanted in Indonesia was yet another trading base from which to exploit the surrounding areas in their competition with the Portuguese for commercial dominance.

Until 1610 Dutch vessels stopped at what would become the Javanese city of Batavia, later the main base in the Dutch East Indies, only for provisions. Likewise, for centuries after a European community had been implanted, still mainly on Java, it remained isolated from much of the surrounding islands and peoples. Apart from the Netherlands, its frame of reference remained most immediately the East India Company bases in South Africa, Ceylon, India, Malaya, and Japan, until the company dissolved in 1799, followed by the loss of most of these bases during the Napoleonic era. The primary identification with the company during the early period was reinforced by the fact that its soldiers and merchants were always the largest segment of the European element in Dutch settlements in Indonesia, which numbered several thousand by the late seventeenth century. Only in the nineteenth century did a settled European community develop which thought of Indonesia as a permanent home. This community was still dominated by a mixed, Eurasian culture. In 1900, three-fourths of the Europeans on Java had been born there. Not until two decades later did European Dutch manners and standards gain sway.[23]

Another characteristic feature of "Dutch" colonial society was the high percentage of other European nationalities present, in the service of the Dutch and independently. Perhaps half the East India Company army was made up of Germans, Frenchmen, Scots, Englishmen, Danes, Flemings, and Walloons. In the early years of the colony Malay and Portuguese were used as the lingua franca, with Dutch culture prevalent only within the company office. Eventually, however, knowledge of Dutch and adoption of the Dutch religion, two of the central defining features of Dutch culture, became the main channels to status.[24] At the same time, few European women came before the late nineteenth century. In fact, East India Company policy for much of the period was to restrict immigration by Dutch women and to recruit bachelors from the Netherlands and have them marry or take Asian women concubines, who, if slave, were first freed, baptized, and given a Christian Dutch or Portuguese name.

This pragmatic strategy, aimed at ensuring the most stable type of service force, is indicative of the pragmatic approach taken concerning racial mixing. A related further measure was the restriction of admission into the Netherlands of Asian wives and children of Dutchmen.[25] Meanwhile, within the Dutch East Indies the Eurasian offspring of the mixed marriages became the preferred marriage partners in the society which developed. One result of this combination of practices was that nearly all members of society were raised by Asian women. Moreover, the racially mixed society as a whole was matrilineal, with Asian-born Dutch sons usually sent to the Netherlands for careers and new bachelor recruits brought in for company manpower.

The social structure which evolved in this Eurasian society resembled more that of the surrounding traditional class societies than that of the Netherlands. Rigid social distinctions were not abolished until 1795. Slaves were always the largest part of the population of Batavia; these were brought from as far away as India and Burma, as well as from other parts of the archipelago, to serve mainly as domestic slaves. As in the New World, there was some hesitancy to employ slaves from the surrounding Javanese population, although slavery was also practiced within it. The late nineteenth century, which brought an end to the slave trade and slavery in the Dutch East Indies as elsewhere, also brought fundamental changes in the nature of Eurasian society there. The brief French and British rule at the start of the century brought hundreds more Europeans, introduced a sharper assertion of the superiority of Western civilization, and ended in 1816 the ties between the different colonies of the East India Company. The Royal Commissioners-General who succeeded the defunct East India Company systematically Europeanized the local society and arranged for the first time that the colony actually be governed from the Netherlands rather than by local elites.

The contours of the distinctive society which developed in the Dutch East Indies could not, however, be totally reshaped by any act of will. For example, although in the early twentieth century the society was defined as "plural," along the well-known Dutch model, with disparate groups living side by side, law could not instantly bend racial and cultural reality shaped by centuries. The peculiar overlapping role for women and children, who, depending on their husband's status, could be Indonesian, European, or a mixture of the two, precluded any neat assignment of roles. Similarly, the current morality which preferred prostitution to concubinage only invited the use of subterfuge rather than changing the behavior. Meanwhile mounting Europeanization in the twentieth century did much to fan the flames of nationalism, which would eventually end Dutch rule.

The relationship which existed between the Dutch East Indies and the Netherlands shows how much the needs of the East India Trading Company which ruled it shaped the society which developed, and how pragmatic, how transient, and at times even how contradictory some policies and practices concerning racial and ethnic questions could be. It will be seen in surveying the other colonies that, while each had its peculiarities, their nature as commercial ventures of the governing trading companies also provided common patterns.

Cape Colony

The implanting of a Dutch colony on the Cape of Good Hope was a direct consequence of the growing importance of the one in the East Indies for the Dutch global economy. The Cape was initially viewed as just a convenient refueling and refreshment station en route to Asia. However, beginning in 1652 a firm colony did take root and it became an important part of the domain controlled by the East India Company from Batavia. Batavia's authority can be seen in the similar policies implemented at the Cape by company officials, some of whom also served in the East Indies. Out of efforts to produce at the Cape as much as possible for reprovisioning the passing ships, an economy based on arable agriculture, wine production, and pastoral farming developed. Cape Colony remained an integral part of the Dutch economic system until the British wrested control away at the end of the eighteenth century. Although by then the British were dominant, from the colony's beginning the makeup of the European population showed a great diversity of nationalities. In addition to the Dutch and British, German, Scandanavian, and French merchants and farmers were prominent. Cape society would also for the first time bring a sizable black African population into the Dutch world. Like the emergence of the colony itself, this too resulted more from expediency than from design.

The development which most shaped Cape society under the Dutch was the introduction of slavery as the basic means of production, with the company itself owning hundreds of slaves.[26] Here it should be emphasized that the first slaves there were not black, and many were not even African. The company brought many from its Asian areas of operation, laying the foundation for the significant "Coloured" population which would become a permanent part of the South African scene. The primacy and intensity of economic rivalry within Dutch society is revealed in the fact that after some initial provision of slaves from West Africa, which fell under the West India Company's domain, friction between the two Dutch companies prevented further exploitation of this logical source.

The reason the Dutch imported slaves was a pragmatic one. The natives of the Cape region, the yellowish or brown-skinned Khoikhoi (Hottentots), were initially respected by the Dutch as independent people employed as hired labor in exchange for rice, tobacco, and alcohol. The Dutch were dependent on the natives, and would have found it problematical directly to enslave them, for the same reasons that it was difficult to use the American Indians for slaves in the New World. For cultural reasons the Khoikhoi turned out to be an unreliable labor force. Traditionally nomadic hunters, they had a distaste for regular menial labor, and the Dutch mistook this for laziness.[27] Consequently, beginning in 1658 the East India Company imported slaves to Cape Colony. They were brought mainly from East Africa, Madagascar, and the Dutch East Indies, and were treated much the same as slaves in other parts of the Dutch empire.

Thus by 1700 the population of Cape Colony consisted of 1,308 whites and 838 slaves. In 1713 the Khoikhoi were nearly annihilated by a smallpox epidemic brought by the Dutch. Later in the century as the Boers (seminomadic, poor Dutch farmers) expanded northward with their sheep and cattle, eluding the relentless assertion of British authority on the Cape, they carried out a deliberate campaign of genocide against the Khoikhoi and Bushmen upon whose land they encroached. They continued this further into the interior after England took over Cape Colony in 1795. In the process, by the early eighteenth century the traditional Khoikhoi society had collapsed as the people became landless laborers on the land usurped by the various European farmers. Now slaves and servants came to be viewed as part of the same broad inferior class, with skin color the defining characteristic. The Dutch also deliberately perpetuated the differences occasioned by language and other cultural traits. Meanwhile the Khoikhoi too viewed themselves as superior to the darker Negroes and other slaves because they were free.[28]

By 1805 the Cape Colony population grew to 25,757 whites, 29,545 slaves, and 28,000 Khoikhoi. The resurgent Khoikhoi, now predominantly a mulatto population, had gradually come to be viewed by the East India Company as a subdivision of the slave labor force. In addition to the Khoikhoi, the Xhosa, a more agricultural people, were hired for some labor, amounting to as much as 30 percent of the labor force. To further augment the labor force at the Cape, the European population employed slavery just as readily as it did seed and other supplies from the East India Company.[29]

The same attitude of expediency which could support exploitation and even annihilation also promoted mingling of the races. While both the East India Company and the church had rules and various proclamations against concubinage, no amount of legislation could prevent it. Meanwhile, not only was there no formal law against miscegenation, extensive mixing was condoned for Dutch males with slave and Khoikhoi females. This ultimately resulted in the Khoikhoi being turned totally into a mulatto population. It was this mixed group which coalesced with the various outsiders to form a part of the population called Coloureds (those of mixed blood). This group was not accepted as more Dutch as a consequence, although the Coloureds enjoyed some advantages from closer association with whites just as mulattoes in other Dutch societies did.

Nevertheless, the legal system made it clear that slaves, Hottentots, and Coloureds were inferior to whites. For example, whites would generally receive light punishment, if any, for murdering one of the others, while the death penalty was certain in the opposite case. Punishment of whites for wrongs against this underclass was most likely when one white injured the slave or servant of another. Then the penalty would be in the form of damages for harming another's property or economic interests. The only breaches in the wall of separation between the Dutch and their slaves and servants in South Africa were intermarriage and conversion to Christianity. Both were firmly discouraged and occurred only rarely.[30]

Society in Cape Colony under the Dutch was never very stable, which is perhaps to be expected for a settlement intended only to serve the economic interests of another far away. Once it was decided to plant a permanent settlement and expand to the interior, Cape society of course also had the kinds of instability inherent in any frontier society. For the Dutch a dominant factor was also the desire to maintain independence from the more numerous and militarily powerful British. This caused the concerted migrations into the interior of the most dedicated Dutch farmers. As for the slaves, their varied origins were an obstacle to any type of real community. Just as their owners spoke many different European languages, the slaves spoke Malay, Portuguese, Khoi, and various other South African languages.

There was always a shortage of slaves, resulting in a constant, if small, import of new labor. Slave marriage was not formally recognized. Only in the final decade of Dutch rule did females amount to

25 percent of the slave population, which as a result was never self-re-producing. High fertility was offset by high mortality and harsh living conditions.[31] Free blacks were prominent in the cities, to which they were almost exclusively restricted. In Cape Town they reached as high as 20 percent of the population in the eighteenth century, and engaged in artisan manufacturing and retail trading. However, although some of them even owned slaves, prevailing restrictions ensured that they could not gain wealth or prestige.[32]

Dutch West Africa

Nowhere was the fact that Dutch colonies were primarily trading colonies more fully demonstrated than with those in West Africa linked to the trade with the Dutch Caribbean and Brazil. The *Nederlandse Etablissementen ter Kuste van Guinea* (The Dutch Establishments on the Coast of Guinea), as the Dutch possessions in the region were collectively called, were a string of forts stretched along some two hundred miles of coastline. These forts were often referred to as "factories," as were the trading bases in various parts of East Asia. Their careers mirrored that of the waning Dutch empire, confronted at every turn by the rising British. After the demise of the West India Company at the end of the eighteenth century, and the Napoleonic interlude, the forts were placed under the control of the (Dutch) Department of Trade and Colonies. Elmina was the most important and enduring. The oldest, Nassau, dated from 1612. Others bore such names as Amsterdam, Leydsaamheyd (Suffering), Goede Hoop (Good Hope), and Crève-coeur (Heartbreak). Over the centuries up to the nineteenth there were half a dozen more, of lesser significance and shorter lived. The names often reflected their having been acquired by the Dutch from other European rivals; and the English would continue the tradition of renaming.

A detailed history of this saga is beyond the scope of the present study. However, because this was an area in which there was long-standing, constant interaction between the Dutch and Africans, it will be useful at least to outline the contours of the kind of society which evolved there over the centuries. The power of none of the Dutch fortresses extended very far into the interior. However, centuries of European presence had created permanent surrounding populations tied to the Europeans either by blood, trade, or other types of symbiotic relationship. The system in place in Elmina in the second half of the nineteenth century may serve as an example, although each fort had its distinctive features.

The Dutch, with some input from the population, chose a symbolic local official who bore the title of *Ohin* (king). The elite element in the social structure was the social group defined as African Free-burghers. The importance of this group was recognized by designation of another official called the *Burgemeester* (Mayor). Also called mulattoes or *tapooyers*, this was the class that was most European in culture and which included merchants and government officials. Those of mixed European and African blood were the most eligible to belong, although blacks who were Christian and otherwise European in culture might also. All the social units, ten in all at this time, were called quarters, and were originally mainly military companies. The other quarters had a captain or *vaandrig* (literally, ensign) as the chief leader. Other leading Elmina government officials were the *Ohin's* judicial and political counsellors, called the *Amafu* and the *Besonfu*, respectively. The Dutch allowed considerable autonomy for the population in regulation of affairs within the society. They also paid an annual fee to the natives as a sort of tribute to their special relationship.[33]

Another common bond between the Dutch and the Elminans was the desire of both to maintain good relations with the Ashanti kingdom inland, both for trading purposes and for military alliance against the impinging British and surrounding hostile African peoples. This type of scenario was also a common one for all of the fortresses along the coast, only with different principals occupying the respective roles played by the Europeans and their native associates. When the English finally displaced the Dutch in 1872 after decades of pressure, most of the forts were only ruins. As usual, this transfer was without the consent of the more than 20,000 African inhabitants of the territories involved. In this instance the people of the town of Elmina dreaded British rule because it would infringe upon freedoms they currently enjoyed in both economic and social practices. When the town of some 20,000 revolted in 1873 after the official transfer, the British responded by bombarding it from the fortress and the sea, into rubble from which it was never rebuilt.[34]

Dutch Brazil

Just as the colonies at Batavia and the Cape of Good Hope arose to support the Dutch rivalry with the Portuguese for the carrying trade in Asia, those which emerged in West Africa and the Americas resulted from Dutch entry into the lucrative new carrying trade in African slaves and New World sugar and tobacco. Brazil would prove the single main market for the imported "black ivory" agricultural labor force throughout the seventeenth century. Already supplying Spanish planters with slaves, the West India Company in the early seventeenth century proceeded to wrest New World markets away from Portugal. The value of the sugar trade had been demonstrated to Dutch merchants, when they had handled about half of the sugar exports from Portuguese Brazil during a twelve-year truce between the Dutch and Spain, from 1609 to 1621.

The decision to gain a foothold in Brazil grew out of the desire to establish Dutch control in a sugar-growing area. After a fifteen-year struggle the West India Company was able to oust the Portuguese from around Bahia and Pernambuco by the early 1630s and set up its own economy there based primarily on sugar. This in turn explains the eagerness to control West African slave supplies and the fact that the conqueror of Elmina was the new Dutch governor of Brazil, Johan Maurits van Nassau-Siegen.[35] After the Dutch had displaced the Portuguese from strategic access points along the African coast and found themselves competing in the region with the English, Swedish, and Danish companies, the West India Company found that the slave trade was more profitable than privateering, which had been its first main competitive strategy. This was true even after the company found it could not maintain its monopoly after 1638. The exploits of naval squadrons led by such colorful figures as Piet Heyn and Cornelis Jol had demonstrated the potential for Dutch success in this enterprise.[36]

The society which the Dutch temporarily conquered from the Portuguese, and which they were to name for a time New Holland, was already highly diverse and usually turbulent. Ethnic diversity was one of its salient features. The Dutch protracted victory was aided somewhat by dissident local Indian allies. A mulatto defector from the Spanish named Calabar in the early 1630s taught the Dutch how to raid the sugar districts with small guerrilla bands, to the great embarrassment of the Portuguese commander Mathias de Albuquerque. Likewise, when the Dutch were finally ousted by the Portuguese again in the 1660s the disgruntled slave and free black population which had evolved there would play an even more crucial role on the Portuguese side. Also, as throughout the Americas, the first century of European presence was attended by steady attrition of the native population from new diseases as well as from the traditional internecine wars between the various local groups. [37]

The European segment of the colony was a population of remaining Portuguese (Catholic) planters, Protestant planters, and Spanish and Portuguese Jewish refugees. During the colony's strongest decade, under the leadership of Johan Maurits, which ended in 1644, some 20,000 slaves were delivered to Pernambuco. The yearly average for the colony for the first quarter of the century, under the Portuguese, had been 2,500. By 1600 blacks formed the largest segment of the population. Whites, 40 percent of the population in Pernambuco in 1630, were thus a much larger part of the population there than in other Western European colonies in South America and the Caribbean. [38] Considerable mixture immediately occurred between the groups, as witnessed by a noticeable "mestizo" (meaning in this colony European-Indian) and mulatto population.

Most of the European population remaining in the territories controlled by the Dutch (Pernambuco, Itamaracá, Paraiba, and Rio Grande) were Portuguese: about 25,000, working mainly in agriculture. Many of those coming from the Netherlands were Jews, and most of these were Sephardic. About a third of the urban population was Jewish, most working as agents, merchants, and financiers in connection with the slave trade and sugar industry. The West India Company used only a few blacks as soldiers, the Portuguese several hundred, but under white commanders. The slaves were seen as vital to maintain the agricultural food supply upon which all forces were dependent. Apart from its own slaves, the company had little control over the master-slave relationship in the colony, although it had some guidelines that it could not possibly enforce. By all accounts slaves were treated brutally. The company did send out expeditions against the Maroons of Palmares, although to no avail. [39] The failure of the Dutch minority regime ever to gain significant loyalty from any of the more populous groups present contributed to its decline after the departure of its strongest leader, Maurits, in 1644. His successor, Wolter Schonenborgh, former mayor of Mauritsstad, was left to fight the uprising of the Portuguese there. Decisive defeat in Brazil in 1654 brought a flood of soldiers home to the Netherlands. The colony passed again into Portuguese hands by treaty in 1661.

New Netherlands

The North American colony of the Dutch actually predated the founding of the West India Company and only intermittently received its careful attention. Nevertheless, New Netherlands' half century of life was an interesting variation as a projection of Dutch society abroad. The region was originally discovered by the Englishman Henry Hudson in 1609, while seeking a new route to Asia for the Dutch East India Company. Although the area was called New Netherlands as early as 1614, the first permanent European settlers were about thirty families of French-speaking Walloons who settled on Manhattan Island in 1624, founding New Amsterdam. Some early maps show the region as New Belgium. The West India Company purchased the island from the Indians in 1626 for sixty guilders and the Amsterdam Chamber of Commerce began to promote colonization around Fort Amsterdam in 1629. By 1630 there were about three hundred Europeans there, still mostly Walloons. In the course of its existence the Dutch colony would be periodically at war with bordering New England and New Sweden, as well as with local Indians, before finally falling to the English in 1664.

Thus this colony too was awash in the swirl of international economic competition. As early as 1615 a New Netherlands Trading Company was founded by Amsterdam merchants. It experienced some success before the founding of the national trading company with its monopoly in 1621. The economy of New Netherlands was initially based on the fur trade with the Indians. The colony became the leading North American source of furs for the first half of the seventeenth century. In its final two decades under the Dutch, the colony grew to around nine thousand people, was centered on an agricultural economy, and had increasingly more commercial ties with the Netherlands. Although the territory stretched for more than a hundred miles along the coast, the population was concentrated in or around just a few towns; the spaces between were still Indian country.

New Amsterdam received a municipal charter and government in 1653, placing its burgomasters and other officials under the colony's director-general, appointed by the West India Company.[40]

As in the case of Cape Colony, the need for provisions led as well to promotion of settlement in the surrounding territories and eventual relaxation of West India Company monopolies on fur trading and fishing. The Dutch government was also concerned to keep a base in North America in light of its intensifying rivalry with England in international trade. Control of the economy did remain centered in Holland, rather than in any local merchant community. However, the declining fortunes of the colony in Brazil in the late 1640s left the company short of funds and cautious of increasing commitments in America. Consequently, although the company retained a monopoly on the trade in African gold and slaves, it opened up the market in other areas to private traders. The ambivalent posture of the company is not surprising considering the fact that it was created more as an instrument of war against Spain than as a colonizing agency.[41]

As much as half of the population of New Netherlands may have been non-Dutch: German, Norwegian, Swedish, Finnish, French, Danish, British.[42] Director-General Willem Kieft, who served from 1638 to 1647, counted eighteen languages spoken in his colony. By 1630 African slaves were also brought to New Netherlands, from the Caribbean and some directly from Africa. However, although there were slave markets in the region of New Amsterdam, most slaves went to tobacco growers in the nearby southern colonies. This northern colony lacked the type of agriculture which welcomed slave labor. At the same time, there was extensive use of indentured servitude by Europeans for existing tasks.

There are no firm estimates of the black population of New Netherlands, slave or free. It is estimated that from 15 to 20 percent of the population of New Amsterdam was slave. Peter Stuyvesant, the Director-General from 1647 to 1664, had forty slaves in 1660, employed in farm labor and domestic work. He was probably the largest private owner. The West India Company was definitely the largest owner of slaves, as it was of most other enterprises. Most of its slaves worked in all-male labor gangs, although there were also female slaves. Slaves carried out much of the construction in New Amsterdam. It is generally agreed that slavery was somewhat milder in New Netherlands than in other European American colonies. The company developed a policy which allowed for limited manumission of its slaves. Some cases of intermarriage between blacks and whites were recorded. The Reformed Church allowed the children of some Christianized slaves to be baptized. Sexual mixing outside marriage occurred more frequently, as elsewhere. In all cases, however, the main consideration was the desire for order and efficiency, rather than humanitarian concerns.[43]

Suriname

The 1667 Breda Treaty, which formalized English possession of New Netherlands, which had been taken in an almost bloodless operation in 1664, also ceded to the Netherlands the colony of Suriname, which the English also controlled but offered in exchange for an end of dispute over control of New Netherlands. The first European colony was founded in Suriname by the English in 1651. Various groups of Europeans had been there, the French as early as the 1620s. The Dutch succeeded for short periods in challenging the British and French for colonization along the Essequibo and Berbice rivers along this same "Wild Coast"; but only the colony centered on the Suriname River proved lasting for the Dutch. Of the Dutch provinces, Zeeland first had most influence in Suriname, through the first military commander and governor, Abraham Crijnssen, who accordingly named the main fortress Zeelandia. The main city, Paramaribo, was at times in the eighteenth century called New Zeeland and New Middelburg.

However, to escape the inevitable heavy financial burden of defending a colony, in 1683 the Zeeland provincial government sold Suriname to the West India Company. As part of the transaction a special chartered Society of Suriname (*Geoctroyeerde Societeit van Suriname*) was created, which was based on shares owned by the company, the city of Amsterdam, and the wealthy family of Cornelis van Aerssen van Sommelsdijck. The latter and his descendants thereby also held the right to the governorship until they sold their share to Amsterdam in 1770.[44] Since Amsterdam merchants dominated trading in both the East and the West, they could best afford to risk capital on the relatively less important Suriname trade. Thus, in contrast to earlier unsuccessful Dutch attempts at acquiring this colony, as a by-product of war with England the Netherlands found itself in possession of a region several times its own size, with some of the same potential as the colony just lost in Brazil. However, this "windfall" colony too would eventually prove unprofitable and a financial burden to maintain.

In 1665, two hundred Portuguese Jews leaving Brazil in anticipation of the imminent Portuguese victory had gained permission to settle and started one of the most stable and important segments of Suriname's society. At the end of the seventeenth century the majority of the white population in Suriname was French (Huguenots) and Jewish. Jews comprised at least a third of the European population until the nineteenth century, many of them speaking Spanish or Portuguese at home, attesting to their earlier ties with the Spanish empire. The diversity of the Suriname colony's origins is imprinted in the native language which developed there. Called Sranan Tongo, it probably originated in West Africa and evolved with local influences in Suriname, incorporating elements of Portuguese, French, and Dutch. It also has been called *Neger Engels* (Negro English), with derogatory connotations.

Suriname would become the one real plantation economy in the Dutch empire; by the beginning of the eighteenth century slaves would comprise over 90 percent of the population. Also by that time hundreds of Maroons had succeeded in organizing themselves into independent communities living in the bush. With the resultant heightened anxiety of the white planters, the social policies established discouraged assimilation across color lines. Slaves were allowed to perform only certain types of labor and were required to wear different clothes and play different music than their masters. They were required to do all the physical labor, down to such simple tasks as filling glasses for drink. They were in most cases forbidden to do mental work such as reading and writing. Obstacles were placed in the way of their conversion to Christianity. Even social intercourse between slaves and black freemen was discouraged; and freemen were still not considered equal to whites. Most Europeans were not allowed to bring wives and children to the plantations; salaries were too low in any case. Sexual intercourse between white males and blacks naturally resulted, thereby making it impossible to maintain the separateness intended. The master's concubine acquired a special name, *Sisi*, and had special status as an intermediary for arbitration with other slaves.[45]

The late distinguished sociologist Rudolf van Lier, himself a Surinamer of mixed Jewish, European, and African descent, was a leading
student of Suriname society through his landmark study of it as a
frontier society.[46] Considering the definitions of society offered by
Max Weber, Émile Durkheim, Pierre Leroy-Beaulieu, Frederick Fur-
nivall, and others, he found Suriname's to be a mixed form, changing
over time, not a "community," but a different type of plural society.
In looking at the relationships between slaves and masters, with special attention to the Jews, he concluded that there were very negative
consequences from the high incidence of absentee planter ownership
after the 1780s. After the Amsterdam stock market crisis of 1773,
between 70 and 80 percent of the plantations in Suriname belonged to
absentee owners.

This meant, according to Van Lier, that the slaves there were
often at the mercy of callous plantation directors who did not even
have the level of regard for the slaves that one would have for his own
property as compared to someone else's. Achieving a slave population
of 50,000 by that time, along with 5,000 free blacks and others, the
colony seemingly never recovered from the economic decline of that
period. In an opposing view, Gert Oostindie argues, in his 1989 history covering 150 years for two Suriname plantations, that the argument linking absenteeism and harshness is illogical because most of
the evidence of slave discontent preceded the time when absenteeism
became the norm.[47] One important consequence of the perception of
economic decline since that time is that Suriname has been viewed
from the Netherlands ever since as a burden.

Although Suriname remained oriented toward Dutch culture
with regard to the official language, administrative structure, and
preeminence of European values, much of the Dutch population left
the colony at the end of the eighteenth century. The West India Company was terminated around the same time; and the Dutch economy
could not overcome the British mercantilist control of the sugar trade
for their own American colonies. The predominantly slave, free
black, and Jewish population would become augmented by new immigrants when contract labor was brought in, especially from the
Dutch East Indies and British India, to replace cheap labor lost
through the ending of the slave trade and the emancipation which
occurred in the course of the nineteenth century. Between the time
of the emancipation in 1863 and the Second World War some 40,000

Hindustani and 35,000 Javanese were brought to Surinam in that capacity.

Although Suriname was part of the Kingdom of the Netherlands, the two societies remained largely separate until the mid-twentieth century. By then the population of Surinamese in the Netherlands numbered only about 3,000.[48] As mentioned in the earlier discussion of immigration to the Netherlands, arrival of perhaps half the diverse population of Suriname in the 1970s has forced renewed interest and examination of exactly how that society does relate to that in the Netherlands. Suriname's assumption of independence in 1975 clarified that for the two countries, but not for the two cultures.

Netherlands Antilles

Taken in possession for the West India Company in 1634 by Johannes van Walbeeck and Pierre Le Grand, Curaçao soon became the major base in the Caribbean for the Dutch fleet, for privateering, and for trading, initially contraband and later legal. It was also the main supply point for all ships coming from the Netherlands to Dutch Brazil and New Netherlands. Within a few years the Dutch also claimed the nearby other Leeward islands of Bonaire and Aruba and also St. Maarten (the southern part), St. Eustatius, and Saba, a threesome the Dutch called their Windward Islands. Some of the islands, St. Maarten in particular, were of commercial interest because of their salt deposits, valuable for the massive Dutch fishing industry. These, along with a number of islands of insignificant size, would later be named the Netherlands Antilles. Taken as a whole, they further illustrate the great diversity of the Dutch world and deserve a much fuller discussion than will be feasible here. For present purposes, Curaçao is of greatest historical importance and will be used here to illustrate the role of the Antilles.

The Spanish had claimed Curaçao since 1527, but had no significant settlement on it. The Dutch found there just a small number of Spaniards and a few hundred Caquetios Indians, who would soon experience the same dismal fate of the other native populations of the region. In 1641 the West India Company began bringing African slaves there for sale and in 1654 it became the main slave depot for the entire Caribbean. Although sugar, indigo, and tobacco were grown on the island, its several plantations were never part of a major agricultural economy. The climate and the island's small size did not favor agriculture. However, transformation of the Lesser Antilles into sugar-producing islands ensured that the slave trade would be the main occupation of the first West India Company for the final two decades of its existence. By the 1670s there were about 150 company employees, 600 colonists, and 2,000 slaves.[49] Dutch became the official language of all six islands. However, in the lower three, Papiamento became the spoken language for most of the population. Like Sranan Tongo, Swahili, and other composite tongues of trading empires, this language is a direct reflection of the layers of historical melding which occurred in its region. In contrast, in the Upper Windward Dutch Antilles English became the main spoken language. On Curaçao another significant lasting legacy of the Spanish rule was that the overwhelming majority of the population was Catholic even under the Dutch.

Curaçao was known for milder treatment of slaves than Suriname. Lending some support for this, there was natural increase in the slave population in Curaçao, while in Suriname birth and death rates were about even. At the time of the emancipation in 1863 the slave population on Curaçao would reach 6,700; there were less than half that many whites, including here also a significant Jewish element. The Curaçao white population was not only smaller but also more stable than Suriname's. Another characteristic of Curaçao's population was a higher proportion of freedmen than in Suriname. By the end of the eighteenth century Curaçao had about 5,000 freedmen, that is, equal to the number of slaves and 2,000 more than the number of whites. Suriname had about 3,000 freedmen, with 2,000 whites.

In Curaçao, however, the freedmen were often materially worse off than the slaves, which is one reason masters were willing to free them. Moreover, because of a curious twist in the role of color, the freedmen did not benefit from their status as much as their numbers should have allowed. Mulattoes were more likely to become free than were other blacks; and in Suriname a mulatto elite did develop later, in the nineteenth century. Sons of common-law mixed marriages were often sent to the Netherlands for education, and in some cases returned to work for the government in Suriname. This became more frequent after the 1773 crisis sent many planters with families home and left the white population almost entirely male. Such a mulatto elite did not, however, appear in Curaçao, at least not during slavery, because of the presence of more white women and maintenance of legitimacy in the white line despite any mulatto offspring there might be. Thus most of Curaçao's mulattoes were uneducated, spoke the native language, and would eventually become Catholic in religion. The Suriname mulatto elite was more Dutch, in language, religion, and other ways.[50]

The importance of Curaçao in the Dutch empire would wane along with the slave trade and rise again only in the twentieth century. The second West India Company, founded in 1674, maintained the trade monopoly of the first until its demise in the 1790s, when control of Curaçao passed directly to the government, as with other colonies. During the Napoleonic wars it fell into English hands in 1800, until given over to the Batavian Republic by the Amiens Treaty in 1802. The Netherlands Antilles developed little sense of regional identity beyond each separate island. At the same time, an attraction to the Netherlands was evident, especially in the Leeward Islands, although significant travel and emigration there for all but a small elite has occurred only since the middle of the twentieth century. Meanwhile, interest in Curaçao within the Netherlands revived only with the advent of the petroleum refining industry there in the twentieth century. It is that industry's decline, coupled with significant Antillean immigration to the Netherlands, and at least some discussion of independence, that has brought the Dutch public to an unprecedented awareness of this part of their kingdom.

The Color Spectrum

The degree of racial and cultural mixture in human evolution and the global nature of the Dutch empire make a discussion of racial terms essential for coherent discussion of changing perceptions of race and color. Even within the Dutch empire words used for racial description sometimes varied in meaning in different regions. This is illustrated nowhere more vividly than in one of the former Dutch colonial areas, Brazil, where in the 1980s statisticians resorted to 136 ways to describe one's color.[51] A tracing of the image of blacks in the Dutch world therefore requires linguistic points of reference.

Words have a power in shaping human society that is often overlooked. It would be well to heed the reminder from the brothers

Grimm on the title page of their nineteenth-century *Deutsches Wörterbuch* (German Dictionary): "im anfang war das wort" (in the beginning was the word). Regardless of the validity of this biblical pronouncement, words do at times have life and force outside human volition. Discussion of the language related to the themes treated here can be as important as the examination of geographic, social, economic, and other factors. Such discussion has two main dimensions. The first concerns the definitions of race and color which evolved in the Netherlands and the empire; the second treats the societal perceptions of people so designated. The latter aspect is what most of the remainder of the present study is about. It is the former that must briefly be addressed at this point.

The clearest path to follow in tracing the evolution of the definition of blacks in the Dutch experience is found in dictionaries and encyclopedias. These compendia of popular usage, which draw also upon the best literary references of the day, harbor echoes of some words no longer heard as well as antecedents and earlier versions of those that have survived. In the sixteenth and seventeenth centuries the dictionaries seemed to celebrate the very act of correct and full written presentation of the Dutch language.[52] By the eighteenth century they were highlighting the breadth with which they covered the terms related to the arts, sciences, industry, and customs. By the nineteenth this all came to be articulated in the dictionaries and encyclopedias under the comprehensive rubric of "civilization." The lexicography thus mirrors the history. The story of the evolution of words describing race and color further bears this out. Just as in the case of the commercial rivalries already mentioned, this is truly an international story. As the author of a leading study of the earliest Dutch-English/English-Dutch dictionaries concluded: "establishment of a network of bi-lingual dictionaries for the modern languages of Western Europe should probably be looked upon as a single process; or, if the evidence of Dutch and English is anything to go by, almost as a single industry, with a complex pattern of international affiliations."[53]

The use of the term "Black" (*swert* and *noir*) to denote a black person was present from the beginning of the United Provinces of the Netherlands.[54] The initial choice of terms used in Dutch to describe blacks appears to have been influenced as much by the French

(Walloon), German, and English as by the Spanish, notwithstanding the place of the Lowlands in the Spanish empire. However, "Moor" and "Neger" from the Spanish legacy came to be the terms most used in the Netherlands. By the same token, "Blanke" became the most popular term for describing whites, as opposed to (the more Germanic) "Witte." In the seventeenth century the word "Moor" from the Spanish legacy already had broadened to include "a blacké Moore, or an Ethiopian"; and "Moor-lands" meant Ethiopia. Alongside that definition in one Dutch-English dictionary was an alternative definition of "een Moor: A Devill, or an ill Spirit."[55] By the eighteenth century the term "neger" (Negro) was equated with "Schwarzer" (Black), "Mohr," and "Mooriaan," although "Moor" was to continue to have an ambiguous meaning, designating also the non-Negroid North Africans and their related cultures.[56]

It should be noted that there have never been precise guidelines for the actual application of these terms in specific cases. In the present study the terms "blacks" and "Negroes," used interchangeably, refer generally to those of predominantly black African descent. It should be noted, however, that just as there were different words for "black" in different parts of the Dutch world, there was also disparity between some of the different societies and cultures with respect to who considered themselves blacks or were perceived as such. The anthropologist Harry Hoetink has pointed out the difficulty of a precise definition in his description of what he calls the "somatic norm," "the complex of physical (somatic) characteristics which are accepted by a group as its norm and ideal." He observes that this "socio-psychological complement of the biological concept of 'race'" is ultimately a composite of the attitudes in a given society toward certain physical traits and accompanying social and economic status. Consequently, a person who because of his or her skin color would be "black" in North America might well be "white" in Brazil if educated and wealthy.[57] The subject at hand is not the resolution of this complex issue, but rather the attitudes toward those who are considered black, regardless of how this is defined.

By the eighteenth century some dictionaries included comprehensive discussions of the definition of blacks, associating the origin of the terms with the region of the Niger River in West Africa, and presenting various scientific theories about how racial differences developed. Such discussion also featured the character and customs of blacks.[58] It also at times sought to explain the relationship between blacks and whites in human history. One volume offered:

> Negroes have possibly been on the earth just as long as Whites. The almost six thousand years which have passed between the first man and us prevent us from knowing if he was white or black. The holy scriptures are completely silent in this regard. However, we may with good reason think that he was white; firstly because Negroes are seldom seen beyond the lands between the tropics. Adam was formed and lived four hundred miles to the North of the Tropic of Cancer. Secondly, seldom, if ever, has the Negroes' color been known to pale through a change in climate, while Whites become yellower as they near the scorching climate. This one observation is sufficient in order to conclude with certainty that blacks must be descendant from whites and must have acquired the darker color which distinguishes them over the course of the centuries. Thirdly, there are far fewer Negroes than whites. Almost all the territories inhabited by Negroes are known; their area is about two million square miles, while the territories occupied by whites comprise more than eight million square miles. And since the former are all desert and totally barren regions, we may reckon that the number of Negroes is at most a twelfth of the number of whites.[59]

In the nineteenth century the widely used P. Weiland *Taalkundig Woordenboek* (Linguistic Dictionary) used examples from popular writings to clarify the definition of "Moor":

> Elsewhere a Moor is a man of black color, with kinky hair and thick lips, like the inhabitants of southern Africa. . . . the phrase, "to scrub a Moor, or Mooriaan," i.e., to do futile work: "Nor will I any longer so diligently wash the Moor,"—H. K. Poot.

"Neger" continued to be used with that same meaning and also spawned a related expression, "negerij" or "negorij," which described any clumping of houses seen to be arranged like an African village.[60] Dictionary entries on these terms grew longer and more confident as the century progressed. One main physical characteristic mentioned in one was "een bijzonder sterk riekend zweet" (a particularly strong, reeking sweat).[61] Interestingly, increasing detail and scientific attention brought more erroneous information:

. . . a race of men belonging to the northwest coast and in the innermost interior of Africa. According to Blumenbach they belong to the Ethiopian race and have a more or less black, greasy and velvety-soft skin; they are of medium height. Their black hair is curly and as fine as wool; their head is small; the jaw and cheekbones jut outward, though the chin is recessed; the lips are thick and curl upward; their eyes are round and white; the nose is broad and flat; they normally have white, even teeth to which they devote much care; they cannot sneeze. They cannot be confused with the Moors of the North Coast of Africa, who are not Negroes. Many naturalists attempt to show that in terms of both material organization and trade practices Negroes can never reach the level of civilization which other, more highly organized peoples, such as, for example, the Celtic tribes, have reached. It may be supposed that when left to themselves they remain on a very low stage of intellectual development. In general Negroes are unfeeling; they very seldom cry and express emotional grief taciturnly, while on the other hand they express the sensual through shouts and song. Thus they are vengeful and appear only, or at least best suited for manual labor.[62]

From excerpts such as these it can be seen that the similar racial ideas of noted nineteenth-century thinkers like Count Joseph Gobineau were actually quite commonplace by then. The brothers Grimm's *Deutsches Wörterbuch* in the late nineteenth century chose to define "Neger" by citing examples from the writings of contemporary luminaries such as Kant, Herder, and Schiller: " . . . die neger von Afrika haben von der natur kein gefühl, welches über das läppische stiege [the African Negro by nature has no feelings which rise above the level of a child]. Kant 7, 435; . . . "[63] One leading Dutch dictionary at the end of the century reflected a continued scientific approach to the definition.

Negroes are also designated as the Ethiopian race (see Races), as are also the Abbysinians, Nubians, Gallas and Somalis, who in many respects differ from the Negroes. The Negroes' color is black; the fumes from their skin have a peculiar, rancid smell which is attributable to the somewhat oily state of their sweat, which generates a sour acid as a result of an unclean lifestyle. . . . Although some tribes are encountered who practice cannibalism, on the whole Negroes are not savages. They practice agriculture and cattle-breeding and various industries; they smelt and work iron, weave and dye cotton goods, and have much aptitude for commerce. They form states, whose government however is mostly horribly despotic. In their religion superstition and fetishism occupy a large space; however Islam is making increasingly greater inroads among Negroes. . . . [64]

The most complete summary of the progression of the definitions of "Moor" and "Negro" at the start of the twentieth century can be found in the *Oxford English Dictionary*, which shows the term "Negro" attached in popular usage not only to people but to fish, fowl, foods, and plants. There was as well the full development of the pejorative "Nigger" and numerous adjectives related to both terms, most of them negative.[65] The most prominent of these terms were also known to educated Dutchmen. In fact, in the *Oxford Dictionary* "Nigger" is said to be an alteration of "Neger." At the same time, in the Dutch language the ancient term "Nikker," which in popular lore meant the devil or various other spirits, had come to be used to describe blacks as well. Meanwhile in the Dutch dictionaries, "blank," although having some negative meanings, continued to describe mainly purity and high quality.[66] In one Dutch encyclopedia of the 1930s half the entry dealt with the unequal status of the Negro in the United States, revealing at the same time an inaccurate understanding of some of the basic facts. No mention is made of their status in the Netherlands or its possessions.[67]

Composed of numerous shades extending from the white Europeans through the yellow Khoi and San of the Cape, the myriad of colors in the East Indies, to blacks in Africa, Asia, and Europe, the color spectrum of the Dutch empire must also be viewed as multidimensional, because the same term may have a different meaning in different parts of the world. By the nineteenth century Dutch dictionaries also included definitions of the terms "creole" and "colored," which also often meant those of black African descent. In their original sense, when applied to people, the Portuguese *crioulo* and the Spanish *criollo* meant anyone born to European parents and brought up in overseas colonies. These terms eventually also came to designate as well those having both European and non-European blood, the related mixed languages and cultures, and even varieties of other animal and plant species. The expression "colored" designated both non-whites in general and those of mixed white and non-white parentage. However, both these terms varied in meaning in different colonies. In Suriname "creole" meant specifically those descended from slaves. In the West Indies in general "colored" described only those of mixed European and Indian or European and African descent and their children. Meanwhile, in South Africa "Coloured" from the eighteenth century applied to people of mixed African, European, or East Indian descent, and sometimes to the Khoi and San peoples whether mixed or not.[68] To further complicate the picture, "mestizo" in Dutch Brazil described those of mixed Indian and European descent, while in the East Indies it meant racial mixture in a more general sense. Mulattoes bore a number of different terms in the West African fortress societies alone. Finally, in one of the most bizarre twists of all, the black Africans in the Dutch East Indian Army were *Blanda Itam* (black Hollanders) and were treated as whites.

The Sum of the Parts

The Dutch world was comprised of much more than its European base. The cultural diversity and dynamism evident in the Netherlands were magnified and manifold in its vast empire. Its ruling class was by definition the bourgeoisie. This presented a sharp contrast to the surrounding conservative "old regimes," which would much more gradually follow a similar course of development toward modernity. The most distinctive feature of this history was the extent to which economics dominated the course of other developments. This was manifest not only in the impetus toward empire, but also in the subordination of the church and social convention to the trading companies in the colonies. Thus for the social structure the concept of class for Dutch society was shaped by economic status and was less rigid than most. Meanwhile, for the colonies, economic expediency eventually outweighed the customs of either the Netherlands or the local areas. A similar pragmatism was evident in the political structures defining the Dutch world. Here was a society equally comfortable under the republican and monarchical regimes, with an infusion of oligarchy in the colonies under the East and West India companies.

In general, there was a great degree of receptivity for the new, regarding the roles of peoples or of things. At the same time, the industriousness of the Dutch exposed them to at least as great a variety of new experiences as any other nation in the world. The character of the Dutch world as a maritime empire would also ensure that the population of the Netherlands would provide a constant flow of information as well as goods to its various components. Not only the government and company officials, but also the thousands of nameless seamen would contribute to this, consciously or not. The fact that perhaps half the sailors were foreigners only further underscores the point.

The most striking overall characteristic of the Netherlands is its modernity. The Netherlands is distinguished among the Western powers as a model of capitalistic enterprise. A visitor to Amsterdam in the 1990s could in a brief stroll through the famous daily open market on the Albert Cuypstraat sample the exotic sights, smells, and sounds which reflect both the legacy of centuries of empire and the more recent "guestworker" elements, all now an integral part of Dutch life. Given the great variety in the Dutch experience, its longevity, and its patently modern character, it lends itself uniquely well to a study of the changing perceptions of race and color in the era of modernization. While I have chosen blacks as the central focus here, both for their conspicuousness and for the potential for comparison with other, related studies, a number of other groups might have been similarly chosen. It is likely in any case that the findings here will have relevance for understanding similar encounters in other societies.

FOLKLORE AS RACIAL GOSPEL

Images of blacks were present in the Netherlands long before there was a significant physical presence. Dutch folklore contains a fascinating array of figures who vividly illustrate this point. This was a result not only of the fact that the emergent independent Netherlands was a former part of the Spanish empire, which was contiguous with North Africa and contained a strong Moorish influence, but also because the Netherlands shared both vicariously and directly in the more general confrontation unfolding between Europe and the wider world. Impressions embedded in the folklore may be the deepest due to their age, and perhaps also the least altered by the modern obsession with consciousness and rationality. Nevertheless, as will be seen, modern developments did have a decisive influence on the forms in which these images have survived.

Black Pete

The American traditional Santa Claus tradition, which did not crystallize until the mid-nineteenth century, is an amalgamation of Father Christmas, brought over by seventeenth-century British settlers, and Sinterklaas, brought by the Dutch to their New Amsterdam.[1] Both of these figures were in turn just two of the myriad offspring of a centuries-old St. Nicholas tradition. As mentioned here in the Introduction, Sinterklaas as practiced in the Netherlands and formerly in Dutch colonies has a component omitted in the nineteenth- and twentieth-century New World adaptation: the Saint has a black companion on his rounds, whose variant names have eventually melded into Zwarte Piet (Black Pete). Unlike the American tradition, Sinterklaas (St. Her[r] Claes) is not observed at Christmas, but rather on the fifth of December, the eve of the day on which St. Nicholas is said to have died. At the end of each November, Sinterklaas appears in Holland in preparation for his treasured visits: Zwarte Piet is at his side. This fabulous duo, whose lineage dates as far back as the Middle Ages, provides a marvelous beginning for tracing imagery relating to blacks in the Netherlands. Their story illuminates a number of the complexities of the subject of color associations and illustrates the impact of historical developments on concepts.

The inspiration for Sinterklaas was the legendary medieval St. Nicholas, the most popular of all the Christian saints, who reached his greatest popularity between the twelfth and sixteenth centuries. The original Nicholas, himself a legendary figure, was a bishop of Myra, in Asia Minor, in the first half of the fourth century. In the Greek Orthodox Church, he was believed to have miraculous powers to protect those threatened by catastrophe. In later centuries, after the Christian faith split into its two main factions, Eastern and Western, the Roman Catholic Church retained Nicholas (in its calendar of saints) and was responsible for his popularity in northern and western Europe too as this region became the center of Western civilization. There he became the patron saint of sailors, which explains his importance in the area which became the Netherlands. He also became associated with benevolence to children (see figure 5).

By the late Middle Ages, he annually commemorated the date of his "birth into heaven" by bearing gifts to all deserving children and punishing the rest with birch switches left for parental use. Dordrecht city records as early as 1360 describe a church-sanctioned St. Nicholas celebration for the children. Records from other areas suggest that such celebration was country-wide.[2] One of the most remarkable aspects of this tradition is the degree to which its essential features have survived unchanged for so many centuries. The splendid 1703 St. Nicholas painting by the Dutch artist Matthys Naiveu includes most of the well-known symbols of the twentieth century. Indeed, St. Nicholas, parading on his white steed through an urban throng, is attired more like the American Santa Claus or an earlier German version than a bishop; and his long, oriental-looking beard is nearly tangled in the heaping bag of toys at his saddle. From available reproductions it is not possible to discern the skin color of the young man who appears to be leading the horse (see figure 6).[3]

In different countries, the St. Nicholas figure had different names but served the same purpose. A similar Christian figure popular in France and Belgium and some parts of the Netherlands is St. Martin.

5. Erve H. Rynders, *St. Nicholas and his servant*. Atlas van Stolk, Rotterdam.

In the Flemish tradition St. Martin also often is aided by a *zwarte piet*. The St. Nicholas legend also absorbed pagan influences. For some, the Germanic supreme deity Wodan (the Norse Odin), an all–powerful deity who was believed to fly through the air on a magic horse each December on the winter solstice, came to be fused with the Saint. The foremost authority on the subject of St. Nicholas, Karl Meisen, discounted pagan origins for the tradition. The Dutchman Adriaan De Groot, among others, insisted that there were both Christian and pagan origins. Given the pattern elsewhere of inevitable mutual borrowings between Christian and pagan rituals, it would seem that De Groot must surely be closer to the truth. There is evidence not only of influence from the Germanic and Celtic folk traditions, but also from ancient Roman and Oriental traditions. The degree of uniformity which the tradition practiced in the Netherlands

6. Matthys Naiveu, *Saint Nicholas*. Swiss Institute for Art Research, Zürich.

achieved by the twentieth century was due to the wide dissemination of *Mannekensbladen*, or *Volksprenten* (children's prints or penny prints), a form of popular print literature widely disseminated in the Netherlands, France, and Belgium, especially in the nineteenth century, through the press and schools. The advent of television, of course, and the commercial incentives related to the celebration brought even greater standardization.[4]

In the Netherlands traces of the dual, Christian-pagan heritage in the Sinterklaas tradition are still evident in some of the more isolated areas. A striking example is the Sinterklazen celebration which still survives on the Waddenzee islands of Ameland, Texel, Vlieland, and Schiermonnikoog. There the folk tradition reveals a winter celebration with some elements which probably preceded the Christianization of the Netherlands. In pagan lore darkness was also the color for death and winter. This lends credibility to the propositions that in some areas of the Netherlands the dark "companion" figures actually predated the Saint and were relegated to a subordinate role only with the increased dominance of Christianity.[5]

Nowhere practiced nowadays in their completely original form, the unique festivals appear a combination of winter festival, puberty rite, fertility rite, and reaffirmation of the local social structure. Masked folk rituals and dances in other parts of Europe during various seasons have similar roots. On the prescribed evenings on Ameland masked, often blackened, men and boys dressed in contrasting black and white trappings would roam the village streets, armed with cudgels and blowing horns, requesting treats from door to door, and ensuring that no house lights were on and no women were out. In the old tradition, if a woman were caught she might be beaten or violated with impunity. Later festivities also featured flirting, dancing, and feasting. Although in modern times the harsh aspects of the game have been softened, the ritual is still observed. In some instances in recent times it has been stylized for tourist consumption. This celebration had many variations, and is also known in other parts of the Netherlands and Belgium. The ghostly, masked figures have variant names. Even on Ameland they are also called *Omes* (uncles). As with Zwarte Piet, chains would trail from the legs of the *klazen* in some locales, recalling as well the Wodan tradition, in which the year's dead are said to be chained until released by the god's annual ride.[6] Thus in its most extreme departure from the standard Sinterklaas tradition, such as on Ameland, this peculiar winter rite could plausibly be viewed as a purely pagan phenomenon.

The survival of the Sinterklaas tradition in the Netherlands was threatened, however, not because of its pagan ancestry, but rather its Christian. That it did survive the concerted attempts of the Calvinist Church and government to root out all vestiges of Catholicism in the late sixteenth and seventeenth centuries testifies to the depth of its hold on the popular imagination. In Amsterdam in the sixteenth and seventeenth centuries the celebration ran for days, with Zwarte Klazen, sometimes called Sunderklazen, making rounds of the neighborhoods, knocking on doors and asking if there were any bad children. From at least as early as the end of the fifteenth century the event climaxed with a Sinterklaas market on the Dam Square on 5–6 December, in which all elements of society participated.

Much to the displeasure of the Reformed Church and city authorities, by the late seventeenth century the array of related booths stretched beyond the square and into other parts of the city. Some of the favorite items which could be purchased were Santa Claus cookies, almond pastry, honey tarts, and marsepein (marzipan). Such merriment in honor of the Catholic Saint prompted the following ordinance in Delft in 1600:

> The setting up of booths on St. Nicholas Eve where goods are sold, which St. Nicholas is said to provide, leads the children astray, and such a practice is not only contrary to all good order, but also leads the people away from the true religion and tends toward atheism, superstition and idolatry, which is not to be tolerated in a civilized Christian Reformed city.

A similar measure in Arnhem in 1622 banned setting out shoes and baking Sinterklaas cake. The authorities responded to continued enjoyment of the all-night revelry which eventually characterized the eves of St. Nicholas, New Years, and the Epiphany with other special ordinances. Among surviving copies are those of 1663 and 1698 in Amsterdam and almost identical ones from Haarlem in 1643 and 1686.[7] Neither the Protestant Reformation in general nor the triumph of Calvinism over Catholicism in the Netherlands was able to root out this "vestige of popery." Small wonder; for the cookie dolls depicting the Saint, other notables, and various sacrificial animals, were themselves graphic testimony to the limits of the Catholic Church's success in curtailing the tradition of edible graven images of Germanic gods and symbols already practiced in this region long before the coming of Christianity. The Reformed Church was going to have to settle for transforming what had been a more formal religious celebration of St. Nicholas into essentially a children's feast.[8]

The historical convergence of the Christian and pagan traditions seems the best explanation of the origin of the Saint's dark companion. In his study of the northern European variations, Meisen found innumerable names and modifications of the same name. Among the most widely used in the Germanies, the Netherlands, Belgium, and Switzerland were Ruprecht the Knecht (servant), schwarzer Kaspar (Black Caspar), schwarze Peter (Black Peter), zwarte Piet, Pieterman, Le More, Pére Fouettard, Schmutzli, Krampus, and Leutfresser. All these terms originally referred to the devil. Ruprecht the Knecht and some of the others were at times depicted as dark, hairy, and with horns. All were associated with darkness and debasement in contrast to the noble, white Saint. Ruprecht is also one of the nicknames for Wodan, which makes the splitting of the Germanic chief deity another possible origin of the St. Nicholas pairs, comparable to the Christian dichotomy between good and evil. People portraying these figures have customarily covered their faces with soot or ashes. In all the societies in question they were used as bogeyman images to instill obedience in children. Some of them were said to wear chains, which aided the Saint in controlling them, and themselves in turn in instilling fear in the children, merely by rattling the chains.[9]

In addition to their preemptive pagan origins, it is possible that personification of the dark *klazen* was for centuries more permissible than that of the bishop because of the difficulty of displaying images of Catholic saints in the Calvinist Netherlands. Therefore, when it became more acceptable to show Sinterklaas, it is not surprising that the *klazen* lived on in the guise of Zwarte Piet, who himself did not appear in graphic illustrations of the Sinterklaas celebration until the nineteenth century. He was, after all, a spiritual force. For contemporary viewers of Jan Steen's famous painting of the morning after the gifts arrived, Sinterklaas and Zwarte Piet were no less present despite the absence of any visual reference to them. It should be noted that in some regions Sinterklaas's *knecht* is called Jan or Jan de knecht. However, an extensive survey conducted in the 1930s showed that in most regions, including Friesland, respondents identified the Saint's companion as Zwarte Piet.[10]

Another evidence of the fusing of pagan and Christian strains is that Zwarte Piet in antique Dutch folklore is the name for the devil. When he first joined Sinterklaas, it was as a servant—caught and chained for the celebration each year. The two would ride over the roof tops and the good Saint would make Piet drop candy and presents down the chimneys and into children's shoes left out for the occasion (see figure 7). Piet also wielded the switches. Even worse, he

7. J. Schenkman, *He looks below*. From *Het Prentenboek van Tante Pau* (The Hague, 1974).

carried a sack in which he would take bad children away. Over the centuries, Zwarte Piet has become a more positive figure, more of a partner. Another part of the Dutch tradition is that Sinterklaas resides in Spain most of the year, just as Santa Claus lives at the North Pole. By some accounts, Zwarte Piet was a Moorish orphan boy whom Sinterklaas adopted and trained as his assistant. In keeping with this scenario, at least since the nineteenth century Sinterklaas parades in Dutch towns have assumed his initial "arrival" by ship in Dutch harbors.

In the towns, Sinterklaas rides in a horsedrawn carriage or mounted upon a white horse, accompanied by marching bands and local dignitaries. Zwarte Piet, a Dutchman or woman in blackface and dressed in the fashion of sixteenth-century Spain, walks alongside holding the reins so that the Saint, resplendent in his bishop's miter and holding his staff in one hand, will be able to wave to all the faithful, which in this case includes Protestants and Jews and others as well as Catholics. In most instances, the parade will have numerous Zwarte Piets who distribute sweets to children along the way. Some of the children may also be made up as Piets. Analyzing all this symbolism, De Groot arrived at a Jungian psychoanalytical interpretation, finding the Nicholas tradition to be full of sexual motifs. Hence, Zwarte Piet is Sinterklaas's phallic servant, carrying a staff which he pounds against objects; riding the houses; going down the chimneys; finding closed ovens in the houses containing sweets; leaving sweets beside the fire, and gifts in empty shoes. De Groot concludes:

> Taken together, St. Nicholas and Black Pete can be seen to represent—as does the Saint riding his white horse—the dyadic unity of flesh and spirit, of animal and man, the integration of instinctual drive and moral mastery.[11]

Regardless of the validity of this interpretation, it points up graphically the relevance of this legend for the present study. An almost identical juxtaposition of European civilization and real black peoples became conventional wisdom in modern times if not before, complete even with the erotic overtones. Therefore, the assertion by some observers, in the debate that has erupted since the 1980s, that Zwarte Piet was not intended to represent a Negro and should therefore have no place in a discussion of racism is not convincing. It may well be, as one scholar has pointed out, that the theme of "the little black boys" can be traced in an hagiography going back through Gregory's *Dialogues* and Athanasius's *Life of Anthony*; but that does not preclude a transfer of negative associations from imaginary figures of no defined race to real people whose appearance is reminiscent of the negative abstraction.[12] A related assertion that the real-life figure upon which Zwarte Piet is based is the chimney sweep, rather than a Moor or Negro, is equally unconvincing. Chimneys and the sweepers arrived in the Netherlands only in the seventeenth century, far too late to serve as model. It is much more likely that chimney sweeps, like blacks, have been at times embarrassed to be mistaken for Zwarte Piet, who was already well established before either of them arrived.[13]

The typical Dutch attitude toward Zwarte Piet is highly positive. Just the mention of him will bring a smile and a twinkle to the eye of even the most somber adult. There are invariably memories from childhood of being warned that Zwarte Piet would come and carry them away if they did not behave. On the other hand, imbued with the charity and understanding for which his saintly master is famous,

8. *A Visit from St. Nicholas.* Atlas van Stolk, Rotterdam.

Piet also is respected for his fairness and ability to reward good deeds. Such a responsible and admired figure should not be identified with the pure buffoon image projected by American minstrel shows, of which his blackface visage is reminiscent. However, at the same time, it seems quite apparent that the Dutch feeling toward Zwarte Piet has to be somewhat ambivalent: respect tinged with apprehension.

Meanwhile, some of the black public witnessed the heightened tension, mentioned in the Introduction, that has appeared as blacks from the former colonies have immigrated to the Netherlands. Some Surinamer men there before the recent influx recall how they would good-naturedly smile and play the role when during the period of the Sinterklaas celebration Dutch children would take them to be Zwarte Piet. However, amid reports of an increasing number of incidents of embarrassment of children in black families, and in the wake of demands from small elements in the black communities urging elimination of this part of the celebration, some groups have begun practicing versions of the celebration omitting Zwarte Piet. A video film entitled "We doen het voor de kinderen" (We do it for the children), made in Curaçao in 1981 by black Antilleans in the Cultural Media Collective, dramatizes this theme, asserting that this tradition is indeed harmful for children's self-esteem. It was shown also in the Netherlands. It appears certain now that Zwarte Piet, born evil, elevated to innocence over the centuries, has again lost some of his innocence.[14]

The Moor

Zwarte Piet was just one manifestation of the most pervasive theme related to blacks in Dutch folklore: that of "the Moor." This theme was expressed in many forms and had a number of quite diverse meanings. Its origins are undoubtedly related to the Netherlands' heritage as a former part of the Spanish empire, which had contained Moorish influence in its population and its armies. The theme of "the Moor" as it developed in the Netherlands, however, though inspired by historical experience, fostered a colorful legacy all its own. It first appeared in Dutch heraldry as early as the thirteenth century, in literature in the fourteenth, and in religious themes and various standard symbols and decorations thereafter. Its role in literature, religion, and art will be treated in subsequent chapters. The present topic is its other uses.

Heraldry

The origin of the widespread European adoption of the *Moorkop* ("Moor's head") as a symbol for family and town coats of arms is highly ambiguous. For example, it is not surprising to encounter such imagery in fifteenth-century arms of the islands of Sardinia and Corsica, sitting in the middle of the Mediterranean, belonging to the African and Moslem world as well as the European, and washed by centuries of foreign conquest from all directions. Much harder to explain is the manifest greater popularity of this symbol in northern Europe than in Spain or Italy. By the time heraldry reached the peak of its development in the fourteenth and fifteenth centuries, this symbol could be found in the far reaches of northern and eastern Europe as well as in the Mediterranean region. Later it could be found as far north as the small community of Marken in North Holland.[15] The

MOORREES.

9. Coat of Arms of the Moorrees Family. Author's collection.

most frequent line of explanation views this symbol as a form of trophy, celebrating the victory of Christendom over the Moslems in
various battles. However, it appears to have been more popular in
Germany than in France, although France played a larger role in the
Crusades.[16]

The presence of this symbol in the Netherlands can be traced in
part to the degree to which the Low Countries' population was constituted largely of families from elsewhere, in part to the importance
of its commercial centers, with linkages to the outside world, and in
part to imitation of fashions current elsewhere in Europe. Nevertheless, it is somewhat astonishing to encounter over a dozen arms with
Moors' heads in an eighteenth-century book depicting crests from
Groningen Province.[17] For some of the Dutch families using this emblem the name itself suggests the reason. Such is the case for the families Moorman and Moorrees (figure 9); that of the sixteenth-century

Vice-Admiral Joos de Moor of Zeeland; and the Van Schwartz family in Drenthe. This, however, calls forth the unanswered question of the name's origin and significance. The coat of arms of Christopher van Schwartz in the eighteenth century features perhaps the most handsome depiction of a "Moor," a standing figure in a golden crown serving as the top piece of the design. At the other extreme is the crest of Jacob Le Maire, a sixteenth-century mariner from Antwerp who explored around Cape Horn. In his family crest are six caricatured Moors' heads and six swine heads.[18] Although heraldic symbols became less frequently displayed after the Middle Ages, they could still be seen in places where the wealthy wanted to announce their presence. One example is the churches, where coats of arms of notable families buried there would hang for centuries. They would also adorn family property, including the luxury carriages in which they rode about.[19]

For most of the families there is no apparent reason for use of the Moor as symbol (see figures 10–13). The Luls family from Utrecht has a coat of arms which is comprised entirely of a Moor's head. What does seem clear is that in most cases it is purely a symbol and has no ethnic significance. One researcher from a Dutch family whose arms bear Moors' heads did trace its origin back to the thirteenth century and participation in the Crusades. According to legend in the Boutmy family, two brothers from the family distinguished themselves in battle in the Holy Land and the one who survived later adopted this family name, which connotes valor in battle. The coat of arms, which goes back at least to the eighteenth century, bears two Moors' heads wearing blindfolds, along with other symbols such as lions and castles. This coat of arms has been used by branches of the family in the Netherlands, Belgium, France, Russia, and Rumania.[20] The meaning of the Moors' heads and blindfolds is not known. One obvious possible meaning, of course, is victory over the Moors. However, Moors' heads and torsos appear in so many forms in European heraldry that no single explanation seems acceptable. Although the blindfolds are unusual, they also appear in a few other family crests in Europe. Some have considered them marks of imprisonment.[21]

The Gaper

Another guise in which "the Moor" appeared in the Dutch experience was in the form of "the Gaper," the favorite trade symbol of the

10. Coat of Arms of the Schuyl van der Does
Family. Author's collection.

11. Coat of Arms of the
De Balbian van Doorn
Family. Author's
collection.

12. Coat of Arms of the Brouerius van Nidek Family. Author's collection.

Brouerius van Nidek.

von Löben Sels.

13. Coat of Arms of the Von Löben Sels Family. Author's collection.

apothecary, druggist, and chemist in the Netherlands from the Middle Ages on to the present. The use of a human head with mouth agape and tongue sticking out has never been fully explained. What is known is that this symbol was employed at times in earlier centuries in western Germany, Italy, and northern France as well as the entire Netherlands. For some reason it became especially popular in the northern Netherlands. In Zeeland there was a small community that carried the name Gapinge until 1868 (now Vrouwenpolder Gemeente). A number of towns had street and house names with "Gaper" in them. Since they were usually made of wood and constantly hung outdoors, few original gapers could survive more than a century or so. Today the number hanging outdoors is quickly dwindling, although the symbol may still also be seen inside in some drugstores. Meanwhile, a few craftsmen continue to carve new heads, while most of the older ones now rest in museums and private collections.[22]

These heads evolved in great variety, often designated as Arab, Turk, Javanese, or Moor, although a great number bore a European visage. Tailored to local tastes, some wore the garb of fishermen, policemen, or jesters. There were even a few women. The faces thus represented a color spectrum from white to coal black and exhibited expressions ranging from innocence to humor or rage. Some were busts with a monkey on one shoulder. Their headwear also displayed great diversity and color, featuring sleeping caps, turbans, helmets, and crowns (see figures 14–16). One of the most striking of the "Moorish" Gapers was that which sat outside the Leiden apothecary De Blauwe Arend (The Blue Eagle) in the mid-eighteenth century, with a golden helmet and red garb contrasting with jet-black complexion and out-thrust tongue.[23]

The most plausible explanation for the curious pose of the Gaper is that it represents the patient opening wide for the doctor and sticking out the tongue for examination. However, clues for completely unraveling the rest of his mystery are hopelessly buried in the sands of time. In a discussion on this subject in a folklore journal in the 1930s, one participant cited one scholar who had pointed out that in earlier times people placed images of monsters with tongues hanging out on buildings in order to ward off evil spirits.[24] Pursuing the question further in the 1950s, another writer offered a quite novel perspective that has some appeal to those aware of changing historical contexts. He surmised that the Gaper represents the assistant who in earlier

14. The Gaper from
the Leiden apothecary
"De Blauwe Arend"
(The Blue Eagle)
in the mid–eighteenth
century.
Municipal Museum "De
Lakenhal," Leiden/The
Netherlands.

15. A Gaper in Ter Aar, near Leiden. Author's photo.

16. A Gaper on Haarlemmer Straat in Leiden, 1986. Author's photo.

centuries had accompanied the quack doctors, the major purveyors of popular medicine who would set up tents at the marketplace, and who were precursors of the later apothecaries with shops. He notes that such helpers were often colored, which would explain why colored Gapers appeared to be the most prevalent. One of their roles was first to draw a crowd to their master's tent by making faces and other antics, and then to entertain in order to allow the medicine man and customers more privacy. The peculiar head outside the apothecary shop is then an allusion to the traditional assistant. In another twist on the entertainment interpretation, one apochryphal hypothesis speculates that the Gapers were placed along the streets to prompt the overly phlegmatic Dutch to healthy laughter, which outsiders felt they lacked in their character. In a similar vein, another cited Bredero's play *Moortje*, in concluding that black heads were so popular for signs because they "gave pleasure to the fairer sex."[25]

One other explanatory element about which there is consensus is that the symbol is directly linked to the Eastern trade. Here the point most often made is that Europeans associated certain spices and herbs as well as advanced medical knowledge with the East. Hence the persistence of Arabs, Turks, and Moors as symbols among peoples who had never seen them in life. It is not certain when the depiction of the Gaper as a Moor began; however, there is evidence that the practice dates at least from the early sixteenth century. For example, an apothecary shop in Oudenaarde in 1609 was called "t Moriaenshooft" (the Moor's Head), and that same name appeared on houses in Amsterdam as early as 1550, and in the next century including that of the apothecary Willem Lambertsen, who lived in "het Gecroonde Moriaenshooft" (the Crowned Moor's Head) on Reestraat. An eighteenth-century gable stone in Maastricht bearing the image of a Gaper includes a similar house name.[26]

The Smoking Moor

The tobacco trade was another which conjured up exotic symbols in the Netherlands. By the middle of the seventeenth century, this commodity was a major element in the Dutch carrying trade and the domestic economy. In addition to managing works for drying, cutting, and spinning tobacco leaves from the Americas, the Dutch were raising and exporting millions of pounds of their own. Evidence of the extent of related enterprises is that by one count around 16,000 people from Gouda alone were employed in the pipe-making industry. The great profitability of this trade overwhelmed the church's efforts to discourage it and smoking became an integral part of the culture, practiced by women as well as men, and with chewing tobacco and snuff soon becoming alternatives to the pipe.[27] There were consequently hundreds of shops throughout the country. Like the apothecaries and druggists, these shops too bore distinctive business signs. In this instance the most prevalent was a human figure of some type smoking a pipe. The most popular variant was the Smoking Moor (*rookende Moor*; see figure 17). As with the Gaper, the reason for this is not completely clear. After all, the original source of tobacco for the Dutch, and still that of the best quality, was the Americas. It is therefore understandable why some merchants used representations of American Indians for their store signs and others pictures of tobacco planters. However, here too the Moor seems to have captured the

17. A Smoking Moor.
The Groninger Museum,
Groningen.

Dutch imagination more completely. He could often be encountered
as a full standing wooden figure in front of the shop or in bust form
on tobacco boxes, packages, or pouches.[28]

The Smoking Moor in the Netherlands, who had similar relatives
all over Europe, was a fusion of history and fantasy which captured
uniquely well the nebulous response in Europe to the exposure to new
worlds and new sensations. With respect to the image of blacks it
brought another example of the growing interchangeability of the
terms "Negro" and "Moor," which persisted into the eighteenth century. At the same time, the odd figure of the Smoking Moor often
showed mixtures of black African, American Indian, East Asian, and
Middle Eastern physical traits.[29] The indistinctness of this symbol for

the tobacco trade suggests that the main prerequisite was that it be exotic, with little importance placed on accuracy or precision. It was enough that it seemed from another world. The Moor had long been the main symbol of trade contacts with the outside world. The black African could be associated with tobacco both because African slaves in the New World cultivated it and because African peoples were thought to be highly sensual.

African Images in Dutch Place Names

The practice of including the term "Moor" in street names began in the Low Countries as early as the sixteenth century. In 1550 Moriaan-straat was named in Antwerp, and under the name "Kleine Moriaan-straat" it came to feature a series of houses bearing names such as "Coninck van de Mooren" (King of the Moors), "Coninginne van de Mooren" (Queen of the Moors), "Moriaens hooft," "Kint van den Moriaen" (the Moor's Child), "Slave van den Moriaen" (the Moor's Man Slave), and "Slavinne van den Moriaen" (The Moor's Slave Woman).[30] Such names can best be attributed to Antwerp's prominent role in world trade at the time. One house on Moriaanstraat was occupied for a time by representatives of the Hanseatic League.[31] A number of the merchant families there had Moors' heads in their coats of arms as well.

A similar naming of houses in Amsterdam around this same time has been mentioned in connection with the apothecary shops. The practice also appeared as far north as Groningen province, where, according to local legend, a room in one of the castles near the town of Pieterburen became known as the *Moorjanenkamer* (The Moor's Room) after a brutal murder was committed there. As the story goes, the provincial governor of North Holland, Diederik Sonoy, was residing as a guest of his son-in-law in Dijksterhuis Castle along with his black servant of twenty years when the mysterious event occurred. During their stay the servant was said to have become attracted to one of the castle's housemaids. It was alleged that he killed both her and her preferred lover in a jealous rage after she rejected him. He was beheaded for his crime on October 20, 1596.[32]

The extent to which it is instructive to speak of an international "Dutch World" during these centuries is attested by the Dutch application of African names in the Netherlands as readily as they applied

Dutch names in Africa, the Americas, and Asia. A recent study published by the Meertens Instituut voor Dialectologie, Volkskunde en Naamkunde in Amsterdam found that the choice of related place names in the Netherlands mirrored a fluctuating image of Africa there as contacts increased from the seventeenth century. As early as the sixteenth century a section of Leiden was named "Klein Egypten"(Little Egypt). This study, by Robert Rentenaar, deliberately omitted city house names and those of cafes, inns, forts, and other establishments because they were so numerous and difficult to explain. However, it does include farms, manor houses, and country inns, especially useful here because most earlier existing information on the subject is from urban areas.

The study identifies thirty-three African names which appear in various form in 121 settings in the Netherlands, spread over the eleven provinces existing at the time of the publication. It treats both official names and those adopted in the folk tradition. When the sample is spread over the provinces, Groningen has the highest percentage, with Friesland next, followed by South Holland. Zeeland and North Holland show only 9.9 percent and 8.3 percent of the total, respectively, compared to 14.9 percent for Groningen. In further comparison of North and South, Limburg has the same number as North Holland, thus far fewer than Groningen and Friesland.[33]

"Egypt" (33) and "Transvaal" (20) lead the list of African names borrowed, followed by "Abessenië," "Bocht van Guinea," "Kongo," and "Sahara." The author notes that as Gypsies appeared in the Netherlands from 1420 on they were at first called Egyptians, and he conjectures that this may have accounted for the place names in some instances. Obviously historical events such as Napoleon's exploits, the opening of the Suez Canal, and the Boer War were also prominent sources. The Cape and Gold Coast, where the Dutch presence was greatest, inspired street and tavern names from the seventeenth century forward. Meanwhile, wealthy neighborhoods in the Netherlands, as elsewhere, were named "Gold Coast," with other African names also used to designate the lower class or undeveloped quality of a site.[34]

One interesting question raised, but not fully answered, by Rentenaar's study is: why did the most dominant trading provinces, that is, North Holland and Zeeland, not lead in this practice of African naming? To be sure, Groningen was a major actor in international trade from as early as its role in the medieval Hanseatic League. Its commercial stature declined after the fifteenth century when the shifts occurring in major trading routes and the rise of the Flemish cities as trading centers diminished its significance. Thus, by the time it became part of the new United Provinces of the Netherlands it had passed the peak of its importance. Another factor working against Groningen was that the size of the modern international shipping vessels increased faster than the Groningers could alter the surrounding waterways to accommodate the larger vessels. Consequently, although Groningen was an important participant in the West India Company and exported goods to Brazil, Gambia, Curaçao, and Suriname, these goods had to be sent first by small boats to Amsterdam. Likewise, most goods from Africa and the New World came indirectly to the northernmost provinces.[35] Nevertheless, many of the leading families of Groningen and the surrounding area, that is, those most responsible for naming places, did have ties with the outside world, either through emigration or through involvement in trade. As in the case of the high incidence of Moors' heads in the coats of arms, these links with the outside world seem to offer the most plausible line for further study.

Bogeymen

Of the various categories of imagery in Dutch folklore, none holds more potential relevance to the formation of attitudes toward blacks than the rich menagerie of bogeymen in the Dutch tradition. The earlier discussion of this side of the character of Zwarte Piet presents the single best example of this. There are as well a number of other interesting figures who should be mentioned, although no others have achieved a degree of universality nor persistence comparable to Zwarte Piet. One close relative is called "De Zwarte Man" (The Black Man), who inspired the following verses:

The Black Man

Groetmoeke would like to read peacefully;
The children grumble and misbehave;

But father threatens: "You must keep still!
Hold your peace, I tell you!"

And Moeke says: "You're making such a fuss,
That the whole neighborhood can hear you;
Just you wait, I'll fix you,
Here comes the Black Man now."

And yo! There he is, black as
A Negro, disguised from head to toe;
He has much of the look of a chimney sweep;
The children are struck dumb with fear.
They don't dare look anymore,
Not one of them still stirs;
They look at him with fearful glances;
Look, how the children, gaze at him!

And when he goes, Mother says: "Children,
What you just saw, remember it well!
The Black Man will come again,
As often as you do bad things."

And he doesn't only come for children,
Whenever he sees their naughtiness,
But for grownups too.
Doors and locks and bolts don't keep him out.

He'll hold a grudge against an adult,
And threaten you only now and then,
Grownups call him conscience,
You just call him the Black Man.[36]

Here we have the classic bogeyman, and he is cast as the symbol for conscience, especially for children. His main objective is the positive one of promoting proper conduct; but his primary means is through instilling fear.

Bogeymen in general serve mainly to enforce social conventions, especially those not readily translatable into a child's logic. Hence in the Dutch tradition there were countless creatures to discourage engaging in such equally diverse activities as running through the grain fields, going out at night, looking in the mirror, eating too many snacks, playing in the woods, and going barefooted. One figure which could be used to discourage a number of these was "Tenensnijder" (the Toe Cutter), who also was known by several similar names. He was said to carry a knife or a spade, with which to cut off the toes of disobedient children. In one version he is featured as a headless and legless, black triangular figure.[37] A variation on this is "Man Zonder Poten" (Legless Man), who is also sometimes featured as black.

Then there are "Pietje Roet" (Little Sooty Peter), who punishes those who play in the street or in the woods, and "Zwarte Hannes" (Black Hans), who forbids sitting on the side of ditches, going outside alone, and laughing and playing in bed. These pitch-black figures, sometimes viewed as synonymous with the devil, emerge from the fireplace and take wrongdoers back with them. A related figure is the "Zwarte Hand" (Black Hand). Women are also represented in this array, in the form of the "Zwarte Wief" (Black Wife). There is also the "Zwarte Ruiter" (Black Horseman); the "Doezeman," black, bearded, large teeth, long fingers; and the "Kopere Ko," a completely black figure who appears rattling chains and copper tins in which he carries off naughty children. Uniquely contrasting apparitions are the ghostly *Blanke Negers* (White Negroes), fishermen who put in at the harbor of Terschelling.[38]

For the present discussion it is fascinating that the only creatures actually referred to here as Negroes are white! However, the likening of the Zwarte Man to a Negro in color shows that the bridge between fantasy and reality may often be very short. As in the case of Zwarte Piet, some looking in the real world for human types with which to associate the black monsters in the world of the imagination are drawn to comparisons using black people. The sketchy tale of the *Blanke Negers* suggests also that there existed some frightening notion about "Negroness" apart from the black color usually associated with it. The question of why various cultures use different colors to symbolize variant qualities is one which needs more study. Its complexity is amply illustrated by a comparative glance at other cultures within the Dutch empire alone. For example, the various styles of *Wayang kulit*, the shadow puppet theater of Indonesia, feature black figures with varying meaning among the profusion of colors offset by shadows and motion.

At the same time, white figures in this tradition also do not always represent good. In the culture which evolved among the Maroons (Bush Negroes) in Suriname at least one religious ceremony involved smearing the face with white clay and the eyes with rum to redden them. One form of festive dance began with the chant "*bakra-boen*" (white is good), which would continue while dancers whirled into exhaustion, becoming "possessed" by the spirits in which they believed. The dancers would dress in their finest; white was one of the favorite colors. One of the most famous dancers, a woman named Api Jaba, whenever she became "possessed" rode around on a white goat. In the folk tales from the African tradition the spirits rarely assume any human form. The Anansi the Spider tales popular in all the African creole cultures is the best example.[39]

Music

Dutch Music

I'm Lubbert Gerritsz, and here I come home.
Say, isn't my outfit fine?
The wide pants, the musty pipe,
The ribbons on the hat?
I never worry about discomfort or sorrow:
I sail from sea to sea.
I have a friend at every port,
A little woman on every route.

In Amsterdam I have a blond.
A soft and gentle sheep;
Brown is my gal from Maassluis,
The one at the Cape is white:
Reddish on the Potomac,
And jet black in Guinea.
I have a friend in every port,
a woman on every route.[40]

Dutch folk music provides another rich resource for expression of attitudes toward race and color. The raucous song above echoes the universal cry of the vagabond sailor. Given the import of maritime commerce for the Netherlands, it also reflects the ready pragmatism of the Dutch in their encounter with the outside world. The Dutch traditional music also contained a more sentimental chord sharply contrasting to the above. This is apparent in a song popular around the end of the nineteenth century, judging from its numerous versions:

Folklore as Racial Gospel

The Indian Flower Girl (or the Beloved Slave)

Do you wish to fly from me, oh stranger,
Across the wild ocean,
Where the smell of the summer fruits
Can no longer refresh you,
Or have you not pledged to me eternal loyalty
Along the peaceful fields?
And now do you want to go give yourself away;
Oh, stay by me in the Land of the Moors.

I will do everything—I will slave for you,
And do all that you command,
I will line your path with roses,
And with palms from the Moors' land;
I will risk my life for you,
As you stroll along the beach.

But I see you already rushing through the sea;
While I weep and wander along the shore
I hear you already counting the days,
Which carry you to your Fatherland;
Well fly away then, unmoved,
to Europe's shore.
If you desire the one who has sworn loyalty to you,
She dies from pain in the Land of the Moors.[41]

The pervasive, nebulous notion of the "Moor" and his land thus runs through the traditional music as well as through the other aspects of folklore treated here. In fact there are musical adaptations of some of the very same themes. In the Sinterklaas tradition, for example, we find:

Here comes the good man Santa Claus
Once again from Spain
On his famous flying horse;
And his servant, the black fellow
Carries a big wide sack
Filled with toys and cookies and cakes.
In the evening as the wooden shoes sit ready
And we hope to go to sleep,
Dear good Santa comes
And brings gifts to children who've been good.

But the one who has been lazy and bad
    will get a grout from him instead.[42]

Tiere, liere, liere,
The little dog sits by the fire;
The cat licks the saucers,
The birds carry the sand;
From behind in the laughter
They fought because the plums were stewing
The cuckoo was always on top.
The cuckoo and the lawreke
Fought around a church!
I heard the bells of Moors' land
From Moors' land to Spain,
Apple from Orange,
Girl from kadeederidee
Brings along the seven sacks
The sacks are for sale,
Ten pounds size
Ten and a half
My cow is no calf
My horse is no pig
Day after tomorrow is St. Nicholas Eve.[43]

Countless variations on these and similar verses form a major part of the annual Sinterklaas celebration in the Netherlands on down to the present day. The figure of the Moor also entered into the broader stream of children's songs. The favorite such piece for untold generations, "Mooriantje al zwart als roet" (Little Moor as black as soot) knows countless renditions. These are but a few:

A Little Moor as black as soot
Once went strolling without a hood
The sun shone on his noggin
And so he carried a parasol.
Shut the door; shut it tight,
Go to bed and kiss your wife.[44]

Little Moor Jan as black as jet
Went out walking without a hat.
And the sun shone on her head
And so she carried a parasol

Folklore as Racial Gospel

Close the door to the house
Go to bed and kiss your spouse.
Little parrot, do you still love?
Yes sir, here I sit
I have eaten up my food
I have left my drink alone
And then to bed have gone.[45]

Little Moor, black as soot
Once went walking without a hood
The sun shone on her noggin ball
So she carried a parasol
Little Moor, are you still there?
Yes sir, Yes sir, I'm still here.
I've eaten up my food,
Left my drink alone,
And to my bed have gone.[46]

The survival of versions of this jingle to the present, in approximately
the same form, and long after the term "little Moor" has lost its original content, testifies to the depth of its roots in the culture. The
combination of the delight in thinking about a little Moor in the sun,
the mildly didactic function of the verses, and the infectious rhythm
and rhyme involved seem irresistible even for those who cannot explain what the lines mean. Viewed in isolation, this cycle of verses'
use of the image of the Moor could be dismissed as insignificant and
random. However, it can now be seen that it is part of a much broader
cultural pattern. Another illustration, one which will be discussed in
more detail in the later treatment of children's literature, is the popular nursery rhyme "Tien Kleine Negertjes" (Ten Little Niggers):

10 little niggers:
On an untracked road:
One fell and broke a leg,
Then there were just 9
(etc.)

This jingle, still sung by teachers and pupils in the Netherlands today,
is generally thought of as a cute, harmless counting exercise. It is an
offspring of the 1860s American minstrel show ditty "Ten Little In-
juns" and its British descendant "Ten Little Nigger Boys."[47] Myriad

Dutch versions were probably directly inspired by earlier German renditions.

Black Music

Up to this point the discussion has been about purely imaginary black personages. A different way in which music influenced popular notions about blacks in Dutch society was through the reaction of the Dutch to the music of blacks once they began to have extensive contacts. This was most clearly evident in the colonies in Suriname and the Antilles, where the Europeans found themselves immersed in the music of field workers, rowers, and urban dwellers. The songs and dances of the slaves and free blacks affected the European image of blacks in two main ways. On the one hand they served to reinforce concepts and stereotypes which were already part of the European culture. On the other, they raised the level of apprehension and misunderstanding in the masters' attitudes toward the subordinate groups.

At the heart of the issue was the strangeness of the African-based cultural forms. This resulted in comparative analysis of the contrasting Western and African music and religion reminiscent of the debates over racial types, continuing on to the present day. Dutch observers and commentators from the eighteenth century forward repeatedly remarked upon the monotone nature of the singing and dancing, which often went together. The music was nearly always described as highly simple, barely deserving to be called music. One writer called it noise lacking melody, rhythm, or harmony and gave this as one reason Spanish music became the favorite in polite society in Suriname instead of native traditions. However, somewhat contradictorily, the slaves are at times described as brutal, thievish, and vengeful by nature and at others as happy-go-lucky.[48]

The African music's "primitive" character and its preference for the minor key are repeatedly tied to its origins in the "oppressive nature of the tropics," an environment viewed as promoting melancholy and superstition.[49] Some Europeans also marveled at the ease with which the Blacks could master the European hymns and street music and especially their facility in choral singing and harmonizing without training. The hymns and other music borrowed through contact with the Moravian and Catholic missionaries, the military, and other Europeans served not only as the only music they did in a major key but also as the basis for improvisation, sometimes derisive, at which they excelled.[50] However, rather than suspecting that this was a sign that their subordinates were at least as accomplished as musicians, if not more so, the Europeans instead concluded that the differences in taste and talent only reinforced their own sense of superiority.

Western-European music was proclaimed to have reached the status of true art and to be the universal standard for civilized music.[51] Hence any African contribution to the popular Spanish American music could be attributed simply to the beneficial influence on the African of association with the European. The blacks who moved to the city were viewed as more refined because they became more European and civilized. The music of the Maroons was then of course the crudest because it was the most African. On into the twentieth century a debate has continued about the concept of "niggerishness," a term used to describe surviving distinctive black cultural traits, and one pressuring members of the black community as well to dissociate themselves from their heritage even if they still found it attractive. One writer cited the displacement of North American jazz in popularity by the Latin American rhythms influenced by it as further evidence of the superiority of the Spanish music.[52]

Alongside the general rejection and denigration of the African music by the Europeans on cultural grounds there ran a stream of apprehension. This has been best summarized by Rudolf van Lier:

> Due to the contradiction now between the belief in their innate superiority and their contempt for the slaves—and their fear of them—the slave masters developed a dualistic reaction pattern that created psychiatric difficulties for them. The impotence which confronted them in cases where they could not impose their wills on the slaves offended their sense of pride and made the ambivalent situation doubly painful. This impotence is strongest when it concerns religious matters: when this was the case slaves went completely their own way. Yet, any attempt to prevent the slaves from expressing their religious practices brought with it great dangers.[53]

The most tangible events the masters feared were slave uprisings and poisoning of masters. There was, however, as well a certain fear of the unknown and unimaginable. In reference to the question of religion Van Lier also reminds us that the Europeans no less than the

Africans still took witchcraft and demons very seriously, even if the prosecutions and burnings for suspected witches commonplace in fifteenth-century Europe were no longer sanctioned. The mere existence of these religious practices which they did not understand by peoples they often oppressed was a serious source of alarm, and one further inducement to Christianize the Africans. The songs and dances of the slaves and free blacks were a constant reminder of both the real and the unknown causes for apprehension.

These fears were stoked in part by reality and in part by imagination. There was, of course, the very real history of warfare between the Dutch government and the Maroons, which though regulated through treaty did not totally end the flight of slaves periodically to join the independent tribes. Such flight was said on one occasion to have been first announced by the following song on the day before the escape: "Mass'ra tama'ra joe no sa si wi mo'ro, miauw!" (Master, tomorrow you won't see us anymore, miaow!). The next day all the slaves on the plantation were gone.[54] The blacks developed their own code songs for various purposes. One visitor asked slaves in Suriname the meaning of the following song, which he often heard sung with a joyous lilt: "Mackareelen zaterdag, mackareelen zondag, mackareelen alle dag, enz" (Mackerel Saturday, mackerel Sunday, mackerel everyday, etc.). He was perhaps far too gullible in accepting the explanation that this was a celebration of the fact that slaves on plantations had a more varied diet than free blacks in the cities dependent upon their own resources.[55]

Another type of historical event giving rise to concern were the periodic slave uprisings in Suriname and surrounding areas. It is almost certain, for example, that by the early nineteenth century the slaves in Suriname and the Antilles got word of the Haitian Revolution, since some even traveled to Europe and back with their masters. It was also rumored that there existed a secret order among blacks and mulattoes in Suriname, which had originated in Africa.[56] Some may have been reassured by this Paramaribo street song still known in the mid-nineteenth century: "Arabi na' Pambo ben senni njoesoe: Soesoetei! no broko hatti o: alla joe kondre de na reti kab à" (Arabi and Pambo have made it known: Authorities! don't be anxious: your whole land is peaceful and orderly). However, it could not be so comforting to be reminded by the black singers that order was so dependent upon their cooperation.[57]

Folklore as Racial Gospel

The slaves appear to have been content to voice their messages in song regardless of whether they were comprehended by the masters or not. At a dance held in celebration of the visit of Prince Hendrik the words sung in endless repetition by a chorus of slave women amid the din of drums and dancing were: "Joe sorrie hin da boen, Joe moessi sorrie hin da ogrie toe!" (You let him see all the beautiful, just let him also see the ugly side). Neither the escorting governor nor the prince understood these ironic lines, which probably heightened the pleasure of the dancing and singing slaves all the more.[58] The slave songs rarely made overt threats or complaints. They rather favored deliberate understatement, sarcasm, and satire. One exceptionally direct protest is the following poignant folksong, which a leading abolitionist claimed was born out of the abuse from slave masters in the early nineteenth century:

1

Have mercy master! mercy! mercy!
Remember earlier times, think how you once loved me!
As you loved me then,
I have still always loved you!
Beat her Bastian, beat her!
The woman fills my heart with wrath!

2

When you came to the land, a white officer,
I had never yet been in love;
As you loved me then,
I have still always loved you!
Beat her Bastian, beat her!
The woman fills my heart with wrath!

3

You took me then from my mother,
And I called you "the handsome white one!"
As you loved me then
I have still always loved you!
Beat her Bastian, beat her!
The woman fills my heart with wrath!

4

You smothered me, your Jaba, with kisses,
As I called out in protest: "stop! stop!"

Was all that just for show?
How can you treat me like this!
Beat her, Bastian, beat her!
The woman fills my heart with wrath.

5

Beg pardon, master, mercy!
Think how you once loved this body!
I beg you, I beg you,
Isn't this enough now?
Beat her, Bastian, beat her!
The woman fills my heart with wrath.

6

Master! master think of the child
Who bears witness to my pure love.
Oh I beg you, I beg you,
Bastian is it still not enough?
Beat her, Bastian, beat her!
The woman fills my heart with wrath.

7

How is it going? Keep beating, I tell you!
The woman fills my heart with wrath!
Keep beating, keep beating I tell you!
Even if it kills her.
Beat her, Bastian, beat her!
The woman fills my heart with wrath![59]

A similar tradition of singing evolved in the Papiamento culture on Curaçao, as witnesses the following song in tribute to Tula, the martyred leader of its most serious slave revolt in 1795. As in the Suriname form, the main verses are sung by a lead singer, with everyone joining in for the chorus.

We're Headed (Now) For Porto Marie

(Chorus): We're headed for
Porto Marie
today we're going to
Porto Marie
(repeat)

(lead):   A long time we've suffered
           under the yoke of slavery,
           but Tula has come and
           wiped out all injustice
           (repeat chorus twice)

(lead)   We've long been in chains
           But Bastian has come
           And broken
           all the chains.
           (repeat chorus twice)

(lead)   Now we're going
           my comrades
           To Porto Marie
           Where we'll set out
           with all the soldiers.
           (repeat chorus twice)

(lead)   There we will celebrate
           our freedom
           Victory is on our side, comrades
           Wecua is with us.
           (repeat chorus twice)

(lead)   We're headed for
           Porto Marie
           today we're going
           to Porto Marie.[60]

While the defiance and self-esteem expressed in some slave songs may have caused concern in some observers, it was probably the dance and its setting which was most troubling. Just the sound of drums in the distance could quicken the heartbeat of a planter uncertain of the occasion. The dances, which usually featured rum, tobacco, and food, could go on for many hours and sometimes for days. Outsiders privileged to witness some of the most guarded rituals reported observing the slaves dance on hot coals without being burned.[61] The government in Suriname attempted to forbid certain dances brought directly from the Coast of Guinea which invoked spiritual possession and were believed capable of casting spells on the slave masters. Slaves caught participating were severely punished and free blacks involved could lose their freedom.[62] The Europeans could not accept the African-based religions as legitimate because although they usually acknowledged the existence of one main God, they also recognized many other spirits, reflecting the diverse origins of the slave population. In Suriname the most prevalent spiritual figure in the dances was the Winti (wind, spirit). Another of many was Jorka, a figure representing death. In the Maroon tradition it was believed that no one dies of a "natural" cause. Death is punishment from God, or the work of some evil spirit.[63]

The dance most common among all the groups of African descent in Suriname was the *banja*, named after the stringed instrument which was originally associated with it, although drums were really the main instruments employed. Another popular one was the *soesa*, which uses hand clapping to set the rhythm and also could be used as a game away from a formal dance setting, where individuals contested their footwork skills.[64] In the Antilles the African dance was usually referred to as the *tambú*, here giving more direct credit to the drum. These practices could not effectively be prevented during slavery because the Blacks were forced into a community, or at least into communal living situations, by the very institution itself. Moreover, the vastly outnumbered ruling class of planters, overseers, and European urbanites knew prohibition of what were often religious rituals would only ensure massive disobedience. After the emancipation, efforts at prohibiting the dances were redoubled, both because of the religious reasons and because massive gatherings outside the control of the authorities were now perceived as all the more threatening now that the population was not controlled by the yoke of slavery. Nevertheless, the practice could not be stamped out. This can be seen, for example, in the accommodation arrived at in Curaçao, where on through the 1980s the *tambú* could receive government sanction by payment of a fee.

Games, Jokes, and Novelties

The manner in which an image is deliberately employed for enjoyment in a culture provides one further vantage point from which to fathom its nature. Dutch humor and games contain elements which project yet further the same notions already discussed here. For example, a nineteenth-century joke book contains two treating the fascination with skin color. One features an exchange between a Dutch

18. Nineteenth-century joke. Leonard de Vries,
Humoristisch album van den 19den eeuw (Laren: Skarabee,
1973), p. 43.

mother and her young son who is pointing at a passing Negro man
(figure 18):

"Hey! I wish I was just as black as that Negro there."
"Why is that, my child?"
"Well, then I would never have to wash."

In the other joke a white woman stands arm in arm with an extremely
negroid man dressed in top hat (figure 19). The caption reads:

A beautiful woman in New York has come up
with the idea of marrying a Negro
in order to accentuate her white complexion.[65]

One game that directly reflects the image of blacks in the folklore
already described is the card game Zwarte Piet. This game is some-

19. Nineteenth-century joke. Leonard de
Vries, *Humoristisch album van den 19den eeuw*
(Laren: Skarabee, 1973), p. 54.

20. Versions of the card game *Zwarte Piet*. Negrophilia Foundation,
Amsterdam.

what akin to the English game Old Maid, with its object being to avoid holding the card bearing Zwarte Piet's image. This game is especially revealing for present purposes because of the way in which racial questions have affected its recent evolution. In earlier decades its card decks bore a wide range of depictions of Zwarte Piet, ranging from caricature of negroid men to formally attired butler figures (see figure 20). However, in more recent publications of the game the Zwarte Piet has become a black kitten or even inanimate. The loser has to submit to having a black stripe drawn on his forehead by the other players.

Toying with the image of blacks has carried over even into the culinary arts, highly significant in a culture so enamored of eating. The edible cookie dolls associated with the Sinterklaas celebration have already been mentioned. Another relevant pastry is the *negerzoen* (Negro's kiss), a small crunchy sweet. Another interesting example is the *moorkop*, which at the very least by its name suggests a reference to Moors. A delicious chocolate eclair topped with whipped cream, it may actually have been named for its resemblance to the facial color pattern on a variety of Arabian horse. However, both its name and the color combination also lead to the association with "the Moor." These pastries probably also entered the Netherlands via Germany, further testifying to the broader European context of many of the concepts considered here.

Images of blacks in Dutch folklore were sufficiently pervasive to represent a kind of subliminal presence which augmented whatever physical presence there might be. The symbolism was there in the festive Sinterklaas celebration; in trademarks for healing and for narcotics, in the form of the Gaper and the Smoking Moor; all around in place names; in food; in recreation; and in music in the twentieth century. Such imagery thus stimulates all the five basic senses and the imagination as well. If the form of the image is often subtle, a clear characterization of it is equally illusive. It is certainly positive at times, and at others revolting. Comparison of these images with those of blacks in other aspects of Dutch culture will be desirable to bring them all into better focus.

ART AS HISTORY

Art's Historical Language

Does a culture's art mirror its history? Even if it does, can this reflection be accurately read by later generations? The present discussion assumes that for Dutch culture both of these questions can be answered at least partially in the affirmative. The main basis of this assumption is the finding that there exist widely accepted, commonly understood artistic symbols whose meanings have remained essentially unchanged over at least the past four centuries. A more specific question which must be asked concerning the present study is: how much can a society's art reveal about groups or individuals who are barely physically present in that society? From the historical evidence it appears that physical presence is not essential for formation of articulate perceptions. At the same time, an actual presence does not ensure clearer perception.

As might be anticipated, there is no consensus on how to interpret Dutch art. However, its early history makes it at least quite clear that there was within this tradition art which was intended to have specific meaning. This is true notwithstanding those schools of artistic interpretation which prefer to focus on form and colors, or which accept the idea of "art for art's sake." A key to understanding Dutch perceptions and interpretations of art may lie in the Dutch variation on the artistic genre called emblemata. Exhibiting features akin to allegorical art and illustrated fables, this form of art flourished especially in the sixteenth and seventeenth centuries. It combined pictures, mottoes, and sometimes versified commentary, and had become highly developed in Italy in the sixteenth century by the time the Dutch adopted it in the seventeenth.

The emblemata genre can count over six hundred authors who collectively produced over two thousand titles, many of which came out in multiple editions. The works of Andreas Alciatus alone, the leading Italian practitioner, enjoyed 170 editions. In the Netherlands Otto van Veen's *Moralia Horatiana* (Horace's Moralisms) appeared in at least 34 editions.[1] The other major emblematists included Roemer Visscher, Jacob Cats, Daniel Heinsius, Pieter C. Hooft, Jan Luiken, and Joost van den Vondel. Visscher gave the genre a peculiarly Dutch flavor when in place of the more standard expression *zinnebeeld* (mental image) he coined the expression *zinnepop* (notion). This was in a sense a deliberate vulgarization of the name in keeping with his intended emphasis on communicating through this art with "Jan en alleman" (Jan and Everybody).[2]

The themes depicted drew largely upon the classical and humanist traditions and were meant to serve as moral guides and practical lessons for living. The emblematists worked in stained glass, jewelry, tapestry, needlework, and architecture as well as the conventional book formats. It can thus be seen that these other forms of arts and crafts, some very popular, also had a didactic function. The Dutch emblems seem especially distinguished by their moralizing tone. This can no longer be doubted by anyone who has read even a page of Jacob Cats on the subject. One work features as frontispiece a beautiful print portraying figures meant to represent all human and other animal types, and highlighting various categories such as gender, occupation, and social class (figure 21). Opposite the print a lengthy, impassioned poem exhorts humankind to rise above the other animals by dint of the power of reason, to pursue the spiritual rather than the material, and to aspire to Christian morality.[3]

From that perspective it can be seen that the genre of emblemata actually included religion and folklore as well as art and literature. Here it is also important to add language, in general. Throughout the literature on the emblematic tradition one encounters the sense that words and visual images were especially closely linked in seventeenth-century Dutch society. It should be kept in mind that this was the very time there was much effort toward developing a distinctive Dutch language. A direct link can be seen in the fact that some of those prominent in the making of the emblems, Cats and Vondel for example, were also playing key roles in the development of the language. There is also ample evidence that, at the same time, the emblemata had a direct influence on seventeenth-century Dutch painting, providing some of its themes as well as its symbols. Exam-

21. Frontispiece from Jacob Cats, *Proteus, ofte minne-beelden verandert in Sinne-beelden* (Rotterdam, 1627). By permission of the Folger Shakespeare Library, Washington, D.C.

ples can be seen in the work of Pieter Bruegel the Elder, Adriaen van de Venne, Jacob Jordaens, and Jan Steen. In fact the lines between the two genres soon blurred as the pictures in the emblems shifted from allegory into scenes more like genre paintings in detail and subject matter. Along with this the accompanying written word changed from Latin and French into the Dutch vernacular.

What is the significance of all this for the image of blacks? First of all, it confirms that looking in Dutch art for reflections of specific historical social and cultural perceptions may prove instructive. Beyond that, the content of the emblematic tradition has broader implications for clarifying the role of all sorts of symbols in the visual arts over the centuries. This was evident from the very beginning to those involved in emblematic art. Andreas Alciatus deliberately created models with which painters, goldsmiths, and those wishing to show status could make badges or trademarks. Caesar Ripa, an important conduit of the tradition into the Netherlands, and the century's major compiler of the vocabulary of standard symbols, could not have been more explicit of his intentions in the very lengthy title of his major work:

> *Iconologia: or Moral Emblems*; Wherein are Express'd, Various Images of Virtue, Vices, Passions, Arts, Humours, Elements and Celestial Bodies; As Designed by the Ancient Egyptians, Greeks, Romans, and Modern Italians; For Orators, Poets, Painters, Sculptors, and all Lovers of Ingenuity.

Of the Dutch artists, Otto van Veen made a notable similar contribution with his publication of a compendium of church and military symbols which had come down to his day.[4]

Thus emblematic art was one link for modern Europe with the ancient roots of Western civilization. The fascination of Italian humanists of the fifteenth and sixteenth centuries with hieroglyphics had fed heraldry as well as emblematic art. This evidence of the survival, however subtle, of elements of pictographic language alongside the alphabetic again highlights the close relationship between words and artistic images which is so prominent in emblemata. It also provides the broader context in which to view artistic symbols appearing over the centuries on down to the present in such variant forms as heraldry, emblemata, genre and portrait painting, trademarks, and commercial advertisements. In addition to art, this is the broader background for the consideration of the various images in folklore, described in chapter two, and those to be presented in the chapters to follow on literature and religion.

The considerable attention given here to emblemata is justified not because blacks were a major theme in them, but rather because of their importance for an understanding that Dutch artists did place deliberate meaning in their work. However, images of blacks did appear in some of these works. Examples from Cats and Ripa illustrate how contrasting they could be. On the print from Cats's work described earlier a "Black Moor" couple are human types on equal footing with the others. In Ripa's *Iconologia* (Iconology), however, among his moral emblems "Africa" is depicted and described as:

> A Blackmoor Woman, almost naked; frizl'd Hair; an Elephant's Head for her Crest; a Necklace of Coral, and Pendants of the same, at her Ears; a Scorpion in her right hand, and a *Cornucopia* with Ears of Corn, in her left; a fierce Lion by her, on one Side and a Viper and Serpent on the other. Naked, because it does not abound with Riches. The Elephant is only in *Africa*. The animals show that it abounds with them.[5]

This of course is a symbol bristling with other symbols of ancient vintage. Could the contrast between these two images be evidence that the Dutch were less biased than the Italians, or that the early seventeenth century was less biased than the eighteenth? These questions, which can probably never be conclusively answered, illustrate the difficulty in reading history through art. However, this also shows how the art is useful in helping to pose historical questions. It would seem that it is indeed legitimate to ask the assistance of art in the effort to fathom history, as long as caution is used. A cursory look through emblemata reveals, for example, that a hoop can represent either endless love or aimless activity. Jacob Cats noted that the very same imagery was at times used to represent something good and at other times something evil.[6] This was also patently the case with the image of blacks in Dutch art.

It was in the realm of religiously inspired visual arts that the earliest concrete manifestation of Dutch awareness of blacks appeared. As early as the fourteenth century European painters began frequently to portray black Africans, based in part on the renewed contacts between the two continents and in part on popular religious and classical secular themes. By the seventeenth century, when the Dutch maritime empire reached its full scope, actual portraiture including blacks was produced on a broad scale. After that century, when the craze for both portraiture and distinctively Dutch art waned as foreign influences intruded on culture as well as on Dutch dominance of the seas, black imagery still continued to abound in prints and in the plastic arts. There is clear evidence that the interiors of even modest Dutch homes by the seventeenth and eighteenth centuries were enhanced by paintings hung on the walls. Meanwhile the Netherlands' role as an international publishing center ensured that prints and illustrations included in books and maps would receive wide exposure there. Therefore a survey of the depiction of blacks in all these media can provide a good indication of the public's perceptions.

Images from the World of the Mind

Religious Themes

Since most art in the early period of Dutch history was religious, it is not surprising that it was in this genre that the first black images appeared. From the late fourteenth and fifteenth centuries in Italy and Germany iconography of the Epiphany developed to include Asian and black wise kings and their retinues. The Holy Roman Emperors, beginning with Charles IV's ascension in 1346, adopted blacks into the iconography of their realm, including the depiction of St. Maurice as a black (see figure 22) and the touting of Gregrory the Moor as the major protector of Cologne.[7] Becoming part of the Empire after Philip the Good acquired Holland and Zeeland in 1428, Brabant and Limburg in 1429, and the bishopric of Utrecht in 1455, the Low Countries too witnessed these symbols along with popularization of depiction of one of the Magi as black. Africans first appeared in Flemish and Dutch painting in the fifteenth century. The *Hours of Catherine of Cleves*, a work executed in Utrecht in 1440, shows the Queen of Sheba (white in this case) accompanied by a black servant woman. Also from Utrecht, the *Eerste Historiebijbel* (First History Bible), 1465, includes paintings of the Baptism of the Ethiopian Eunuch, the black bride of the Song of Songs, and the Adoration of the Magi.[8]

Other good examples are in the works of Rogier van der Weyden, Hugo van der Goes, and Geertgen tot Sint Jans (see figure 23). Van

22. Anonymous, Statue of St. Maurice, ca. 1240–50, Cathedral of St. Maurice and St. Catherine, Magdeburg. Menil Foundation/Hickey & Robertson, Houston.

der Weyden included blacks in the background in his St. Columba altarpiece, executed around 1460. Van der Goes's Adoration altarpiece, now located in the Hermitage in St. Petersburg, features an especially handsome, boyish black king. Van der Goes drew figure studies of black Africans, as would later, notably, the German Albrecht Dürer (see figures 24–25) and the Flemish painter Peter Paul Rubens. In tot Sint Jans's exemplary early work on an altarpiece for the Order of St. John in Haarlem, titled "Julian the Apostate Ordering the Bones of St. John to be Burned," a black spectator stands out.[9] Another black spectator, mounted, richly attired, is also featured in Cornelis Engebrechtsz's Crucifixion of Christ (1509).

The Adoration of the Magi, featured in thousands of works, was the single most popular religious theme featuring blacks in sixteenth and seventeenth-century European art. The black king was usually depicted as the youngest, presumably symbolizing Africa as the con-

23. Geertgen tot Sint Jans, *The Adoration of the Magi.*
Rijksmuseum, Amsterdam.

tinent just beginning to participate in world affairs. The black king
was also often strikingly handsome, to a degree which led a recent
scholar to bemoan "finding among these thousands of Adorations
only a very small number of representations in which the features are
not sweetened to some degree. . . . "[10] For present purposes, of

24. Albrecht Dürer,
*Portrait of the Moorish
Woman Katharina.*
Florence: Uffizi Gallery.
Photo Marburg/Art
Resource, New York.

course, the existence of such a convention is welcomed. It evidences
a rare instance of a widely projected positive image of blacks and in-
vites examination of the question of why this occurred. Flemish and
Dutch artists executed some of the most distinctive of these images.
Examples can be seen in Adorations of Jacob Jordaens (1644), Hans
Memling (1464), Gerard David (15th c), Justus van Gent (15th c),
Jacob Cornelisz van Oostanen (15th-16th c), Pieter Bruegel I (16th c),
Hendrick Goltzius (16th c), Lucas van Leyden (16th c), Jacob de
Gheyn, Hieronymus Bosch (ca. 1510), Peter Paul Rubens (1606),
Rembrandt van Rijn (17th c), Matthias Stomer (1650), Cornelis de
Vos (17th c), Pieter Quast (1644), Nicolaas Wieringa (1664), Jan
Mostaert, Hendrick ter Brugghen, Abraham Janssens, Pieter de
Kempeneer, A. Goubau (1670), Johannes de Cock (1704), and many
others (see figures 26–29).

It is plausible to view the Dutch contributions to this tradition as
simply imitation of the prevalent styles. However, these works exude
a vitality that demands recognition of their originality and sensitive

25. Albrecht Dürer, *Study of a head of a black man*. Graphische Sammlung Albertina, Vienna.

regard for the subjects treated. The artists in question appear to have been quite deliberate in their portrayal, and not just mechanically following convention. There remains, therefore, a valid question as to why Dutch artists during these centuries chose to personify Africa in such a favorable light. In comparing works which bore this motif between the fifteenth and eighteenth centuries, it is also possible to discern a change in quality as well as quantity. The most beautiful and most powerful images are the earliest, with Memling's and Bosch's Adorations representing unsurpassed majesty. How astonishing it is when first viewing these works to discover that the renowned, handsome sixteenth-century black figures of Rubens and Rembrandt are surpassed in intimacy by these fifteenth- and sixteenth-century pieces of Memling and Bosch, which have an almost photographic quality. The decrease in the number of works treating this theme can probably be attributed to the secularization of art along with other developments in society. The changes in character of the works are surely related in part to changes in artistic styles and to the decline

26. Jacob Jordaens, *The Adoration of the Magi*. Photo Rijksbureau voor
Kunsthistorische Documentatie, The Hague.

27. Hendrick Goltzius, *Adoration of the Magi* (1594). Print Room, Plantin-Moretus Museum, Antwerp.

28. Hieronymus Bosch, *The Adoration*. Museo del Prado. Menil
Foundation/Hickey & Robertson, Houston.

29. Peter Paul Rubens, *The Adoration of the Magi*. From the Art Collection
of the Folger Shakespeare Library, Washington, D.C.

toward the end of this period in what might be described as distinctively Dutch art. However, these changes may also have to do with changing European perceptions of blacks, which will be pursued further throughout the present study.

The Baptism of the Ethiopian Eunuch, a theme inspired by the text describing Philip the Deacon's encounter in the book of Acts, was another extremely popular one in European art, especially from the fifteenth to the seventeenth centuries. This theme, which can be traced in Christian iconography at least as far back as the third century, also attracted many Dutch artists (see figures 30–32). Many artists executed more than one version; and this was also one of the themes on which pieces were mass-produced by master artists assisted by apprentices. Less fettered by a traditional conception of the scene described, the Baptism found itself at times barely perceptible on expansive landscapes more characteristic for art of later centuries and at other times it is the sole action on the canvas. The "Ethiopian" varied in his physical features: at times definitely negroid, at others Cushitic or somewhat Asiatic. Good examples may be seen in the works of Abraham Bloemaert (16th c), Maarten van Heemskerk (1572?), Rembrandt (1626), Pieter Lastman (1620), J. A. Marienhof, Frans Francken II (16th c), and Albert Cuyp (17th c). Like the Adoration theme, that concerning Baptism symbolized inclusion of blacks in the civilized and Christianized world.

Baptism related to the "Ethiopian," which, remember, in early modern Europe was used to describe Negroes in general as well as Ethiopians, actually suggested two different biblical injunctions which were in some respects contradictory. The one was the philanthropic evangelical charge, the other the Old Testament negative use of an Ethiopian's color in an analogy concerning salvation. It is difficult to say which of these meanings these paintings conveyed to the public. The relevance of this question is quite clear given the existence of a popular saying in Dutch culture which translates roughly as "a washed Moor." This is based on the biblical text of Jeremiah 13:22–25, which denies the possibility of a leopard changing its spots or an Ethiopian his color.

As noted in one of the dictionary quotations in the discussion of lexicography in chapter one, this phrase in popular lore came to be an expression of futility. Further research reveals that the Dutch drew this symbol at least in part from the emblemata tradition which it

30. Rembrandt, *Baptism of the Ethiopian Eunuch*. Rijksmuseum Het Catharijneconvent, Utrecht.

shared with Italy and France. It can be found in variant forms in a number of the editions of Andreas Alciatus's book of emblems published from the mid-sixteenth to the early seventeenth century (see figure 31). In the Netherlands Jan Luikens in the early eighteenth cen-

Alciatus	Emblemata	Padua	1621

Motto
*Impossible
The *impossible

Picture
A *Moor (*Ethiopian) is seated on a block in front of a fountain. He is flanked by two men who try to *wash the *colour from his *skin.

Subject
*Futile *labour
The *impossible

Impossibile.

E M B L E M A   L I X.

A BLVIS AEthiopem quid frustra? ab desinis: nulla illustrare nigra amea potest tenebras.

Epigram
Why are you *washing (abluo) in vain the *Ethiopian (Aethiops)? Give up.
No one can *light up (illustro) the *darkness (tenebra) of black *night (nox).

		Paris	1536

Epigram
There are a thousand things for which there is no *remedy (remède). No matter how hard you try, you will not be master of them. Therefore if you seek to be above reproach, do not try to make a *Moor (Maure) *white (blanchir). *Light (clarté) cannot be born at *night (nuit). An inveterate *vice (vice) remains.

		Paris	1542

Epigram
No matter how long and well one *washes (waschen) a *Moor (Mohr), it does not help a hair. The *night (Nacht) is so full of *darkness (Finsternis) that it cannot be made *bright (klar) with any *light (Licht). Similarly, take note that natural *vice (Laster) and what *time (Zeit) has aged can never be eradicated, no matter what *art (Kunst) one uses.

31. Andreas Alciatus, the emblem for *Impossible*. From Peter M. Daly, ed., *Andreas Alciatus*, v. 2 (Toronto: University of Toronto Press, 1985).

tury featured it as the theme of a beautiful etching and elaborate verse in his collection of emblems entitled *De bijkorf des gemoeds* (The Beehive of the Emotions). It is interesting that popular usage chose to focus on the "Ethiopian" rather than the leopard. The association of

32. Jan Luiken, *De Mooriaan*, from *De Bykorf des Gemoeds*
(Amsterdam: 1711), Photo Folger Shakespeare Library,
Washington, D.C.

washing with cleanliness was stymied in this instance by the religious
ambivalence on this score, underlined by the popular notion that this
kind of "color" could not be changed.

A related and even older religious theme bearing a negative con-
notation for blacks was that concerning the Hamitic legend. Based on
varying interpretations of a chapter in the Old Testament book of
Genesis in which Noah supposedly condemned the descendants of
one of his sons to perpetual servitude, this theme enjoyed intermit-
tent popularity over the centuries in later Moslem and Christian traditions as well. Its role in Dutch culture will be treated more fully in
chapter five. In European art it was conventional to depict Ham's
descendants as negroid. A thirteenth-century parchment from Soest
is an early example of this in the region of the Netherlands.[11] Illustrations done for Bibles and paintings on this theme usually focused on
Noah and his sons and therefore only hinted at a different sort of

33. Jacob Jordaens, *Moses and Zippora*. Rubenshuis, Antwerp.

progeny for Ham by giving him curlier hair and darker complexion
than his brothers. Maarten van Heemskerck was one Dutch artist
who gave special attention to this theme. Illustrations for Josephus's
history of the Jews featured some distinctively black figures. The
story of Moses and the Egyptians is the prime example. On this same
theme, Moses' marriage to an Ethiopian woman, described in the
book of Numbers, inspired one of the most powerful paintings involving blacks in all of Dutch art: Jordaens's *Moses en Zippora* (figure 33).

34. The Queen of Sheba. Prayer Book of Catherine of Cleve. The Pierpont Morgan Library, New York. M. 917, f. 109.

Another occasionally illustrated biblical event with a black is the rescue of the prophet Jeremiah from a dungeon by the Ethiopian eunuch Ebed Melech. A more famous story, the visit of the Queen of Sheba to King Solomon was first depicted in the Lowlands in Flemish art and then carried over into that of the new Dutch Republic in various art forms (see figure 34). In a painting by Erasmus Quellinus, *The Queen of Sheba offering gold and precious stones to King Solomon*, the

Queen is black, as she is also in later versions found in Dutch art. In the Christian and Islamic traditions the Queen has usually symbolized ministry to those outside the faith. In the Judaic she has also been viewed in some instances as a daemonic, occult figure.[12] Other biblical stories which did not specifically mention blacks were also depicted by artists with black figures. One popular throughout Europe was the scene with Bathsheba in her bath, often featuring a black servant girl. Rubens and Cornelisz van Haarlem are among artists in the Low Countries who depicted this theme.

Secular Themes

At the start of the sixteenth century Hieronymus Bosch became the first Dutchman regularly to depict blacks in themes other than the Adoration and in secular art. In his surrealistic *Garden of Earthly Delights* blacks and whites mingle freely in committing forbidden acts. In one background scene a mixed couple makes love.[13] Bosch's work may be seen both as an example of the Low Countries' tradition of nonconformity and as an expression of the intense religious fervor which was part of the Dutch worldview. The eventual formation of the Dutch Republic amid the throes of the Protestant Reformation made religion even more prominent. One consequence of this is that religion remained such an overwhelmingly important criterion for establishing identity that a trait such as skin color was insignificant by comparison. Any assessment of Dutch racial attitudes must also bear in mind the strong sense of superiority inherent in the Reformed Church's Calvinism. Nevertheless, paradoxically, a more secular worldview continued to grow apace alongside the new religious thrust during the sixteenth and seventeenth centuries.

Blacks continued to appear in the secular art which now appeared just as in the religious art. This was not really an innovation since the themes presented in this were often from the classical Western tradition which had always used some blacks as symbolism. An example of a direct depiction of a classical scene is Abraham van den Tempel's 1651 work *Stedemaagd ontvangt de Neering* (The Town Protectress receives the Emissary).[14] At the very center of the piece a black servant girl cradles the train of the heavily gowned city protectress. The work of the engraver and painter Hendrick Goltzius exemplifies the continuation of the classical themes in the mannerist style. His works, replete with human figures personifying various elements of the cos-

35. Hendrick Goltzius, *Dawn*; Detail from *The Creation*.
Print Room, University of Leiden.

mos, often featured a black figure, usually female, to lend balance to
the composition as well as the concept projected. In a detail from one
titled *The Creation*, a black woman stands under a cloak of darkness
as a white male figure steps out into a glorious, contrasting light (figure 35). In another, celebrating the glory of Rome, the same nubile,
dark figure personifies Africa paying homage at the feet of a helmeted
Roma (figure 36).

Peter Paul Rubens's work *The Four Parts of the World* has seated at
its very center a pensive, attractive young black woman personifying
Africa, amid its several nude figures drawn in the conventional style
for gods and goddesses (figure 37). The personification of the parts of
the world was probably the most popular of all the formats for modern allegorical art. It would appear in tapestries, sculptures, and statues as well as paintings, prints, and emblems. Perhaps the most
elaborate rendition of all is the 1798 engraving of Thomas Koning

36. Hendrick Goltzius, *Roma*. Print Room, University of Leiden.

37. Peter Paul Rubens, *The Four Parts of the World*. Kunsthistorisches Museum, Vienna.

based on J. G. Visser's work. Titled *De Wereld* (The World), it includes four columns topped by human figures representing Europe, America, Africa, and Asia. On each column lands and peoples are listed. At the very center of the work stands a statue of a crowned female figure representing the world standing on a globe. Clustered about her feet is a multitude of people bearing features and apparel reflecting the diverse cultures and climes, while in the background various flora are set against a canopy of celestial elements (figure 38).

Jacobus Waben, in the early seventeenth century, offered a more down to earth *Allegory with the World as a Woman*. Here in the foreground "Vrouw Wereld" (Lady World) is shown receiving indecent amorous advances from a lavishly attired suitor while music and revelry proceed in the background with a figure symbolizing death looming over the company. To the left of the composition sits a Smoking Moor, clearly representing worldly temptations and evil. Hendrick Noorderwiel's 1647 work *De Huwelijksfuik*, based on J. Cats's poem about marriage, has one black cherub. One of the most colorful of the secular allegories is Abraham Hondius's *Kosmische Al-*

38. J. G. Visser, after Th. Koning Engraving, *The World*, 1798. Atlas van Stolk, Rotterdam.

legorie. In this one a dark, crowned negroid male figure is one of four representing one of the four parts of the day along with others signifying the four winds, all highlighted by a morning and evening star in the background (figure 39). Other striking seventeenth-century allegorical pieces are Cornelis Nobertus Gysbrechts's *Vanité au Nègre* and Cornelisz de Vos's *Wealth Crowning Agriculture*. In the latter the black figure is a bystander clad in armor.

There are also works of unclear intent which seem to fall somewhere between allegory, emblemata, and historical illustration. An example is Nicolaes Berchem's work *A Moor Presenting a Parrot to a Lady*. In the background is a bustling harbor. At the center of the piece a lavishly attired black man offers a parrot, another native of the tropics, to a white lady whose most prominent piece of jewelry is a Christian cross on her necklace. Here is a work which allows for a broad range of interpretations based on symbolism of a social, political, economic, religious, or erotic nature. Who can say what the artist

39. Abraham Hondius, *Cosmic Allegory*. Öffentliche Kunstsammlung Basel, Kunstmuseum, Basel.

really intended? Nevertheless, there can be little doubt that such a work, emerging out of this unashamedly didactic artistic tradition, would leave the viewer with some impression concerning the juxtaposition of the contrasting cultures represented principally by the Moor and the lady (figure 40).

From the World of Experience

Blacks first began to be fairly noticeable in the Low Countries in the sixteenth century. By the next century they became fairly commonplace as slaves, servants, and seamen in Dutch port cities.[15] The Dutch perception of blacks, earlier based largely on imagination, could now be tempered by direct experience. In art this new awareness now became mirrored in their appearance in portraiture and in scenes from everyday life. Meanwhile what these scenes reflected then was the lifestyle resulting from Dutch commercial success and assertion of political sovereignty. The religious themes so pronounced in art of the previous centuries gave way in the seventeenth and eighteenth

40. Nicolaes Berchem, *A Moor Presenting a Parrot to a Lady*. Wadsworth Atheneum, Hartford, Connecticut. The Ella Gallup Sumner and Mary Catlin Sumner Collection.

to those related to business and science. Indeed, artists themselves increasingly performed as businessmen. This is not to imply that the art was always an accurate depiction of life. On the contrary, this was often deliberately not the case.[16] The art does, nevertheless, reveal much about the artists' and the society's reaction to their new experiences.

The largest category of paintings in which blacks figured were the countless portraits of Dutch burgher families, groups, and individuals. The Lowlands produced more of this type of art than any other area in the world. England was the only other country that even comes close in this regard to the Netherlands and Belgium.[17] These portraits were intended to celebrate achievement and to leave a lasting record for posterity. Therefore, the blacks who appeared in them, as well as other real and contrived figures and objects, often served as symbols. The most frequent pose of the black figure was the role of servant. Hundreds of family portraits included a black servant boy or girl. It is rare to encounter depiction of an elderly black. They appeared in a wide variety of poses, although some basic patterns of composition were repeated with formula-like frequency. One format showed the servant in intimate contact with the principal figure, as in a number of portraits by Adriaan Hanneman, Jan Mytens, and Caspar Netcher in the late seventeenth century. Hanneman, for example, depicts a black servant boy placing jewelry on the wrist of a mistress, a rare instance during that period when it was acceptable for a black man to touch a white woman (figure 41).

Another standard pose features the black servant holding a parasol over the head of the mistress or master, seemingly out of place in Antoni van Dyck's portrait of the Marchesa Elena Grimaldi set against a backdrop of cloudy sky (figure 42). Fr. van der Mijn's 1742 portrait of Jan Pranger presents a more realistic, but less imaginative, common scene with the black as valet or butler standing in the background. The most patented and most ancient of all the poses has the servant offering food or flowers to the master or mistress, as in F. Hagen's late seventeenth-century portrait of Susanna Vernatti (figure 43). When carried to its logical extreme the cliched use of a black servant as symbol featured just a bust or head of a Negro among room furnishings. A step short of this are numerous pieces where the obligatory black plays no active role in the scene and is visible only in bust relief (see figure 44). One example is the 1676 Lambertus de Hue portrait of William III of Orange, Stadholder of the Netherlands and King of England. An even more graphic illustration of this background effect is the portrait of Gustaf Willem Baron van Imhoff by Philips van Dijk. Here a turbaned black boy holding a bird stands to the rear and off to the side from the baron. The lower part of his figure is masked by a world globe and flowing drapes, while he and the bird seem just as plausibly part of a classical sculptured wall relief immediately behind them (figure 45).

41. Adriaan Hanneman, Maria Henriette Stuart.
Mauritshuis Museum, The Hague.

The prosperity celebrated in these pictures was built on action, not the kind of sedentary behavior depicted in these portraits of leisure. There was also an attempt to project this dynamism in artistic form. This was accomplished most forcefully in the numerous portraits and engravings of such heroes as Admirals Michiel de Ruiter and Cornelis Tromp and of Stadholder William III. In these a black servant usually holds the helmet for the armored warrior dressed for battle on land or sea. The most striking of these is L. Visscher's engraving of Tromp. The black boy standing elbow-high at Tromp's side, cradling a plumed helmet half his size, appears almost to be crushed downward by the armored limb cocked to allow the admiral to prop his hand on his armored hip. Tromp's other hand rests on a world globe and telescope while in the background his fleet engages in battle (figure 46).

One of these martial portraits is perhaps the most abject, servile

42. Sir Anthony van Dyck, *Marchesa Elena Grimaldi, Wife of Marchese Nicola Cattaneo*. National Gallery of Art, Washington; Widener Collection.

43. F. Hagen, Susanna Vernatti. Photo Iconographisch Bureau, The Hague.

44. John Smith, after Gottfried Kneeler, Willem II Hendrik Prins van Oranje Nassau. Rijksmuseum, Amsterdam.

45. P. Tanjé, after Ph. van Dijk, Gustaf Willem Baron van Imhoff. Photo Iconographisch Bureau, The Hague.

46. L. Visscher, engraving, Cornelis Tromp. Atlas van Stolk, Rotterdam.

portrayal of a black in all of Dutch art. This is the 1693 portrait of Admiral Gilles Schey by Jan Weenix. Here the armored admiral stands beside the usual globe, his telescope in one hand and the other pointing contemptuously at a kneeling Negro who stares upward at him with helpless resignation. At the same time a dog at the admiral's feet snarls at the Negro, seemingly with equal scorn, as a battleship takes on provisions in the background against a gloomy sky (figure 47). The message in this portrait takes on greater force when considered

47. Jan Weenix, Admiral Gilles Schey. Netherlands National Maritime
Museum, Amsterdam.

within the context of the emblematic tradition. The scene contains all
the conspicuous signs of worldly success for the Dutchman, which
would imply divine blessing in the Calvinist religious tradition.
Meanwhile the black servant whose kneeling figure underscores this
mastery is rejected by the dog, who in the Bible is usually mentioned

only in an unfavorable light. The age-old positive image of the dog as man's loyal friend in this instance further lowers the worth of the Negro.

In a Weenix portrait of Dirk Schey executed the same year, a black, possibly the same model, accompanies the master on a hunt along with two dogs.[18] This time standing, but slightly bent and with hat in hand, he epitomizes the stereotype of the docile Negro which was taking hold in the West and would live on for centuries. Thus the selective depiction of blacks as servile in this rich tradition of portraiture, perhaps at the time just one means of accentuating Dutch prowess, helped to obscure the full scope of activities and status of blacks in that century, and to further crystallize a negative stereotype.

Family portraits presented the artist an even greater temptation to improvise, given the difficulty of actually having so many subjects pose at once. In fact, many compositions included people deceased at the time of the painting. It is therefore not surprising that many of these works display artificial backgrounds such as would later become standard for photographers' studios. This can be seen in the works of Roelof Koets, for example his picture of the Adolf Werner van Pallandt family around 1698. The liveried, jet-black groom holding a white horse in the background is on the wall. Jan Steen's depiction of the Van Goyen family around 1665 is likewise almost entirely fabricated, including the room and its furnishings. This is not really surprising, since Steen was one of the artists strongly influenced by the emblemata tradition. The black servant, like most other items in the scene, symbolizes rather than reproduces the lifestyle which the artist wished to chronicle.[19]

Cornelis Troost, one of the few outstanding eighteenth-century Dutch artists, at least on two occasions painted himself at work painting in a commissioned family portrait. One of these was that of an unidentified family in 1733, in which there is also a black servant, in this case serving hot chocolate.[20] Michiel van Musscher's 1687 portrait of Thomas Hees provides an especially cogent example of deliberate composition. This piece, whose purpose was to commemorate the diplomatic career of Hees in the Barbary States, includes many souvenirs from the region as well as his slave boy Thomas, whom he had brought home with him. This piece is remarkable in the extent to which the slave seems just as much a part of the family as Hees's two nephews (figure 48).

Another distinctively Dutch form of group portraiture was the

48. Michiel van Musscher, Thomas Hees. Rijksmuseum, Amsterdam.

49. Bartholomeus van der Helst, *Company of Captain Roelof Bicker*. Rijksmuseum, Amsterdam.

Art as History

50. Cornelis Troost, Stadhouder William IV's Inspection of the Cavalry, 1742. Rijksmuseum, Amsterdam.

schutterstuk, the formal pictures of the town militias. One of the most famous of these has a black figure right in the middle. In B. Helst's *Company of Captain Roelof Bicker*, which hangs in Amsterdam's Rijksmuseum directly opposite Rembrandt's *Night Watch*, a diminutive, cloaked black servant huddles close in the shadow of Captain Bicker (figure 49). It is notable that in the works describing this piece every figure in the picture is identified or mentioned except him. Considering the prominence of this painting, this omission makes it a good illustration of one of the most pervasive characteristics of blacks in Dutch painting: they seem often to go unnoticed, at least by the conscious eye. Perhaps at the time of the painting this might be explained in terms of class status rather than color. But why have generations of art historians also ignored the servant?[21]

One more astonishing example of this is Cornelis Troost's painting of Stadholder William IV's inspection of the cavalry in 1742 (figure 50). At the very head of the ceremonial column, mounted on a strutting black stallion rides a colorfully uniformed black man. Yet no sources on this work discuss this figure, including a very recent book

51. Two Soldiers and a Canteen hostess. Artist unknown. Photo
Rijksbureau voor Kunsthistorische Documentatie, The Hague.

devoted to Troost which includes this painting. A drum hanging at
his mount's side suggests that he is a drummer. This figure forms
such an important element in the composition on the basis of his location, posture, and color, it is amazing that he receives no notice. A
little-known painting from the nineteenth century provides another
surprising suggestion of a greater presence of blacks in the Nether-

52. Jacob Jordaens, *Kitchen Scene*, tapestry. École Nationale Supérieure des Beaux-Arts, Paris.

lands than is generally supposed. By an unknown artist, it shows a military canteen hostess from an artillery unit pouring wine for two of the unit's soldiers standing at her shoulders. One of them is a smiling black in the uniform and insignia of the unit (figure 51).[22]

Blacks appeared as incidental actors in all aspects of Dutch life captured on canvas during the heyday of Dutch genre painting, and not only as servants. Jordaens featured one in one of his several pieces titled *Gezicht in een Keuken* (Kitchen Scene; figure 52). Blacks also appear in serious landscapes such as those of the brothers Philips and Pieter Wouwerman in the seventeenth century.[23] In Matthys Naiveu's *Twelfth Night: Buffoon and Others Dancing* at the start of the eighteenth century one of the dancers is a Negro. Blacks are also shown in the seamier side of Dutch life, as attests Christiaen van Couwenbergh's gripping work from 1632, *Rape of a Negress* (figure 53). At the same time, scenes of compassion were not unknown. Especially

53. Christiaen van Couwenbergh, *Rape of a Negress*, 1632. Musée de la Ville de Strasbourg.

54. Henri Bource, *The Drowned*. Photo Rijksbureau voor Kunsthistorische Documentatie, The Hague.

55. Peter Paul Rubens, Negro head studies. Musées Royaux des Beaux-Arts de Belgique, Brussels.

striking in this regard is the later, 1866 depiction by the Belgian Henri Bource of the death scene for a shipwrecked black sailor receiving tender care in the home of local villagers (figure 54).

As the presence of blacks increased in the Netherlands they increasingly became the main subject of works of art as well as parts of works such as those discussed thus far. Spectacular early instances can be found in the work of Peter Paul Rubens. Following the example set early in the sixteenth century by Albrecht Dürer, who executed sympathetic portraits of black men and women, Rubens's series of Negro head studies showed a similar fascination with the subject (see figure 55). His pupil Van Dyck followed this interest. Rembrandt too left immortal, realistic portraits of Negroes from the seventeenth century. His *Two Negroes* is the most noted example (figure 56). His own interest in the Negro form for figure study is also reflected in his 1658 etching of a nude *Reclining Negress*.[24] Rembrandt's pupil Gerard Dou also left memorable works of this nature.

56. Rembrandt, *Two Negroes*. Mauritshuis Museum, The Hague.

A lesser-known seventeenth-century artist who executed some of the most compelling portraits of blacks to date was Albert Eeckhout. In the employment of the West India Trading Company in Dutch Brazil, he executed hundreds of scientific drawings of flora and fauna for Governor Johan Maurits, including detailed portraits of the local populations. Maurits brought the collection to the Netherlands at the end of his service in Brazil and later sold most of the pieces abroad. In 1654 Frederick III of Denmark acquired some of them, including a number of those depicting different types of blacks in Brazil. The most extraordinary of these portraits, appearing on the cover of the present study, is that of a Congolese envoy sent along with three others to Governor Maurits at Recife by King Dom Garcia II of the Congo and the Count of Sonho in 1643. The realistic portrait presents the very dark Negro in European trappings intended as gifts from Maurits to the two African rulers, whose envoys had also brought gifts. The costume depicted included a black velvet coat trimmed in gold and silver, a silver-plated saber, and a plumed, beaver felt hat with a gold and silver band (figure 57). Accompanying this portrait were those of two African boys, more modestly dressed, who were perhaps servants to the envoys. Another similar portrait, of an African woman holding a sword, may also belong to the same group.

Most colorful of all were two works titled *Negerstrijder* (Negro Warrior) and *Negerin met kind* (Negro Woman and Child) (figures 58 and 59). In the first Eeckhout presents an African armed in the fashion of the Fetu people on the African Gold Coast. The second presents a mother and child who appears to have European and African ancestry. As with contemporary painters in the Netherlands, Eeckhout did not hesitate also to embellish his scenes with additional symbols of the lifestyle, notwithstanding the accuracy of his drawings of the natural surroundings. His rendering of the figures and faces are exceptionally attractive.[25] Another artist who worked in Brazil under the patronage of Johan Maurits was Frans Post. His only known works completed during his seven years there were several landscapes; but these are some of the most memorable in all of Dutch art. Human figures on these appear only as indistinct miniatures, but still convey, like Eeckhout's, a positive, realistic tone.[26]

By the eighteenth century a new stage in the acknowledgment of the presence of blacks in Dutch society was signaled by their being named in art, and not just appearing as anonymous figures or symbols. Wide circulation of prints from the F. van Bleyswyck engraving of the black predicant Jacobus Capitein in the 1730s was a novelty (figure 60). However, it was one which contributed to a broadening of the image of blacks. Clearly a further projection of the emblematic tradition, and in many respects a propaganda piece, it might have been intended simply as a trophy attesting the power of Christian

57. Albert Eeckhout(?), Congolese envoy to Recife in Dutch Brazil. National Museum of Denmark, Department of Ethnography, Copenhagen.

civilization over presumed savagery. However, this stately, wigged, and robed figure with a Bible in his hand and shelves of learned tomes at his shoulder also announced through the composition's oval frame that blacks could rise to new heights in European society.

In the nineteenth century another new role for blacks in the

58. Albert Eeckhout, *Negro Warrior*. National Museum of Denmark,
Department of Ethnography, Copenhagen.

59. Albert Eeckhout, *Mother and Child*. National Museum of Denmark, Department of Ethnography, Copenhagen.

60. F. van Bleyswyck engraving, Jacobus Capitein.
Stichting Iconographisch Bureau, The Hague.

Dutch world would be reflected in portraits: the role of soldier. Most
of these were of the anonymous variety. The best are by Ernest
Hardouin and August van Pers. Each of them, independently, executed portraits titled *Afrikaansche Soldaat* while working in the Dutch
East Indies, where the Dutch employed a few thousand African
troops in the foreign legion (figures 61 and 62). Hardouin's shows the
soldier in battle, fierce, with bayonet fixed and a slain enemy on the
ground. Pers's by contrast shows an African soldier in dress uniform,
accompanied by his local wife and child.[27]

Dutch painters of the late nineteenth and early twentieth century
continued to produce studies of blacks, reflecting both the interest of
the Netherlands in the wider world and a growing presence of blacks
in Dutch society. Examples can be found in such works as Pieter
Josselin de Jong's *The Lemon Seller*, Cornelis Maks's *Familiegroep*, and

61. Ernest Hardouin, *African Soldier*. Photo and Print Collection,
Koninklijk Instituut voor Taal-, Land- en Volkenkunde, Leiden.

Isaac Israels's 1915 *Negerbokser*. Maks's portrait of an unidentified
family is especially interesting. Executed around 1905, this painting
of a racially mixed family, including a black man, his Dutch wife,
their three children, and a white governess, reflects the extent to
which the complexion and complexity of the Dutch empire had
begun to reach home. Maks was to use many black subjects in his

62. August van Pers, *African Soldier*. Photo and Print Collection, Koninklijk Instituut voor Taal-, Land- en Volkenkunde, Leiden.

later paintings, for example, several studies of mulatto women and one striking portrait of a Negro soldier in a British colonial army uniform. Meanwhile another development which would ensure even more attention to blacks was the emergence of black artists. One at the beginning of the century was Ed Frankfort, whose paintings and drawings expressed many moods from the lives of blacks.

63. Nola Hatterman, *Negro Band*. Rijksdienst Beeldende Kunst, The Hague.

The most impressive of all the art depicting blacks during this period, however, was by Nola Hatterman, an Amsterdamer who moved to Suriname because of her artistic interests. Her powerful, softly textured works appear to snatch and freeze the spirit of an actual moment in time, and project an extraordinary sense of vivacity (see figure 63).[28] Other examples of twentieth-century artists who excelled in depiction of blacks in their work are Theo Goedvriend, Kees van Dongen, and Lily Smulders Eversdijk.[29] As the century progressed there have, of course, been ever growing numbers of black artists in Suriname and the Netherlands Antilles as well as in the Netherlands itself. However, their work is only now beginning to be widely shown, preserved, and catalogued. Frank Creton and Eddy Goedhart are notable Surinamer artists (see figure 64).[30]

It is by now evident from what has been presented here that many of the very same images have found expression in every conceivable form of the visual arts. The patterns and styles in the depiction of

Art as History

64. Frank Creton, *The Street Barber*. Courtesy R. E. Clements, Peize, The Netherlands.

blacks in the more plastic arts are quite similar to what has been outlined for painting, engraving, and other illustration techniques. For example, from earliest times the same relevant biblical themes described in these categories were also expressed in mosaics, tapestries, sculptures, statues, and all manner of decoration for buildings, furniture, transportation vehicles, and other implements. The same is true for the various secular themes involving blacks. With respect to the religious themes, as might be expected, the black Magus also played his role in crêches in the Netherlands. Meanwhile the story of the Queen of Sheba was woven into tapestries and molded into the decorative relief panels for ships.[31]

In secular allegorical art the theme of the different parts of the world was also popular for tapestries and sculptures. The curious 1704 statue by Johannes Claudius de Cock of a Negro boy wearing a fortress as a crown probably is meant to represent Africa (figure 65).[32]

65. Johannes de Cock, *Africa*. Rijksmuseum, Amsterdam.

Africa is also often represented in other sculptures where Negro types are arrayed along with other people and animals. Artus Quellinus's grand frieze on the gable of the seventeenth-century town hall of Amsterdam is the most obvious example. Here an African mother stands with her son on one side holding a tropical bird while on the other she holds a lion at her hip while a serpent encircles her leg. Forming their background to the rear is a huge elephant (figure 66). This group, clearly reminiscent of "Africa" in Caesar Ripa's *Iconologia*, is just part of a much larger dramatization of Amsterdam's commercial links with all parts of the world.[33]

The embellishment of building exteriors and interiors with images of blacks continued in many forms through the centuries. The visitor to Dutch cities who never looks high up along the buildings misses an entire dimension of the cities' character and history. The pace of modern life and the restricted field of vision of modern conveyances obscure the intended perspective of scenes prepared for viewing from boats and on foot. In Amsterdam one focused on the ground level will miss the hundreds of myriad heads of humans, animals, and mythological creatures, whispering tales long forgotten and now swept away on the wind. In addition to the Gaper emblems discussed earlier, many house exterior decorations included Moors' heads, along with other human types, animals, and other symbols. Some can still be seen in Amsterdam and other cities to this day.

In some instances the decoration is just a delicate relief. In others heads or busts actually protrude, as in the case of the African couple over the entrance of the Theological Seminary of the University of Amsterdam on the Herengracht (figure 67). The practice was not restricted to Amsterdam, however. At Nienoord Castle in the town of Leek near Groningen a highly decorative grotto built around 1700 has walls completely covered by a mosaic of shells and two carved wooden Moors' heads with movable eyes and chins. On the exterior is a stone Moor's head, which, according to legend, was cast in tribute to a faithful servant who saved the master's children from drowning. In nearby Groningin one eighteenth-century grand house featured on its facade two black mermaids (figures 68 and 69).[34]

In Amsterdam the gaudiest example of this type of decoration is the huge relief on the gable of a seventeenth-century house on the Rokin, number 64–64ᴬ, not far from the Dam Square (figure 70). In earlier centuries there was nearby the opening to an alley called the

66. Artus Quellinus, *Africa*, terra-cotta model of detail from the
Amsterdam Town Hall gable, ca. 1650–1657. Rijksmuseum,
Amsterdam.

67. Entrance of the Theological Seminary of the University of Amsterdam on the Herengracht, Amsterdam. Author's photo.

68. A Moor's head at Nienoord castle near Groningen. Author's photo.

69. Black mermaids on a grand house in Groningen. Photo Collection, City Archives Groningen.

70. Gable decoration on an Amsterdam house from the seventeenth century, Rokin Street 64–64^A. Author's photo.

Mooresteeghie, now closed off. The decoration features a black figure recalling to mind the nondescript type pictured in the margins of the early modern atlases. He holds a fishing net above his head with one hand and a golden bow in the other. Archival records show that in 1610 the property upon which this house came to be built came into the possession of one Bartholomeus Moor, which probably explains the chosen decor. A similarly opulent display of exotic decoration crowned the house at number 187 on Amsterdam's Oudezijds Voorburgwal. On this gable are portrayed a seated Negro on one side of the gable and an Indian on the other, with bales of tobacco at their backs (figure 71).[35]

Also in Amsterdam are some of the most subtle and beautiful examples of African themes in building decoration. An eighteenth-century blue tile wall mosaic gracing the wall in a hall of the Rijksmuseum has almost the appearance of a three-dimensional photograph. The black servant who waits table in the scene has a dignity reminiscent of the black Magi in the paintings of the centuries before (figure 72). Another mosaic in the museum done in a completely different spirit also has a bright quality, although more ambiguous. This

71. Gable at Oudezijds Voorburgwal 187, Amsterdam. Photo Lion Versloot.

72. Willem van der Kloet, detail from blue tile wall mosaic, 1707.
Rijksmuseum, Amsterdam.

seventeenth-century Delft tile mosaic done in a humorous vein
starkly contrasts with realistic paintings from the period. Its exquisite, cartoonlike figures representing black Africans and Asians flit
amid a rich array of colorful plants and animals in a somewhat surreal
fashion harking back to Bosch's *Garden of Earthly Delights*, but far
more innocent (figure 73).

Moving now to a different part of the Netherlands, still another
variety of decoration has been preserved at Amerongen Castle museum near Utrecht. Nine pairs of black arms serving as candle holders

73. A seventeenth-century Delft tile mosaic.
Rijksmuseum, Amsterdam.

74. The Moor's head as decoration for helm handles.
Rijksmuseum Zuiderzee Museum Enkhuizen.

protrude from the walls of the castle's main hallways. One large arm
extends from each side of the main entrance hall; eight smaller pairs,
two on each wall, are located in the upper hallway. The castle, which
dates from the thirteenth century, also contains two statues of black
servants approximately four feet high. No full explanation of this
decor is available. However, it appears that it was intended at least in
part to accord with Italian styles.[36]

Another major area of Dutch life in which images of blacks were
used in decoration was in connection with the maritime industry.
Mention has already been made of a part in religious themes in this
regard. Moors' heads could be found as well on helm posts, atop oar
handles, and decorating other implements (see figures 74 and 75).[37]
Similar decoration could also be found on some land transportation vehicles. The National Coach Museum at Nienoord has a luxury coach

75. A Moor's head as decoration for flagstaff handles. Rijksmuseum
Zuiderzee Museum Enkhuizen.

76. Examples of stereotyping memorabilia. Negrophilia Foundation, Photo Pierre Verhoeff, Amsterdam.

of the Van Loon family which bears the Moor's head insignia from the family coat of arms.

One final general category of items which should be mentioned here is composed of the myriad use-objects which have been made in the shape of peoples. With respect to blacks this has been a popular fashion in the West since the ancient world, but especially so in recent centuries. Moreover, it has been particularly fashionable to make these objects in caricatured and ridiculous form. The Netherlands has shared in this tradition, borrowing much directly from Germany, England, France, and America. It is therefore possible to find minia-ture embodiments of many of the various figures and concepts treated in the chapter on folklore, with Zwarte Piet being the most obvious example (see figures 76 and 77). The use-objects range from practical items such as ashtrays, coin banks, and other containers to

77. Examples of stereotyping from post cards, children's books, and popular literature in the Netherlands, France, and Belgium. Negrophilia Foundation, Photo Pierre Verhoeff, Amsterdam.

dolls and other toys. The coin banks in the shape of blacks might well be fashioned to promote fund raising for missionary work. However, the "Alabama Coon Jigger," an American dancing windup toy, could also find its way to the Netherlands in the early twentieth century. A sizable, special collection of related material collected primarily in the Netherlands has been amassed by two Antillean artists in Amsterdam.[38]

Popularization and Standardization

As was the case with painting, the earliest widely distributed prints and illustrations were those related to religion. A popular illustrated biblical history was that of Flavius Josephus, which was available in German and Dutch. It featured illustrations of distinctively black figures for the story of Moses and the Egyptians.[39] Another biblical event with a black occasionally illustrated in various forms was the rescue of the prophet Jeremiah from a dungeon by the Ethiopian eunuch Ebed Melech. He is described in one print on this theme, captioned in old Dutch, as a "Moorman." Representing a slightly different art form, a remarkable seventeenth century woodcut from Ghent presents a tableau of the Epiphany with one of the Magi black in its three different scenes (figure 78). The Saint Nicholas legend was another religious theme frequently given expression on woodcuts (see figure 79).[40]

The oldest and most enduring medium for popular illustration was the *volksprent*, a pictorial literary genre developed more fully in

78. A seventeenth-century woodcut from Ghent. From Emile H. van
Heurck and G. J. Boekenoogen, *Histoire de l'imagerie populaire flamande et
de ses rapports avec les imageries etrangeres* (Brussels: G. van Oest & Co, 1910).

the Netherlands than anywhere else. Produced in its earliest form in
the sixteenth century as woodcuts, by the nineteenth century it had
evolved into a printed single-sheet format comparable to the broad-
side and penny paper and prefiguring the twentieth-century comic
strip. Over the centuries their topics ranged from the pious and profound to the profane, and in the nineteenth century they were mainly
humorous. In the nineteenth century they may have been the single
most popular standardized print medium. The volume of *volksprenten*
reached its fullest development in the nineteenth century with the
expansion of such printing houses as Brepols & Dierckx Zoon, which
enjoyed wide distribution of its works in Belgium and the Netherlands. German publishers also contributed to this industry. Black
characters were represented in a number of didactic as well as in entertaining compositions.

An eighteenth-century sheet of Dutch proverbs, including equiv-
alents of "hitting the nail on the head," "a bird in hand is worth two
in the bush," "if the shoe fits, wear it," "shutting the barn door after

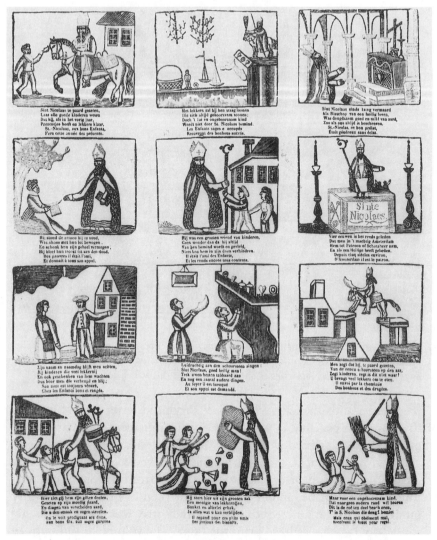

79. A children's print from the first half of the nineteenth century. *Leven van Sint Nicolaas*. Atlas van Stolk, Rotterdam.

the cows are out," and "a bull in a china closet," also features "Het is den mooriaan geschuurd," the "washed Moor" mentioned earlier in connection with the "Baptism of the Eunuch" theme. In it two white men are washing a coal-black man (figure 80). As noted in one of the dictionary quotes in the discussion of lexicography in chapter one, this phrase was an expression of futility. Here the theme from Jere-

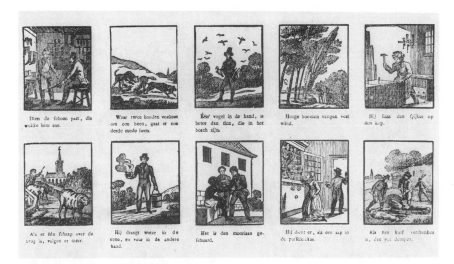

80. An eighteenth-century sheet of Dutch popular sayings.
Atlas van Stolk, Rotterdam.

miah and that of the baptism of the Ethiopian were manifest in the popular consciousness in yet another guise. Printers and booksellers, often one and the same, also used the *volksprent* format for educational matter. An example is a sheet showing various ethnological types in male and female couples in their real or imagined native costumes (figure 81).[41]

It was in the nineteenth- and early twentieth-century travel and adventure strips that black figures became most commonplace in the *volksprenten*. This tradition in the Netherlands was reinforced by counterparts in neighboring countries. One German creation combined the Saint Nicholas tradition and the exotic travel fad to produce "Knecht Ruprecht in Kamerun."[42] Here the Christmas servant during an idle period decides to travel to Africa laden with gifts for the children there. His stay is short, however, as the savage children in frame after frame destroy the lovely toys with spears, teeth, fire, and pummeling. In one frame a white girl doll is roasted over a spit. This strip illustrates the role these could play in reinforcing the stereotypes which by then had become part of Western culture. A Belgian strip, "Marius Castoulade chez Ménélick/Marius Castolade bij Ménélick" (Marius Castoulade Visiting Menelik) provides a further example (figure 82). In this case there is more humor and the blacks displayed are less brutal. However, it ends with the hero meeting the Ethiopian

EGIJPTENAARS   ABISSINIERS   NEGERS VAN DE SENEGAL   INW VAN SAHAR

NEGRS VAN GUÎNÉE   NEGERS VAN KONGO   HOTTENTOTTEN   KAFFERS

INW VAN NATAL   INW. VAN MONOMOTUPA   INW. VAN ZANGUEBAR   INW. VAN MADAGASKAR

SEMIOLEN   INW. VAN JERUSALEM   ALGERIJNEN   MAROKKANEN

81. Various ethnological types: male and female couples in their real or imagined native costumes. Atlas van Stolk, Rotterdam.

82. A popular nineteenth-century *volksprint*. Brepols & Dierckx Zoon.
Atlas van Stolk, Rotterdam.

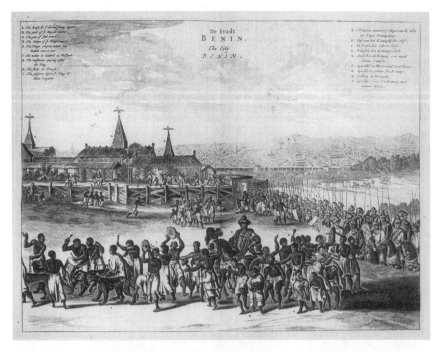

83. The city of Benin in the 17th century. From Olfert Dapper, *Naukerige Beschrijvinge de Afrikaensche Gewesten* (Amsterdam: Jacob van Meurs, 1676).

emperor Menelik only to discover that he was a Negro he had earlier encountered selling candy in Marseilles. When asked to explain this, Menelik replies that it was done in order to learn good French and fine manners.[43] This theme will be treated further in the discussion on literature.

No people have been more fascinated by serious travel literature than the people of the Low Countries. Travel literature, geographical studies, encyclopedias, and other reference books were a major source of public education especially in the centuries before it became generally available. In much of this literature can be found presentation of images of blacks along with all the other human types. This too was accompanied by prints and drawings, such as the allegorical pieces on Africa discussed earlier.[44] Perhaps the best known authors of early travel books with relevant illustrations were Olfert Dapper in the seventeenth century and Willem Bosman in the early eighteenth. Dapper's work includes two magnificent prints deserving special mention.

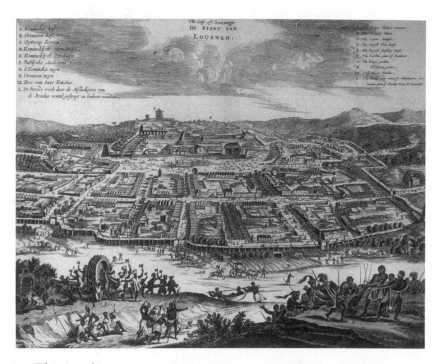

84. The city of Loango. From Olfert Dapper, *Naukerige Beschrijvinge de Afrikaensche Gewesten*.

One is of the city of Benin, the other the city of Loango. Done in the form of city scapes, apparently drawn from life, they also include graceful portraits of African people (figures 83 and 84). Although he never himself went to Africa, Dapper published related materials of such high quality that a museum named for him and devoted to pre-colonial Black African art was opened in Paris in 1990.[45]

One of the most handsome reference works of this type was the *Groot Prenten-Boek* (The Complete Print Book), published in Amsterdam in the early nineteenth century by B. Koene.[46] This work, which was designed to guide the youth in learning to read, draw, and paint, presents archetypes such as those on one page where fish types occupy one-half of the page and a "Hottentot's brood" the other. The latter are described as "grimy, filthy, and ugly" and one is shown preparing animal intestines to eat (see figure 85). This image of the Khoikhoi is a sharply negative contrast to the less widely known L. Portman 1772 etching of a Hottentot, based on W. Alexander's draw-

85. Illustration on Hottentots from an eighteenth-century children's reference book. Atlas van Stolk, Rotterdam.

Een Hottentot.

86. L. Portman's etching of a Hottentot, based on W. Alexander's drawing. Print Room, University of Leiden.

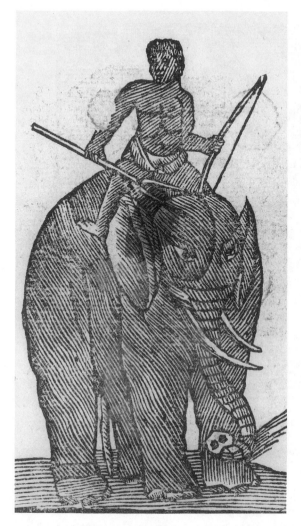

87. A "Moor" driving an elephant, from a nineteenth-century children's reference book. Atlas van Stolk, Rotterdam.

ing (figure 86). In the same *Prenten-Boek* a "Moorish" elephant driver astride his mount shares a page with a goat, with each given his respective rhyming caption (figure 87). Atlases often featured rich marginal illustrations which for many readers were as much of an attraction as the maps. Mapmakers, including Willem Janszoon Blauw, would borrow from existing works by artists such as Hendrick Goltzius.[47]

Some illustrations of life in Europe also contained blacks. A black man with no legs who moves about with crutches and an improvised platform appears in a set of wood frames depicting the various kinds

88. *Consequences of the Racing Business*, Drawings on everyday life. From H. van Heurck and G. J. Boekenoogen, *Histoire de l'imagerie populaire flamande*.

of injuries sustained in the racing profession (figure 88).[48] Blacks at times also appeared in pieces treating science. In the Boerhaave Museum in Leiden is an unusual French print from the eighteenth century showing a parlor demonstration of electricity, which was a fad for some time in the European upper classes. At the center of this experiment stands a Negro boy holding a bottle of water into which a metal rod is thrust by a young lady who stands on a stool and with her other hand holds a second rod which is attached to a device through which a young man generates a current with a crank (figure 89). Blacks in Europe were also targets of humor in illustration. C. J. Visscher's bawdy *Toonneel des Werelds* (The World's Stage) in the mid-seventeenth century borrowed Negro faces from Pieter

89. *An Experiment with Electricity*. Museum Boerhaave, Leiden.

Bruegel's etchings to go with the rhymes for his characters *Bruyntje Springh-in 't Bed* (Brownie Jump-in-the-Bed), *Flip de Duyvel* (Flip the Devil), and *'t Moye Molletje* (Pretty Molly) (figures 90–92).[49]

In the nineteenth century two major historical developments related to blacks came to be celebrated in illustrations as well as in other

90. C. J. Visscher engraving, after Pieter Bruegel, Brownie Jump-in-the-Bed. From *Toonneel des Werelds. Ondeckende de Ongestuymigheden en Ydelheden in woorden ende wercken deser verdorvene Eeuwe.* Print Room, Plantin–Moretus Museum, Antwerp.

91. C. J. Visscher engraving, Flip the Devil. From *Toonneel des Werelds.* Print Room, Plantin–Moretus Museum, Antwerp.

92. C. J. Visscher
engraving, Pretty Molly.
From *Toonneel des Werelds*.
Print Room,
Plantin-Moretus Museum,
Antwerp.

ways. The first was the broadening scope of missionary activity by
the Dutch religious organizations. Prime targets of Dutch missionary
activity were, of course, Black Africa and especially the Dutch possessions in the Americas. This led, for example, to annual illustrated
calendars and maps as well as periodicals devoted to the mission. Such
a calendar might include scenes depicting pagan practices around the
globe as well as others showing natives under the sway of the Christian faith. The other main event was emancipation of slaves of African origins in the New World. The collection of sketches by Charles
Rochussen inspired by Harriet Beecher Stowe's *Uncle Tom's Cabin*
nicely captures the tone of many of the other illustrations prompted
by emancipation. A related calendar was titled "Uncle Tom's Almanak 1854." With a calendar in the middle, around its borders are
scenes from the novel. A joyous print on the same theme shows a
freed couple with arms uplifted in praise and their children burying
the cast-off chains (figures 93–95). An 1874 illustrated song sheet
printed in tribute to the silver jubilee of the reign of King William III
included a scene celebrating the emancipation.[50]

Historical developments also dictated that by the nineteenth cen-

93. "Uncle Tom's Almanak 1854." Atlas van Stolk, Rotterdam.

tury there would be more interest within the Netherlands than ever before in the peoples in the wider Dutch empire that had materialized over the past few centuries. Drawings of the Dutch West African fortresses made their way into Dutch literature. Increased direct contact sometimes resulted in more accurate depiction of some of the

94. Title page for drawings on *Uncle Tom's Cabin* by
Charles Rochussen. Atlas van Stolk, Rotterdam.

peoples abroad. A series of drawings by Thomas Bray and others by
A. Borret portrayed Negro life in Suriname. [51] The collection of one
hundred lithographs compiled by P. J. Benoit depicting blacks, Indians, and Europeans in the early nineteenth century contributes further refreshing realism and beauty to the body of illustrations of the
population in Suriname (see figures 96–102). [52] Finally, at the close of
the century some of the colored peoples of the Dutch colonies were
deliberately brought to the Netherlands on some occasions so that
they could be seen firsthand by all. One major such occasion was the
1883 International Exhibition in Amsterdam, when eleven blacks
were in the group borrowed to represent the peoples of Suriname.
Charles Rochussen captured this group in drawings which were published along with a related article (figure 103). [53]

With the expansion of the reading public brought by increasing
literacy, popular, illustrated fictional literature also grew by the nine-

95. *Emancipation*, Atlas van Stolk, Rotterdam.

teenth century. This too would come to reflect the mounting cultural
diversity in the Netherlands and her empire. This can be seen, for
example, in a mid-century English novel available in the Netherlands,
one of whose main pictured characters is a mixed African and Portuguese servant boy who travels with his master from Brazil to the

96. The Dutch West African fortress at Elmina, from the land side.
Netherlands Maritime Museum, Amsterdam.

Dutch East Indies.[54] Illustrated magazines were also very much in vogue. This provided the major outlet for Dutch artists like Charles Rochussen. An example of the kind of subject related to Blacks which might appear can be seen in an 1891 issue of Elsevier's *Geillustreerd Maandschrift* (Illustrated Monthly), one of the most successful of these magazines. In this issue appeared a play based on the life of Admiral de Ruiter, who had a black servant boy named Jan Companie.[55] Another form of literature which saw great proliferation in the nineteenth and twentieth centuries was children's literature. Here the most popular theme for present purposes was that of Sinterklaas and Zwarte Piet. Numerous Sinterklaas storybooks published in the nineteenth and twentieth century were adorned with beautiful lithographs as well as with less formal drawings (see figure 104).[56] Other types of children's books also included blacks in presenting a world of increasing cultural diversity. Some of the most handsome drawings in this regard in the early twentieth century were those of Cornelis Jetses (see figure 105).

Illustration is, of course, not limited to literature. Another widely disseminated pictorial medium since the nineteenth century is the postcard. Here too themes related to blacks have enjoyed great popu-

97. Drawing by Thomas Bray portraying Negro life in Suriname.
Atlas van Stolk, Rotterdam.

larity. The scope of topics and styles is panoramic. Indeed, there are
hardly any of the various forms of art that have been treated here that
have not found expression as well on postcards. For those not familiar
with Dutch culture, cards devoted to the Sinterklaas theme are especially unusual. Since the persistence of this theme is related in part to
its commercial value, it is not surprising to find it as well in all forms

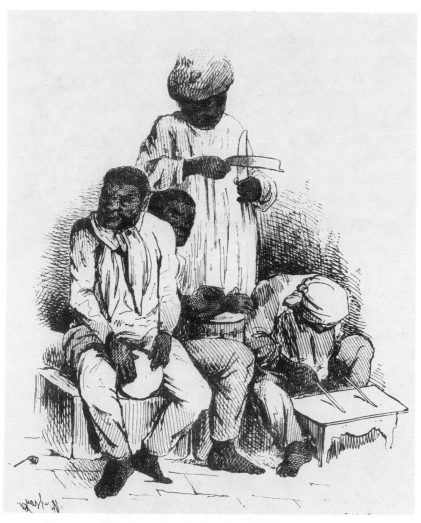

98. Drawing by Thomas Bray portraying Negro life in Suriname.
Atlas van Stolk, Rotterdam.

of graphic advertising, including such items as wrapping paper, in
addition to all kinds of publications. In the depiction of Zwarte Piet
these advertisements have ranged from presentation of darkened European faces at one extreme to crass stereotypes of blacks at the other.
Black faces and bodies also became frequent trademarks for all sorts
of products, but especially for raw materials, foods, and cleansers (see

99. P. J. Benoit, Three Creole and African tradeswomen. From P. J. Benoit, *Voyage a Surinam: Description des Possessions Neerlandaises dan La Guyane* (Brussels: Société des Beaux-arts, 1839). In the collections of the Moorland-Spingarn Research Center, Howard University, Washington, D.C.

100. P. J. Benoit, Three Negro artisans, a Creole slave, and a slave boy. From *Voyage a Surinam*, Moorland-Spingarn Research Center, Howard University.

101. P. J. Benoit, High Class People on their way to church. From *Voyage a Surinam*, Moorland–Spingarn Research Center, Howard University.

102. A. H. A. H. M. Borret, *Diverse people of Surinam and their Occupations* (late nineteenth century). Photo and Print Collection, Koninklijk Instituut voor Taal-, Land- en Volkenkunde, Leiden.

103. Charles Rochussen drawing of Representatives from Surinam
at the 1883 International Exhibition in Amsterdam. From G. P. H.
Zimmermann, "De Surinaamsche Inboorlingen op de Tentoonstelling,"
Eigen Haard Geillustreerd Volkstijdschrift (1883), p. 414.

figures 106–108). A random sample of the collection of some fourteen hundred items of memorabilia depicting blacks, mentioned earlier, reveals the following general categories of products employing
blacks on their trademark: tobacco, coffee, liquor, cleansers, rice fa-
rina, candy, shoe polish, metal polish, and tooth paste.[57]
    The advent of photography in the nineteenth century introduced
new dimensions to standardization of art and to the evolution of the
image of blacks. This topic is too large to be given proper attention in
the present study; however, it has a significance which demands at
least a brief description of its relevance. First, photography brought
the potential for detailed reproduction of other types of imagery as
well as one further means of capturing an original in a variety of
styles.[58] Second, its ease of reproduction meant a wider dissemination
of relevant visual information. Finally, later related innovations, resulting in the art of film and in the television industry, contributed to
a revolution in communications and in culture formation that has direct bearing on the evolving image of blacks as well as on all other
attitudes. As numerous studies have shown for other Western socie-

104. J. Schenkman, *St. Nicholas and His Servant*. From *Het Prentenboek van Tante Pau* (The Hague, 1974).

ties, these media can and have been used consciously and unconsciously to create and influence attitudes toward peoples as well as toward things and ideas.[59] As with the other forms of art discussed here, the messages in these media have been in turn influenced by historical developments.

105. Cornelis Jetses, *Where Do Butterflies Come From?* Wolters–Noordhoff Archive, Groningen.

106. Trademarks for Belgian polishes around 1930. Negrophilia Foundation, Photo Pierre Verhoeff, Amsterdam.

The material in this chapter raises some of the most complex questions of all for the topic at hand because of the power of visual imagery and the way in which it often serves as a medium for imagery of other types. We also tend to attribute to the visual the highest degree of reality. The assumption that what we see is more reliable than what we think and what we feel underlies such sayings as "seeing is believing" and "a picture is worth a thousand words," while it is equally plausible that in both cases the opposite is true. Can we trust the visual not to distort the ideas from folklore, religion, literature, and other perspectives? Is there a common enough language of symbols and aesthetics for a broad audience to read a common message in the images? As has been shown here, the visual art has power through both what it shows and what it omits. With respect to the question of racial perceptions it also raises all sorts of thorny questions about the psychology involved, the powers of suggestion, and the didactic role of art, whether conscious or unconscious. It would seem that art must be viewed as more a prism than a mirror of history.

While all of these questions need much further study, it is at least clear from what has been presented here that, while there are striking positive images of blacks in Dutch art, common patterns in their depiction tend more to support familiar, negative stereotypes in Western culture in general. It is also evident that the standardization and

107. A trademark for cigars around 1930. Negrophilia Foundation, Photo Pierre Verhoeff, Amsterdam.

dissemination of visual imagery that became more possible in the modern period magnify the range of those stereotypes proportionately. It may be that this is just a reflection of the obvious fact that for most of the history in question blacks were a tiny minority, and outsiders with whom Dutch society was not yet familiar. Yet this does

108. Trademark for Dobbelmann's "Buttermilk Soap," 1910. The little white girl says to the black girl: "Don't you wish you also had washed with Buttermilk Soap?"

not rule out racial bias. Perhaps the more literal expression of attitudes that can be found in literature and the views on human worth in the religious thought should inform this discussion. It is to those areas that we now turn.

DUTCH LITERATURE'S DARK FACES

Belles-Lettres

IN LIGHT OF THE early presence of imagery concerning Blacks in Dutch folklore and art, it is not surprising that similar elements also appeared in literature from its very beginnings. The evolving imagery in literature paralleled that in folklore and art, chronologically and thematically. Moreover, due to the overlap in these three forms of expression, literature often was inseparable from folklore and art. As in the folklore and art, it is through the pervasive theme of the Moor that blacks also entered the literature. The earliest manuscript is the Arthurian romantic tale *Morien*, which dates from the early fourteenth century in its Dutch language form. This story of a black knight who is a son of one of the knights of the Round Table and a Moorish princess is just one of several European versions:

> He was black, . . . his head, his body, and his hands were all black, saving only his teeth. His shield and armour were even those of a Moor, and black as a raven. . . . Had they not heard him call upon God no man had dared face him, deeming that he was the devil or one of his fellows out of hell.[1]

Here it can be seen that religious distinctions are very important. However, even more notable is the perception of the black skin color as sinister.

The most common theme in Dutch literature on blacks is the Dutch experience with African slavery. The works sometimes stated or implied opposition to slavery. The earliest notable work of this nature was the 1617 play *Moortje* (Little Moor) by G. A. Bredero. In it are the lines:

Inhumane practice! Godless Knavery!
That men sell men into chattel slavery!
There are some in this city who ply such trade.
In Fornabock; but it will not escape God's gaze.[2]

This did not, however, prevent Bredero from presenting his lover a black girl as a gift. Bredero is thus an early example of the ambivalence which would continue in Dutch society concerning ethical principles and practices related to slavery. This would be apparent both in the lives of various thinkers and in their works.[3] Bredero's *Moortje* also projected one of the stereotypes concerning Blacks which was popular in Western culture:

I've been told and have taken it to heart
That the Moors are inclined toward the ladies for their part.[4]

A mid-seventeenth-century work which carried this play on sexual stereotypes even further was C. J. Visscher's ribald *Tonneel des wereldts*, with its set of rhymes accompanying drawings of Pieter Bruegel. Amidst its lampooning of priests and nuns this work also brings to life such black characters as the following two, mentioned in the previous chapter:

Brownie Jump-in-the-Bed

My skin is like a mole's
My hair as black as jet
My teeth like ivory
My curled lips

My round breasts are hidden reefs.
And as for my lap,
It challenges the whitest wife:
Thus many a man seeks
To spend his time with me.

Flip the Devil

With black sheep's wool is my head crowned
I am a Devil for the Dutch women.
My nose, a flat beak, exhibits a horrible beauty.
Such are suspicious in squeamish eyes.
I delight my nice Mooress nonetheless.
She takes care of me and calls me playmate.[5]

The work that set the tone for novels about slavery was written by a British lady with a Dutch name; but its setting is Suriname. Mrs. Aphra Behn's *(Oroonoko) The History of the Royal Slave*, first published in London in 1688, was the main prototype for the "Noble Savage" imagery in the Netherlands. The story was apparently based partly on events either experienced by the author or recounted to her. Its hero, an African prince, had a "Roman" nose, "fine," un-negroid lips, and spoke French and English. He was tricked into slavery by unscrupulous Europeans who lured him onto their ship as their guest. In Suriname he was still venerated by the other slaves for his royalty. Eventually he tried to flee captivity with his wife. When they were caught he killed her to protect her from further life as a slave, but was subdued before he could commit suicide as he intended. He was tortured and dismembered for his defiance.[6]

The best example of the "Noble Savage" imagery in Dutch literature came a century later with the novel of Elisabeth Maria Post, *Reinhart of natuur en godsdienst* (Pure Heart or Nature and Religion), published in Amsterdam in 1791–1792. Reinhart, the hero, is a "good" slave master. The novel is strongly antislavery in tone and presents a sympathetic picture of Violet, a male slave of Reinhart. Reinhart denounces slavery because to him it violates natural law, which demands individual liberty. Reinhart is also shocked by the contradictions he finds between the Christian beliefs and actual practices of colonists in Suriname. However, his reason for going there was to rescue his mother in Holland from financial ruin, and he soon compromises his beliefs for this higher motive. He becomes a slave master, but treats his slaves well and encourages others to do the same. This concession to the established order did not, however, obscure the fact that at one point in the novel he stated that he would not be surprised if the slaves revolted. This line in Post's work was an uncomfortable reminder to the Dutch public of the revolts which had occurred by then, especially in the 1760s.[7]

An anonymous novel, *De Middelburgsche avonturier* (The Middelburg Adventurer), published in 1760, brought new depth to the analysis of colonial society and the place of blacks in it. The main character, Lodewijk, is from Zeeland and has experienced financial ruin and imprisonment, until freed by a clergyman. In Amsterdam he meets a Jewish gentleman, Wilhelmus, who is desperate to escape an intolerable domestic situation, and who has been offered a plantation by relatives in Suriname. The two set out for there to make their fortune. From the outset they listened to suggestions from the slaves for improving their own lot and maximizing profits for the plantation. The venture was a huge success and ended only after Wilhelmus died and Lodewijk returned to Holland out of loneliness after selling the plantation. The two principals were thus portrayed as "good" masters, albeit using business rather than humane criteria for their actions. The author uses the technique of expressing some ideas through black spokesmen, as is also done in *Oroonoko*.[8]

Another anonymous novel of this period presents a rare case of a master who was good for humanitarian reasons. Its title is *Geschiedenis van een neger, zijn reize met de heer N . . . van Surinamen naar Holland* (The Story of a Negro, His Trip with Mr. N. from Suriname to Holland), published around 1770. For a change, the Negro is the main character in this story, which shows some influence from the real life of Jacobus Capitein, which will be detailed in the next chapter on religion. N. is a Huguenot who comes to Suriname through Holland. He becomes a plantation owner by marrying the widow of a planter. When the family takes a trip to Holland, an unusually gifted male slave is allowed to accompany them. On the way they stop at an island where a Huguenot leader has set up a religious utopian community. The slave is allowed to become a Christian minister and assumes the name Thomas. Upon arrival in Amsterdam he becomes a severe critic of the society he confronts because of all the evil he sees. Finally, he marries N.'s daughter, Agnes, with her father's blessing, despite the racist objections of society.[9]

Yet another writing in which a black character was the principal figure appeared in the Amsterdam periodical *De Denker* (The Thinker) in 1764. The author submitted what was purported to be a letter which he had edited, allegedly written by a black African named Kakera Akotie. The latter had supposedly been a free man mistakenly enslaved while on a ship bound from West Africa to Suriname. His relatives had managed to arrange his release through official channels, and he had written the letter in question while in Amsterdam en route back to Africa. Somehow the letter, an account of Kakera Akotie's experience of slavery, had miraculously fallen into the hands of the "editor." The letter was full of strong reproach for the white colonists, detailing all the usual cruel abuses against the slaves and ending with a prediction that one day the slaves would take their revenge in a massive uprising. The "editor," however, ends his offering with the comment that this letter calls for appropriate rejoinders from Dutch plantation owners. He suggests arguments along the lines of Montesquieu's *Spirit of Laws*, which provides satirical justifications for slavery based on economic necessity and physical traits of the Africans. It is left to conjecture whether he or his audience understood them as satire.[10]

There were a number of other Dutch periodicals in the late eighteenth century which featured pieces concerning relations between the Dutch and blacks, for example, the *Neerlandsch Echo* (Dutch Echo) in 1770–1771 and *De Koopman* (The Merchant) from 1768 to 1776. At the same time, black subjects were also treated in other forms of Dutch literature besides novels and feuilletons. In 1771 there appeared a play entitled *Het Surinaamsche leeven* (Life in Suriname). In it the unknown author, who used the pen name "Don Experientia," denounced the conduct of the German, French, and Dutch colonial administrators.[11] A somewhat different message received expression in the next decade in the poetry of Paul François Roos, a Dutch planter-poet who wrote from Suriname. He championed freedom for the emerging United States of America and for the Netherlands; but he tended to romanticize black slavery. In his satirical pseudoletter "Schets van het plantaadje leven" (Sketch of Plantation Life) he describes the planter's lunchtime:

> I see lunch being served.
> A retinue of girls stands crowded around a dish.
> While another, with hand towels at their bosoms,
> Up they stand. Yes, my friend, I live like a prince.
> The slave is attentive to my wink; my words are commands.
> A squire can live like a king.
> I demand a clean pipe, tobacco, and a glass of wine
> This must already have been prepared as I was asking.[12]

In another work, "Myn neger jongen Cicero" (My Negro Boy Cicero), Roos supports one of the planters' arguments for slavery by having a slave assert that he would not change places with freemen in Africa, Poland, or the Netherlands.

> I shall tell you considerably more about it.
> When I was able to accompany my master
> To the freedom-minded Netherlands,

I thought: so, now I'll learn
How to appreciate freedom's worth,
While slavery is banned there,
I found I was fooled; for the free poor
Are worse off than slaves.

These contrasting outlooks concerning slavery suggest the complexity of this issue for those who gave it serious thought.[13]

By the late eighteenth century deep involvement in the slave trade was a long-accomplished fact for the Netherlands; now colonial society became a frequent setting for literary fiction and the issue of how to relate to slavery was more pressing than ever. Not only African slavery, but slavery in general gained attention. In 1780 there appeared in Batavia the novella *Kraspoekol; of de droevige gevolgen van eene te verregaande strengheid jegens de Slaaven* (Kraspoekol; or the Sad Consequences of an Excessively Severe Slavery) by Willem van Hogendorp. Its plot featured the murder of an unusually cruel mistress by a wronged slave. The mixed reception it received in the Netherlands can be gauged from a description of an English observer who was present in The Hague in 1801 at the attempted staging of the story as a play by Hogendorp's son Dirk:

. . . six months after the publication of this play, with his name to it, he attempted to have it represented on the stage at The Hague, on the 20th March 1801; but the East India Gentry, not thinking it proper to exhibit the most illustrious actions of themselves and their noble ancestors upon a stage to vulgar European spectators, went to the play provided with little half-penny whistles and trumpets, and kept up such a tremendous whistling and trumpeting from the very moment the curtain began to be drawn up, that not a syllable of the play could be heard—and, if these Gentlemen could, they would also have extinguished the candles, to keep in darkness what themselves and their ancestors never intended for the light. In short, the play, after being thus interrupted the whole of the first act, was broken off before the second, when the manager was obliged to give up the entertainment. . . . The next day the ignorant part of the audience was so curious to know the secrets which these East India Gentlemen had been thus industrious to conceal, that the bookseller (as he told me himself) sold infinitely more copies of the play that day, than all he had sold the whole of the preceding six months, and had he ten times more, they would not have answered the numerous demands.[14]

Another good example is a German novel by C. G. Salzman, translated as *De geschiedenis van Simon Blaauwkool* (The Story of Simon Blaauwkool), published in Amsterdam in 1813. Like *Reinhart*, set in Suriname, the story chronicles the exploits of a young German who worked his way up in the colony to owning a plantation (ultimately through marriage). He too was noted for his humane treatment of the slaves while surrounded by other whites who insisted: "These are not men . . . they are dogs, and if they are not thrashed enough, they cannot be curbed." The Dutch translator, a cleric named William Anthony Ockerse, noted that the starkly negative portrait painted of the Dutch planters was exaggerated. He also objected to the singling out of the Dutch planters for blame.[15]

Also, by the late eighteenth century growing abolitionist sentiment, led by the movement in England, helped tilt public opinion in the Netherlands further against slavery. Here it should be noted that it was only in Great Britain and in parts of the United States of America that abolitionism ever developed as a mass movement. Elsewhere it remained a concern of elites, with the plight of African slaves attracting little popular interest. Although neither the abolitionist movement in the Netherlands nor opposition to it ever really became strong, some of the resultant literature was.[16] Good examples can be seen in the writings of two representatives of that peculiarly Dutch tradition of the preacher poets: Nicolaas Beets and Bernard ter Haar.

Beets is especially interesting, for his attitude showed an element of change over time. In his best-known work, *Camera Obscura* (Dark Chamber), first published under his pseudonym "Hildebrand" in 1839, he treats the racial color question in the short story "De Familie Kegge." Satirizing bourgeois values in general, using a colored family which had moved from Suriname to the Netherlands, Beets also has the family head, Kegge, express contempt for Negroes.[17] Meanwhile, the one black character, a male servant, plays his patented role as silently as do his counterparts in Dutch paintings. Since *Camera Obscura* was one of the most widely read Dutch novels in the nineteenth century, its view of various elements of society must have enjoyed some influence. Hildebrand's characterization is also useful here in illustrating how the attitudes concerning color may have been accepted by those of color in the Dutch world as well as by the rest.

Beets wrote *Camera Obscura* while still a divinity student in Leiden. In his later life he was one of the most strident champions of abolition in the Netherlands. Regardless of his specific attitudes on color, he was against slavery:

> Oh Netherlands mighty and righteous!
> Break our yoke:
> Bring, bring your poor Negro slaves
> Now finally, finally out of oppression.
> Though we are Blacks,
> We have hearts
> Just like you.
> Good if your hearts are better,
> Then loosen ours from the pain!
> We suffer so! [1853][18]

Bernard ter Haar also lent his voice to the call for freedom at mid-century, like Beets perhaps buoyed more by developments in the United States than those in the Netherlands. Before later writing about slavery in Suriname, he was inspired by Harriet Beecher Stowe's *Uncle Tom's Cabin* to write a number of pieces. One tribute included:

> America! Dare you call yourself the Land of the Free,
> Where Liberty's most beautiful temple stands?
> While the Negro slave, writhing in his chains, lies dying at your
>   feet?
> Do you dare proclaim God's peace on the African,
> Whose back you have ploughed up with lashes and wounds?
> [1853][19]

Assuming that the calls of these popular preachers touched a responsive chord in their audience, there must have existed a significant public sentiment affirming at least that blacks should not be enslaved. There were as well other prominent supportive voices in popular literature. For example, Eduard Dekker, whose work *Max Havelaar* vied with Beets's for the honor of most popular of the century, echoed similar sentiments. It is also interesting to note that in one passage of this work he used the term "Nigger" in referring to slaves in the East Indies, showing Dutch awareness of the universality of this term, which originally was coined to underscore the contempt of the Europeans for the black Africans.[20]

Twentieth-century Dutch writers have also continued to feature blacks in various roles in fiction. Louis Couperus, like Dekker a civil servant working on East Indies affairs, presented many black slaves in his novels set in the Roman era, for example *Antiek toerisme* (Ancient Tourism), published in 1911. They often fit either the primitive or sensual stereotypes. At the other end of the century Guus Kuijer's 1989 novel *De redder van Afrika* (The Savior of Africa) treats the life of Jacobus Capitein, thus offering a black as the sympathetic main character.[21]

The negative view of blacks characteristic of most Dutch literature generally became amplified in that which was produced in the new languages which developed in the colonies. However, once the authors writing in these languages came to include those of African descent, this also brought a more sympathetic treatment. It should also be noted that these languages themselves—Sranan, Papiamento, and Afrikaans—represented an African influence on Dutch literature and culture. Even Afrikaans, which is derived largely from a Dutch dialect, owes some of its rhythm and many concepts to the original Khoisan patois. Nevertheless, the stereotyped image of "Cape Coloureds" and its impact on racial attitudes helped shape and reinforce the prejudices which developed. There was direct continuity between the stereotypes applied to the Khoi in early travel literature and those designating the Coloured on through the twentieth century.[22]

Sranan did not exist before 1651. It evolved as a contact language between slaves and masters and between slaves of variant origins, and of course became the native tongue of those born in Suriname. In the late nineteenth century the first writers to stress African-Surinamer racial identity wrote in Dutch, because their intended audience was the educated elite. A notable example is Carl P. Rier of Paramaribo, a black Baptist minister who wrote mainly historical and practical tracts. By stressing in them the need for self esteem, national unity, and triumph over adversity he articulated what would come to characterize the Afro-Surinamer literary tradition, which would be taken up by such later writers as A. Koenders, Johanna Schouten-Elsenhout, and Edgar Cairo.[23]

Although Sranan was considered lower-class until the middle of the twentieth century, it became more respected due to the rise of nationalist sentiment and the quality of Creole poetry. The first partly Creole published poem was written in 1783 by the Dutchman Hendrik Schouten, a friend of Roos, who likewise was married to a colored woman, and who earlier wrote in Dutch a poem called *De geele vrouw* (The Yellow Woman) defending his wife against the prevailing prejudice.

The Yellow Wife

A wife who minds the virtues and her duties,
Out of genial joy sometimes sings a tune.
Plays the clavicymbal and sometimes lustily leaps
To enlighten the enslaved minds

Who bold in home-making and pure in cooking arts
While shunning stinginess, is still frugal,
And when the need calls gives generously
With a wise management of everything rarely seen.

Who, however, is still now sometimes scorned, despised, envied,
Through base scandal-mongering in honor wrung from regret,
And through mean spiritedness denounced for unchasteness

In order that . . . my terrible tongue becomes my part
I did not hush this calumny, each mortal must know
The virtuous woman was yellow instead of white![24]

The theme of miscegenation and clash of cultures would reach its fullest development in the twentieth century, and with special poignancy in the work of the Antillean writer Cola Debrot, whose maternal great grandmother was a colored Creole.[25] His novel *Mijn zuster de negerin* (My Sister the Negress), published in 1935, was the first Antillean work of fiction in the Dutch language. His last novella, *De Vervolgden* (The Persecuted), explores the sixteenth-century conflict between the Spanish and the Indians in the Caribbean. Borrowing from Shakespeare's model in *The Tempest*, treating European civilization's confrontation with "the other," he scores the European assumptions of spiritual, racial, and moral superiority. In this and his other writings, in contrast to Shakespeare's unhappy resolution of the predicament, Debrot proposes a synthesis of the diverse cultural values in place of the conventional European subjugation of all others.[26]

Debrot's hopeful scenario has not, however, been realized in either literature or life in the Dutch colonies. Suriname still struggles with these cultural issues even after independence in 1975, while in the Antilles the late 1980s witnessed talk of "coming cultural revolution." Its leading voice, the black Curaçaoan linguist and writer Frank Martinus Arion, asserts that it is precisely through replacement of Dutch by the native language, in this case Papiamento, that cultural maturity and independence will come to the former colonies. As director of the Instituto Lingkwistiko Antiano, Arion set as his primary goal the formalizing of this folk language, comprised of Spanish, West African, Portuguese, Dutch, and English elements, and having it adopted as the official language of instruction in the schools. In his view this would contribute to an increase in literary activity by native writers, which would inevitably enhance the image of native culture.[27]

At the same time, responding to the growing black presence, black themes can be encountered ever more frequently on stage and screen and in the communications media in the Netherlands proper. Vignettes from the historical experience joining African and Dutch history continue to fascinate. An example is the story of the African slave boy Jefke, who was a gift to the Antwerp Zoo in 1845, in exchange for a lifetime pass to what was at the time a very exclusive institution. Baptized as Jozef Möller, he became a popular zoo caretaker and a mascot-like figure in the community. He was married in the Ape House to a Dutch servant girl who later bore him a daughter. He died in 1882 at the age of 48, deeply mourned. A year earlier a historic fire in the Ape House in his care had cost the lives of 79 apes. In 1990 this story inspired a satirical play entitled *De nacht van de brandende apen* (The Night of the Burning Apes) by the Flemish writer Tone Brul.[28]

Travel Literature and Scientific Writing

Travel literature and geographical studies were present in large volume in the Netherlands from a very early date, due both to the importance of Amsterdam as an international publishing center and to their popularity. Consequently, just as was the case with dictionaries and encyclopedias, these works played a major role in shaping the initial formulation of Dutch images concerning blacks, at least for the reading public and those influenced by it. A prime example is the physician Olfert Dapper's compendium of geographical knowledge, mentioned in chapter three in connection with its remarkable prints. Commissioned by the city of Amsterdam and titled *Nauwkeurige Beschrijvinge der Afrikaensche Gewesten* (Exact Description of the African Regions . . .), It was published in Amsterdam in a Dutch edition in 1676, in French in 1686, and became one of the most popular references of the century and a standard source for many later works in the Netherlands and abroad. In the frontispiece an enthroned king looks more Persian than African and his surrounding subjects are a variety of imaginary types. At the other extreme stand the marvelous prints depicting the cities of Benin and Loango in almost photographic detail.[29] However, the overall impression left by Dapper's work as well is a negative one due to the sundry misinformation which its text repeats concerning cultures about which the author had no firsthand knowledge. In contrast to the exceptional engraving from Dapper's work mentioned above, most illustrations and texts in similar works revealed an ignorance of both the appearance and the mores of the peoples of Africa, Asia, and the Americas, and in general showed a highly Eurocentric outlook. The Dutch in the seventeenth and eighteenth century seemed predisposed to imagine blacks as Dutchmen in African clothing, just as they were unclear on how to depict their own Zwarte Piet, whose "Moorish" features varied widely and who dressed in European clothing.

Nevertheless, a persistent preference for the exotic and bizarre which was pronounced in the visual arts appears to have carried over into the literature.[30] Another illustrative travel narrative was the well-known work of the early eighteenth century by the Dutchman Willem Bosman. Bosman, who had served as a Dutch official in Elmina in the late seventeenth century, began his characterization of the natives with:

> The Negroes are all without exception, Crafty, Villainous and Fraudulent, and very seldom to be trusted; . . . they seem to be born villains: All sorts of baseness having got such sure-footing in them, that 'tis impossible to lye concealed; and herein they agree very well with what Authors tell us of the Muscovites.[31]

Perhaps this last gratuitous comparison at least suggests that Bosman was not viewing the African in purely racist terms. Nevertheless, these views by an observer who, unlike the authors of many such compendia, at least had resided in the region treated, helped perpetuate misinformation which would be repeated in later influential travel literature, such as the works by J. D. Herlein and Philip Fermin.[32] Bosman's book in another place also paraphrased a view expressed earlier in an account by J. W. Focquenbroch, which would realize numerous editions and be even more popular than Bosman's:

> As for the misses, alias Negresses and mulatto women, I find these so deathly, shameful, indeed dreadfully ugly, that if I was a dog I would not want to piss on them, so that I would be in a clean state to leave this country again.[33]

In contrast to this, a travel account treating the Cape Colony Khoikhoi published in 1790 provided real-life support for the literary myth of the "Noble Savage." The author, François Le Vaillant, was born in Suriname, of a French father and a Dutch mother. In pursuit of his hobby as a naturalist, he spent four months in the interior of southern Africa with the Khoikhoi, whom he learned to admire. The two-volume work he published as a result contradicts a number of popular misconceptions of the time about this people. In one chapter he extols the virtues of his favorite servant, one Klaas, in terms epitomizing the "Noble Savage":

> Klaas was now my equal, my brother, the confidant of my hopes and fears; more than once has he calmed my agitated mind, and reanimated my drooping courage.

The tone of Le Vaillant's work, however, was exceptional for such accounts. Moreover, the public seemed to prefer the more fantastic descriptions. After the first quarter of the eighteenth century the most popular works were Dutch translations of English and French books.[34]

In the seventeenth and eighteenth centuries, to the Dutch awareness of blacks through folklore, art, and belles-lettres was added a new, scientific interest. The purveyors of the Age of Reason could hardly neglect such an intriguing subject as the nature of the differences between peoples and cultures. The letters of Anton van Leeuwenhoek provide an excellent illustration. Writing from Delft in 1684, the famous naturalist described his microscopic analysis of skin samples he took from the arm of a black Moorish girl. Comparing these to earlier examinations of his own epidermis, he drew an analogy between the human surface skin and the scales of fish. He was particularly fascinated with the question of the source of the color in black skin, noting that the "scales" when viewed individually were transparent and only took on color when lying on top of each other. Notwithstanding a few conjectures which are erroneous by modern standards, Leeuwenhoek correctly concluded that the pigment originates in the deeper layers of the skin. He therefore rejected the view he knew to be held by many Dutchmen that

> The Moors become black merely by rubbing their bodies with a certain oil, for they say the children are red when they come into the world, just like our children. But just as it is impossible to dye the wool or the hair on the body of a sheep, a horse, or any other animal so that it retains this colour, because the hair is shed, so also it is impossible to dye the scales forming the epidermis, so as to keep it black, because the scales are constantly shed.[35]

Scientific inquiry into the distinctions between races was, of course, just beginning. Many aspects of the question are still not answered. In Holland the question surfaced again in 1765 in a scientific treatise by Claude Nicolas Le Cat entitled "Traite de la couleur de la peau humaine en general, de celle des negres en particulier" (Treatise on the Human Skin in General and That of the Negro in Particular). While this was published in Amsterdam, its French author was the retired chief physician and surgeon of the Hotel-Dieu, the main hospital in Rouen. In his work Le Cat advanced a theory which contradicted the prevailing belief of the time that blacks were a separate species with black bile accounting for their color. Following a different current of ideas, Le Cat posited the existence of a substance he called *ethiops*, which he said existed in varying degrees in all living creatures. He based his hypothesis in part on his own experiments with frogs. *Ethiops* as he described it bears striking similarities to what later came to be called melanin.[36] Le Cat thus accepted the basic concept—one which some earlier thinkers had mentioned in various forms—that was eventually adopted as the most valid for explaining skin color. The Dutch reading public of the time therefore had access to the most advanced thinking on this subject.

Of course, this does not mean that this interpretation would necessarily gain acceptance. One Dutch writer in 1787 commenting on the color of black children in Suriname asserted with an air of great authority:

A [black] child comes into the world completely white; thus none distinguish him from a child born of a white woman. About the third day there begins to show more or less a black color on the fingernails, over the flesh, and on the male sexual organ, on the skin which loops down over the sack of manhood. Within two days this color deepens; the entire child becomes browner, and then completely black; until within fifteen days his natural black color is achieved.[37]

As late as the mid-nineteenth century the agronomist Maarten Teenstra would still be countering white Surinamers who claimed

That it must be forbidden for Negroes to walk upright (on their hind legs), among Whites, since they are the Devil's creations, and an ultimate mocking parody of the creation of man.[38]

An important scientist in the Netherlands who made a major contribution to this discussion was the distinguished anatomist and zoologist Petrus Camper (1722–1789). Camper was one of the true pioneers of modern physical anthropology, and is perhaps the most misinterpreted of all. A talented scientific artist, Camper came upon his most noted contribution while attempting to develop a method for drawing people more accurately in terms of their natural forms. Of special interest for the present study, it was his irritation with depictions of the black king with European features in the many Adoration of the Magi paintings he had seen that prompted him to try to provide other artists guidance on how to draw human figure types for which they might not have models on hand. This led him in the 1760s to undertake intensive empirical study of human skulls and those of other animals, especially apes. Like some earlier scientists, he found that quantification of the physical characteristics of different racial groups aided in their classification. His most original contribution is a criterion he called the "facial angle," the angle at the intersection of a horizontal line drawn from the ear opening to the base of the nose with a vertical line from the edge of the incisor teeth to the most protruding part of the brow above the eyes.

Camper illustrated his findings with a series of profiled heads, showing the last on the right, an ideal Greek statue type, having a one-hundred-degree "facial angle." This index then descended, moving to the left, through the Roman statue, the general European, the Kalmuck, the Angolan, the orangutan, the monkey, and in theory on through the vertebrates to a bird's bill or fish.[39] However, quite the contrary of what some contemporaries and especially nineteenth-century scientists surmised, Camper did not intend his scale to represent a kind of chain of being reflecting qualitative measurement. Nevertheless, the subsequent history of craniology and craniometry shows just how persistent and compelling this notion has been. One of the most popular related ideas, resisting overwhelming evidence to the contrary, is that intelligence is proportional to brain size. For example, this was advanced prominently by Samuel Morton in the United States in the mid-nineteenth century and by Paul Broca of France in the late nineteenth. Even after its convincing refutation by the American anthropologist Franz Boaz in the twentieth century, the theory was still resuscitated by some in the 1960s and 1970s, most notably by Arthur Jensen. Its twentieth-century champions added a fixation on standardized testing data to the earlier absorption with measurements and numbers.[40]

While it is true that on his scale blacks fall between Europeans and the apes, Camper explicitly denied that this meant they were inferior to whites. He attributed variance in his "facial angle" to differences in the structure of the jaw, rather than the size of the brain cavity. Moreover, he wrote in no uncertain terms that "we are white Moors; we are human beings identical in every respect with the blacks."[41] Having dissected and investigated the cadaver of an Angolan boy in Amsterdam in 1758, Camper established that the blood and brains were the same color as those of whites. Regarding the physical difference between the races, including skin color, he accepted the approach of those who argued that environmental factors which take centuries produce the changes. Although he learned from studying fetuses that white is the common color, he observed that color came immediately with birth. A prolific researcher on a broad range of subjects, he conducted much empirical study of skulls, sexual organs, and other anatomical parts of many African types along with those of other humans. Comparing them to apes as well, he concluded that blacks were not closer to "lower" animals than were whites, as some were contending at the time.[42]

Nevertheless, the English doctor Charles White in 1779 used Camper's scale, in part, to launch his theory on the chain of being, which placed Negroes as the intermediary between great apes and white Europeans. A similar distortion was represented in the adaptation and recalculation of Camper's data by Georges Cuvier, who linked the differences to mental development, and whose ideas would become especially popular in the early nineteenth century. Even such anthropologists as James Cowles Prichard and Friedrich Tiedemann, who were in agreement with Camper's actual views, helped perpetuate the false image of these views by repeating and then attacking them. Thus, incomplete reading of Camper's findings and misappropriation of them by racist doctrines served to leave a flawed impression of this supporter of monogenesis and human equality, and opponent of slavery.[43]

In the burgeoning new sciences of the Enlightenment the French took the lead through the *philosophes'* role as disseminators of knowledge. Some of their publications too first appeared in Holland. For those imbued with the Enlightenment spirit, the new scientific outlook knew no national boundaries. Hence the findings of Frenchmen were not necessarily French ideas. In keeping with this, it was as natural for the literate late eighteenth-century Dutchman as for a Frenchman to look to the *Encyclopédie* for the most advanced information on any subject covered. The article there by Le Romain on "Negroes (Commerce)" may therefore provide an indication of the current liberal view on the subject. Le Romain's first point was that the slave trade was "loathsome and contrary to natural law." However, he goes on to note which areas of Africa provided "the best Negroes." He identified these as Cape Verde, Angola, Senegal, the river Gambia, etc. He then repeated some popular European views which may be found in a number of other sources from the period. He stated that in African slave markets,

> One sees sons selling their fathers, fathers their children. Still more frequently one sees Negroes who are not linked by family ties put a price of a few bottles of brandy or bars of iron on each other's freedom.

And further on:

> These black men . . . find a certain relief in America which renders their animal existence much better there than in their own country. This improvement makes it possible for them to withstand the work and to multiply abundantly.

In a more direct analysis of the Negroes' character, he continued:

> Even if by chance one may meet upright men and women among
> the Negroes from Guinea (the majority are always depraved), most
> of them are disposed to immorality, vindictiveness, thievery, and
> lying. . . . As far as creole Negroes are concerned, their education
> has given them notions that make them somewhat better. Yet to a
> degree their original nature still shows through: they are vain,
> scornful, proud, and love finery, gambling, and women above all
> else. The women are in no way better than the men and follow the
> ardor of their temperament without any restraint. On the other
> hand they are capable of keen feelings, affection, and fidelity. The
> Negroes' faults do not affect all of them and one meets with some
> individuals who are very good.[44]

Thus it can be seen that "enlightened" opinion too contributed to
projecting a basically negative image of black Africans. The educated
Dutchman, who could be expected to know French literature, found
decidedly negative images there in the works of such famous writers
as Racine, Corneille, and Molière.[45] Moreover, Le Romain had probably relied heavily on Willem Bosman's writings. In contrast to
Camper's work, other biological theories evolved toward the end of
the eighteenth century which supported racial bias. The *philosophes*,
Voltaire for example, favored the theory that whites and blacks are of
different species, which is directly contradictory to Camper's position. This notion was appealing to some humanists because it challenged the biblical account of creation.[46]

It was ironic that the same scientific outlook which inspired the
Enlightenment and decried human bondage encouraged theories
which sought to dehumanize a large part of humankind. This would
become much clearer in the full-blown racist theories of the nineteenth century, which would evolve in part from this earlier debate.
One final mass medium, newspapers, which in the Netherlands date
from the early sixteenth century, reflected some or all of these views
found in the belles-lettres, scientific, and travel literature. In the
twentieth century a black press also came, with such publications as
De Banier van Waarheid en Recht (Banner of Truth and Justice) beginning in 1929 in Paramaribo, and later in the Netherlands the Surinamese *Ons Suriname* (Our Suriname) and the Antillean *Noticiero*
(Reporter).[47]

Children's Literature

Children's books were an especially important means of transmitting certain images of blacks to a mass audience. This type of literature, which could boast some three hundred books in the Netherlands by the 1780s, had a specific intention of teaching as well as entertaining. For this, in addition to native currents, the Dutch drew upon a general European stream of development.[48] From the native traditions one prominent theme was of course the Sinterklaas and Zwarte Piet tandem. Many versions can be found in books throughout the nineteenth century, and they continued to show the same ambiguity concerning racial identity that surrounded the notions of "Moor" and "Negro." Most of these books could just as properly be discussed under the category of art since they are really books of wonderful popular prints accompanied by verses. They are included here under literature because they did usually appear as books and because of the verses. One of the most popular series of Sinterklaas prints and verses is that by J. Schenkman, which was first published at mid-century and many times subsequently. His also show the modernization of the tale:

Arrival of St. Nicholas

See, there comes the steamboat
    From Spain again!
St. Nicholas also comes along!
    I already can see him!
How the streamers blow
    The boat back and forth!
His servant stands and laughs,
    And already calls to us;
"Those who've been good get goodies;
"Those who've been bad get a switch"

Zwarte Piet also features prominently in the arrival parade:

The Stately Entry of St. Nicholas

There he rides through the city,
    Dressed as a bishop.
His servant carries the treasure chest.
    Heh, see how he sweats!

Flowers are strewn all around!
  Everyone celebrates and cheers.
While St. Nicholas himself
  Bows most congenially;
However, one hides and tries to escape him.
  It is William, a cutup;
But he is seen at once.

The series' prints show the fabulous duo visiting the bakery and the bookstore to stock up on gifts; checking their list of children and their conduct; and visiting children of various economic classes and behavior:

St. Nicholas at the Bad Childrens'

Heh, heh . . . Ole St. Nick
  Is far from shy!
There he stuffs two smarties
  Plump in his sack!
It is wages swiftly delivered
  And richly deserved.
He doesn't like to punish children,
  For he is their friend.
Oh Bishop! Forgive them
  This one time,
Please, show them mercy,
  They won't do it again.

In the print accompanying this verse Zwarte Piet is stuffing a protesting naughty boy into a sack, which Sinterklaas also holds with one hand, while in the other he holds a second struggling candidate for the sack.[49]

The more traditional Sinterklaas, without the modern trappings, also survived in some late nineteenth-century books:

Sinterklaas

. . . With his servant—
There he comes,
With his splendid outfit on,
Red stockings on his legs—
Ride on away through the streets;
And the children stay there,

Looking at those exquisite togs,
With his sack
Already on the roof. . . . ..[50]

In most illustrations of the arrival parade Zwarte Piet walks alongside
while Sinterklaas sits astride a white horse. However, a few show Piet
mounted as well and featured almost as an equal in the accompanying
verse:

And then!

St. Nicholas travels around, so quiet and unnoticed
Until he learns all that he wants to know;
Then, he goes home and writes in the big book,
What toy each will get, and goodies, sometimes a book!

His steamboat was about to sink
Santa Claus didn't care much for that,
He then went to all the shops in the city,
Bought goodies here and books there from all of them.

And everything pretty and tasty, cases and baskets,
It makes the mouth water for everyone who sees it,
Then brings his servant to the houses, where then the children's
friend
Distributes it to each according to what he deserves!

Thus his celebration arrives, toward which already many weeks
The children have watched out for with longing;
Then the Saint makes his rounds with this servant Piet,
From nightfall to the early morning.[51]

As can be seen, these verses exhort adherence to the societal
norms of behavior, with some special attention to the virtues associated
with book learning. The main characters in other moralistic tales
were also tailored to teach. By the late eighteenth and nineteenth centuries typically Dutch figures like Sinterklaas and Zwarte Piet were
joined by those from imported sources such as LaFontaine's fables,
Grimm and Mother Goose fairy tales, and imitations of popular
translations of German stories. The best example of the latter was the
best-seller *Struwelpeter* (*Piet de Smeerpoets* or Peter Greasy Hands),
written and illustrated around 1845 by Heinrich Hoffman. This figure in his turn was an adaptation of Gavarni's *Enfant terrible*. Another
nineteenth–century story featured a black character who seems to

combine elements from "Moorjantje" with some from the medieval St. Nicholas legend:

The Story of the Black Boys

Three lads came leaping
And mocking a Negro boy,
Whose skin was as black as soot,
Who had lips as red as oxen blood
And teeth handsomer, so it seemed,
Than the finest ebony.
"Hey, look!" called Karl to Louis,
"That dummy has a parasol!"
"He sure does!" said little Piet,
"Surely the summer sun won't hurt him!"
"Aw, you know," they all cried then,
"Such a Negro boy has no sense of decency,
"As you can see from all he does!"

St. Nicholas, the big boss,
Happens along with rapid strides
And meets the threesome along the way.
A big inkwell stands beside him!
"Shame!" he cries, with a stern voice,
"I've overheard your mocking
"And am very annoyed with you.
"Say, bad boys, aren't you ashamed?
"You're bringing this Negro much grief;
"He has never done anything to you,
"Therefore, let him go his way as well!
"His skin is black, yes as black as soot,
"But his heart is as pure as snow!"
But Karel, Lodewijk, and Piet
They didn't heed this scolding
And thought in their boyish delusions:
"What business is it of that old Saint what we do!"

And see, St. Nicholas, not slow,
He grabs the boys by the collar
And raises them up in his arms
Like a child would a little doll,
And casts them for their wicked ways
Into the just-filled inkwell.

"Awk! Awk!" they all loudly whined,

De historie met den Zwarten Jongen.

Drie knapen kwamen aangesprongen
En spotten met een negerjongen,
Wiens huid zoo zwart geleek als roet,
Die lippen had als ossenbloed
En tanden, fraaier, zoo het scheen,
Dan 't allerfijnste elpenbeen.
„He, kijk!" riep Karel tot Louis,
„Die gek loopt met een parapluie!"
„Dat zeg je wel!" zei kleine Piet,
„Hem deert de zomerzon toch niet!"
„Och, weet je!" riepen allen toen,
„Zoo'n negerknaap kent geen fatsoen,
„Dat ziet men wel aan al zijn doen!"

109. "The Story of the Black Boys." From *Het Prentenboek van Tante Pau* (The Hague, 1974).

"Dat is een mooie grap!" zegt Piet.
"Maar flinke jongens treuren niet!"
"Komaan, een pretje moet er wezen!"
Roept Karel zonder angst of vreezen.
"Kijk, kijk, daar gaat de nikker heen!
"Wij allen volgen vlug ter been!"
En zoo gezegd is, wordt gedaan:
Eerst Piet, toen de and'ren achteraan,

En 't negerknaapje, droevig lot,
Werd door de knapen weer bespot
Maar toen Papalief bij hen kwam
En elk eens bij de ooren nam,
Toen was het einde van de pret:
"Een stroobos krijgt gij elk voor bed,
"En geen van u wordt er verschoond,
"Vóórdat ge waar berouw betoont!'

110. Further illustration from "The Story of the Black Boys." *Het Prentenboek van Tante Pau.*

"Now we also look like Negroes!
"Alas! Alas! no complaints would help this.
"We will remain Negroes forever!"

"That is a nice joke!" said Piet
"But smart children, don't you worry!"
"Come on, this must be fun!"
Karel shouts without fear or fright.
"Look, look, there the Nigger goes away!
"Let's all follow right in stride!"
And as soon as they'd said it, they acted:
First Piet, then the others behind him,
And the Negro lad, a sad fate,
Was again mocked by the boys.
But when Papalief [Daddy Dear] came by
And took each of them by the ears,
That was the end of that fun:
"You each get a spanking before bed,

"And none of you will be excused,
"Before you show sincere repentance!"[52]

This story was clearly intended to serve as a lesson in behavior, to
teach that it is wrong to tease one who is in some way different. However, an unmistakable, though unintended, message is that it is a horrible fate to be black. This same point is expressed more directly in a
humorous tale from the early twentieth century entitled "Hoe dat ik
in een neger veranderde" (How I Changed into a Negro). In it the
narrator has a nightmare in which his face became blackened through
an encounter with a black man.[53]

The most popular of the rhymes about Blacks was "Tien kleine
Negertjes" (Ten Little Niggers). Usually illustrated with comical car-
icatures, this jingle was highly popular both in book form and as a fun
song.

Ten Little Niggers

10 little niggers:
On an untracked road:
One fell and broke a leg,
Then there were just 9

9 little niggers:
One had a mishap
A coconut right on his head,
Then there were just 8

8 . . . the elephant snatched one of them,
He started to tremble from fright.
The others soon ran away
Then there were just 7

7 . . . They went on a lion hunt
But had no success
The angry lion chased one away,
Then there were just 6

6 little niggers:
One got a stomach ache
He went home as fast as he could,
Then there were just 5

5 little niggers:
What fun they were having!

One was not allowed to play, went home
Then there were just 4

4 little niggers:
One is lost, and look,
They haven't looked for him,
Then there were just 3

3 little niggers:
But one could not continue
Because he fell into the water,
Then there were just 2

2 little niggers:
One ran away really fast
Because a porcupine scared him.
Then there was just 1

The one then beat a drum
And . . . all at once
There they all were
Again together and big as life!

This is one of the milder versions of the rhyme. Most early versions showed closer kinship to the more violent German, English, and American ancestors from which it sprang. Here, for example, is an older, English version:

Ten little nigger boys went out to dine;
One choked his little self, and then there were nine.

Nine little nigger boys sat up very late;
One overslept himself, and then there were eight.

Eight little nigger boys travelling in Devon;
One said he'd stay there, and then there were seven.

Seven little nigger boys chopping up sticks;
One chopped himself in half, and then there were six.

Six little nigger boys playing with a hive;
A bumble-bee stung one, and then there were five.

Five little nigger boys going in for law;
One got in chancery, and then there were four.

Four little nigger boys going out to sea;
A red herring swallowed one, and then there were three.

Three little nigger boys walking in the Zoo;
A big bear hugged one, and then there were two.

Two little nigger boys sitting in the sun;
One got frizzled up, and then there was one.

One little nigger boy living all alone;
He got married, and then there were none.[54]

An alternate frequent ending in Dutch versions has the one survivor marrying to produce ten once again. Regardless of the various means by which the ten are disposed of, what is most striking about this jingle for the present discussion is its gentle implication that Negroes are creatures of a different sort. Like "Moorjantje" they are reduced to miniature size; at the same time they are reduced to simple objects to be counted. Another rhyme published at the end of the nineteenth century reflects this same type of diminution and depersonalization. Titled "Van twee zwartjes" (The Two Little Blacks) it is a supposedly humorous account of a minor mishap caused by a little black boy who is fishing, which resulted in a black woman falling in the water. Throughout its nineteen verses the characters remain things rather than people.[55]

The mood and images reflected in the "Tien kleine Negertjes" jingle and the story of the "zwarten jongen" (black boys) spawned an entire subgenre of popular adventure series in the Netherlands, called the *beeldverhaal* (picture story). In its full scope, this genre, an off-spring of the earlier *volksprenten*, may properly be seen as analogous to the comic strip literature which developed in the United States and which is often intended for adults as well as children. The first professional comic strip drawer in the Netherlands was Henk Backer, who began his strip "Tripje en Liezebertha" (the names of the lead characters) in 1923. In the 1930s P. Koenen began a strip called "De lotgevallen van Pijpje Drop" (The Adventures of Pijpje Drop), which featured a black family in the leading role. The strip "Bolletje en Bonestaak," started by A. M. de Jong and G. van Raemdonck, was remarkable for posing questions concerning the assumed superiority of Western civilization when juxtaposed to others.[56] However, the most popular black comic strip character in the Netherlands is Sjimmie, from the series "Sjors en Sjimmie" created in 1950 by Frans Piet. Although he evolved over the decades into a less starkly caricatured appearance and a more equal leading character, Sjimmie was by definition a helpless figure, dependent on Sjors to solve all the silly situations he would get himself into. This role as humorous butt of the jokes would continue to be the most consistent one for the black figures.

Another example from the 1950s are the books by Piet Broos, with such characters as Piempanpoentje, Pompernikkel, and Piepeling visiting exotic regions. The appeal of these series did not die with the influx of a significant black population into the Netherlands in the 1970s, as witnessed the books of H. Arnoldus featuring Oki, Doki, Tup, and Joep.[57] A special fascination with ancient Egypt in particular, evident for centuries in the Netherlands, would continue to inspire strip adventures on into the 1980s. This was the subject of a special exhibit at the Leiden Museum of Ancient History in 1989. One noteworthy aspect of the samples displayed of drawings over the centuries is the tendency to depict the Egyptians as "white" in most instances.[58]

A Surinamer student of anthropology who was educated in the Netherlands was inspired by her impressions of the comic strip figures to undertake a systematic study of the image of blacks, their culture and society in Dutch children's books. Her findings have been published in abbreviated form. Reviewing some eighty selected books, she concludes that the literature, when not overtly derogatory, generally projects basic Eurocentric assumptions which it believes should properly be reflected in the literary images. Blacks are consistently depicted as inferior and animal-like, cannibalistic dwellers of wild lands, lacking in culture. Their native societies are described either as tyrannical or as totally chaotic.

Thus all of the usual stereotypes regarding blacks in Western civilization show themselves in this literature in varying degrees. Their language, outward appearance, and subordinate status are suggested as proof of this in the plots and characters of the stories. There are clowns, but no true artists. Music and dance are presented as evidence of wildness rather than creativity.[59] A later study by two other authors focusing specifically on school books arrived at similar conclusions. They find that some of the most basic texts have racist content advanced through such fundamental subjects as geography, history, and biology. The authors conclude that the solution to this problem lies in the implementation of a multicultural, truly "intercultural," educational program, one which does not perpetuate the assumption of Western superiority over all others.[60] Even a cursory examination of some of the books critiqued shows that this analysis merits serious consideration. The generations of the Dutch public exposed to such literature could hardly help experience some type of influence in the formulation of their ideas about different races and cultures.

At the same time, evincing the rich diversity of Dutch culture, there was in some literature directed at the youth a deliberately positive portrayal of blacks. One striking example is a story titled *De Zwarte Man*, whose central figure turns out to be an angel of mercy rather than the bogeyman of that same name. The story begins with a miller rescuing a lost "Moorish" stranger from the freezing cold and bringing him home to feed him and provide him with a warm night's rest. Just the sight of the stranger struck fear into the miller's children:

> *However they ate very little that evening and asked permission to go to bed; for the black man with snow-white teeth was so frightening to them that they were even afraid to look at him.*

Later the grateful "Moor," who turned out to be a servant of a general of a nearby army, provided the entire family protection from all warring factions until hostilities moved beyond that region. He then departed, refusing to accept an offered half of the miller's fortune in gold as reward.[61] A story very similar to this one, said to be an account from the Haitian Revolution, appeared in a magazine in 1823. In this instance a loyal slave, although supporting the revolt, hides and saves a respected white mistress and her family. The credibility of the report is enhanced by the use of names of the Europeans involved. However, remarkably, the heroic "Negro" remains nameless.[62]

From the late eighteenth century forward a host of weeklies and other magazines oriented toward the young sought to instruct on the latest knowledge concerning the outside world and its peoples. A 1799 article on Africans and Americans presented very current geographical and anthropological knowledge. It asserted that environmental conditions largely determined the color and the level of cultural development of the African peoples, and attributed any corruption they exhibited to the influence of what it considered the false religious beliefs from Mohammedanism, to the slave trade, and to alcohol from Europeans. It is noted that Europeans who lived long on the African coasts themselves began to resemble Africans. The article described great variety among African peoples and found some of them beautiful and others ugly, using clearly European standards of beauty.[63] While this author found the handsomest Africans to be those in the region of Senegal and the "ugliest" to be the "Kaffirs and Hottentots," a more tolerant piece on "De Kaffers" in another magazine a quarter of a century later described them as "not unpleasing." It should be noted, however, that those he defined as "Kaffirs" were distinguished from Negroes, and were described as the most like Europeans, although with dark skin. This later article also pointed out that this was not the name they called themselves, in fact that they could not since their language had no "r" sound. This point exemplified a general approach which at least espoused objectivity and viewing the people on their own terms.[64]

Just as the fictional *volksprenten* and adventure stories written for children were presented in serial form, so also was historical matter. A series on Suriname in one of the youth magazines of the early 1840s began:

> We Netherlanders may speak with a certain pride about Suriname, our most important West-Indian possession. When one recalls the condition of this region over the past two centuries, that is since Europeans began to settle there, and compares this to the present, the differences are surprisingly great. Thick, almost impenetrable forests, where nature, under the influence of the plunging, perpendicular sun rays, exhibited all her fertility in covering the interior. A few Indian tribes, here usually called Caribs, roamed there. They led a very poor life and found their sustenance in tree fruits, a few food plants, and in game birds and creeping and four-footed animals with which these forests swarm. They are totally unacquainted with the privileges of civilization; they destroyed each other in constant fighting. . . . The whole colony, though in recent times, through various causes, having waned in prosperity, is still a pearl in the Netherland's crown.[65]

Considering the historical fate of the Caribs and other Indians of the region and the endless warfare among the Europeans, it is noteworthy that the author seemed oblivious to the irony of his views. On the other hand, later issues of the same magazine include a grisly description of a slave ship and the "middle passage," complete with a diagram, and are highly critical of the alleged continuation of open slave markets in Suriname.[66]

Dutch Literature's Dark Faces

Thus the image of blacks disseminated through literature, which of course included folklore and art, augmented those spread through folklore and art through nonliterary means, and further ensured that there were attitudes concerning blacks in the Netherlands long before there was a significant actual presence of blacks. It is also apparent that, although there was some positive or neutral literary imagery, it was, on balance, negative. When literacy increased and when blacks arrived in greater numbers in the Netherlands, and became even more often the subject of writings, thought about blacks became more constant. It did not, however, become more positive.

IN THE EYES OF GOD
BLACKS AND DUTCH RELIGIOUS TRADITIONS

Even now, in the late twentieth century, the skyline in the Dutch countryside is dominated, not by the remaining fabled windmills, but by churches. The more recently arrived Lowlands-scale skyscrapers (*wolkenkrabbers*) cannot begin to compete with the grace and beauty of the old city churches. The windmill may be a more fitting symbol of the material accomplishments which made this paragon of modern capitalist, commercial societies great. However, the churches, some of them over four hundred years old, attest the power and persistence of the spiritual base of Dutch society. They remain a lasting symbol of the power of religion, which played a particularly decisive role in the original definition of Dutch cultural and national identity as the United Provinces emerged out of the religious wars of the Reformation period. Any consideration of Dutch attitudes toward others must include close examination of the role of religion in shaping those attitudes.

Formulation of such an examination is highly complex. It should first be noted once again how the Dutch religious traditions intertwined with folklore, art, and literature, and have therefore already been part of the discussions in previous chapters. The religious beliefs evolved under the sway of the same historical and cultural forces already outlined. With respect to institutionalized religion, there has never been a formal state church in the Netherlands, although the Dutch Reformed Church has been favored by law at times. And, although the religion most closely identified with Dutch culture, Calvinism has at its highest point of adherence counted just over half the population. In the early seventeenth century it represented only about 10 percent of the populace in the Netherlands.[1] Catholicism has remained the main rival for influence, followed by other Protestant faiths, Judaism, Islam in the postwar period, and lesser-known religions. The discussion here will center on Christianity in its various forms, since it was the Christians who dominated Dutch society and who had the most influence in shaping standards of all types.

The task of analysis at hand remains nevertheless formidable because of the seamless web of contradictions the subject contains. Part of the difficulty derives from the general character of religious tradition and practice. For example, what is one to make of the fact that even today separate worship by different racial groups is the main pattern throughout the Christian world, including communities with seemingly good racial relations? A plausible argument can be made that the main reason is the strength of tradition in religious practices rather than manifest conscious or unconscious racial attitudes. Perhaps the present discussion can throw some light on why this tradition came about. A reminder of how deeply rooted this attitude is in the Dutch tradition is the fact that the Dutch-implanted Reformed Church in South Africa only in the 1980s declared the concept of racial superiority to be un-Christian. Even then, its leadership continued to speak against racial mixing and would not denounce the system of apartheid. On the other hand, the Dutch branch had long opposed apartheid. Another area of contradictions concerns the ambiguity of biblical themes pertaining to blacks, which lend themselves to both positive and negative interpretations.

Still another paradox is the idea of "the Chosen," which the Calvinists have embraced just as ardently as the Jews. This concept, exclusive by definition, seems clearly to condone a sense of inherent superiority over all others. Nevertheless, there were instances where both of these religions admitted Blacks in the Dutch colonies. In Suriname in particular there were cases where slaves or free blacks came to Christianity after having lived under the Jewish faith due to previous ownership by a Jewish family. Thus, adherence to the concept of predestination provides no simple answer to the question of its impact on attitudes toward blacks. At the same time, however, some Calvinists arrived at much more humane positions concerning blacks than did leading proponents of rationalism and modern science.[2] Indeed, further complicating the picture at various times, while elements in the church participated in slavery, some of the same ones, along with others, also promoted abolition and missionary work.

Biblical Motifs

For the present discussion the central, inescapable issue within Christianity is the question of whether blacks are equal to whites in the sight of God. Among Dutch Christians there was little debate over the meaning of the biblical statement that God created man in his own image. Therefore, beliefs concerning blacks' inferiority raise the question of whether the various churches and Christians recognized the full humanity of blacks. If they too are in God's image, on what bases could unequal treatment be justified—especially after the notion of equality also became secularized during the Enlightenment?[3] The genesis of the basic questions which fueled discussion of this issue in the Netherlands can be traced through Dutch history in the evolution of related biblical themes, which have already been discussed, such as the Adoration of the Magi, the Baptism of the Ethiopian Eunuch, the legend of the Hamitic Curse, the Queen of Sheba's visit to Solomon, and Moses' Egyptian wife. A consideration of the first three of these will be sufficient for present purposes. The order in which they are discussed here parallels that of their rise to consciousness in the Netherlands, rather than their age or sequence of appearance in the Bible. Since the occurrence of these themes in art, folklore, and literature has been treated in earlier chapters in this present study, the discussion here will center on their place in religious thought and belief.

Adoration of the Magi

The deliberate inclusion of Caspar the black king in the Dutch celebration of the Epiphany reflects a high regard for Africa and the black Africans he symbolized. This was a continuation of attitudes shown in the medieval period when black saints were proclaimed in parts of Europe. The statue of St. Maurice in the chapel of St. Kilian at Magdeburg and the seventeenth-century bust and older relics of St. Gregory the Moor at the Church of St. Gereon in Cologne testify to the strength of these notions and to their proximity to the Netherlands. Both these legendary figures were of ambiguous African origins until the thirteenth century; but thereafter they were frequently featured as black.[4]

This special recognition aimed not only to acknowledge the contribution of African martyrs to the Christian cause, but also to affirm the relevance of Christianity to all peoples and races. In considering the historical fate of black Caspar in the Dutch religious tradition, his relative decline after the seventeenth century may have resulted from more than just the relative decline of Dutch art. Simon Schama in his work on Dutch culture, in discussing the centrality of biblical scripture to the genesis of the Netherlands, observes that Calvinists held a higher regard for the Old Testament than did Catholics, who preferred the New. There were, of course, no Protestant saints to lend dignity to those whose heritage might be associated with them. At the same time, with Catholics forced into a subordinate status in the Netherlands, even while a majority, modifications of standard practices based on New Testament motifs might be expected. The declining recognition for the black saints may simply have been a natural consequence of the waning significance of the Holy Roman Empire, which was their main sponsor. However, this is a subject which requires more intensive study, focusing on Germany.

Baptism of the Ethiopian

For your many sins your skirts are torn off you,
   your limbs uncovered.

Can the Nubian change his skin,
   or the leopard its spots?
And you? Can you do good,
   you who are schooled in evil?
Therefore I will scatter you like chaff
   driven by the desert wind.
This is your lot, the portion of the rebel,
   measured out by me, says the Lord,
   because you have forsaken me
   and trusted in false gods.

                    Jeremiah 13: 22–25

This passage, in which a "Nubian's" (more popularly translated as "Ethiopian's") skin color is mentioned in a discussion of sin and punishment, came down in the popular lore of Western civilization as a stigma against black skin color. It may well be, as Frank Snowden surmised in his study of the ancient view of blacks, that the reference here was simply to color as a neutral, immutable trait, and not to racial or moral qualities. Snowden further points out that Origen, St. Augustine, and other Church Fathers articulated an interpretation of scripture using Ethiopia as a symbol of the mission to spread the faith. This culminated with Theodoret, who explained the baptism of the Ethiopian eunuch by Philip the Deacon in the book of Acts as affirmation that it was, indeed, possible for the Ethiopian to "change his skin," at least figuratively, through Christianity.[5] However, in its travels through the Greek and Roman world and into early modern Europe, the inescapable negative implications of this proverb also persisted. After all, the celebrated "cleansing" also reiterates the "evil stain." It became a popular theme in Christian iconography from the third century forward.[6] The countless paintings and drawings on this theme by Dutch artists of the sixteenth and early seventeenth centuries had to carry this mixed message to the viewers.

The well-known penchant in Dutch culture for cleanliness makes this theme all the more significant. Discussing this in his broader study on Dutch culture in a chapter titled "Cleanliness and Godliness," Schama indirectly touches upon yet another close tie between this theme and blacks: "The brush stood as a heraldic device for the new commonwealth, cleansed of the impurities of the past. To have been slaves was to have been dirty. To be free is to be clean."[7] By the sixteenth century the concept of slavery for Europeans had become associated primarily with blacks. This surely sapped some of the power of the positive symbolism in the baptism of the Ethiopian. This may also help explain why this theme ceased to be a popular one in Dutch art as the Dutch plunged ever deeper into the African slave trade. If black skin was a sign of evil, if "cleanliness is next to Godliness," as the saying goes, and if for the Calvinists "cleanliness" was one of the conspicuous signs of being one of God's elect, this placed black slaves in compounded peril, and all blacks in an inferior light.

Application of this theme to real life can be seen in the experiences of two figures prominent in eighteenth-century Dutch colonial history. The first was the predicant Jan Willem Kals, who served in Suriname in 1731–1733 for the Dutch Reformed Church and gained notoriety for championing the rights of Indians and Negroes. His collected writings, published in 1756, include an account of his encounters while in Suriname with two pious Negroes with surprising knowledge of the Bible. In one of these, named Trouble, he aroused tears of joy when telling of Philip's response to the Ethiopian eunuch when the latter requested baptism: "Look, here is water: what is to prevent my being baptized?"[8] The second example from the eighteenth century was that of the famous African predicant trained at the University of Leiden, Jacobus Elisa Joannes Capitein, whose portrait, widely circulated in the 1740s, bore the following inscription:

> Viewer behold this MOOR! His skin is black;
> But his soul is white, for JESUS
> himself is his priest. He goes to teach
> faith, hope and love to the Moors,
> so that they, made white, may
> all the more honor the LAMB along with him.
>
> Bran dyn Ryser[9]

This rhyme and the picture it accompanied reflected a full-blown actualization of the positive thrust of the proverb about the Ethiopian and might very well have been inspired by the emblem by Jan Luiken presented in chapter three. The caption under that emblem is from Psalm 24, verses 3 and 4, and exhorts the true Christian to maintain clean hands and a pure heart. At the same time, the engraving of Capitein implicitly addressed the debate current at the time over whether blacks could or should become Christianized. It was not universally accepted either in the church or in society as a whole that blacks had souls and were equal human beings with whites.

Capitein was celebrated in Holland not only for his academic and religious achievements, but also because of a vocal stand he took on the issue of slavery. The paper he wrote to complete his studies at the University of Leiden was a ringing justification of slavery as a necessary avenue to salvation for black Africans! Drawing upon the tradition of theology distinguishing between the spiritual and physical world, which can be traced back to St. Augustine and was popularized in the Netherlands by the seventeenth-century predicant Godefridus Cornelisz Udemans, Capitein argued that those insisting upon physical in addition to spiritual freedom were Christian fanatics.[10] Consequently, while he gained great favor among the merchants and plantation owners, and others who supported slavery, he did not contribute much toward resolving the related religious questions. Regarding the question of human equality within the faith, Capitein was clearly on the side of equal status for blacks. However, the popular image of Capitein, as reflected in the inscription accompanying his portrait, was an equally forceful assertion of the assumption that blacks were inferior because of their color and their heathen status. Capitein's case would contribute further to the debate when his brief career as a predicant in his African homeland proved to be a miserable failure. (This will be discussed in more detail in chapter six.)[11]

The Hamitic Legend

Since slavery in modern European history came to mean almost exclusively enslavement of black Africans, the Hamitic legend played an especially important role in the shaping of perceptions of blacks. The convergence of this legend as well as that on the Ethiopian's baptism with the historic advent of the African slave trade represents just the type of historical fusion and confusion that can help explain the depth of modern racism's roots: myth confirmed by the historical illusion of white superiority. Capitein, in his defense of slavery, also accepted the tradition concerning the biblical curse of Ham as the origin of slavery. His view appears to have been representative for eighteenth-century religious circles, although the issue was still debated. It appears that it was precisely in the eighteenth century, from Capitein's time forward, that the legend first gained wide currency in the Netherlands.

A half century after Dutch involvement in the slave trade had reached its highest volume, the timing of the popularity of this tradition on the origin of slavery is probably related to the fact that this was also the period when opposition to Dutch involvement increased, perhaps in response to the rise of abolitionism in England.[12] The inconsistency in the Hamitic legend had not escaped the notice of earlier thinkers in the Netherlands. The legend is illogical because the relevant biblical text states that Noah placed a curse on the descendants of only one of Ham's sons, Canaan. This became distorted and confused in later lore and literature.[13] Udemans had noted this inconsistency in his handbook for shippers, merchants, and colonial officials of the Dutch East and West India trading companies, published in 1638 in the Netherlands. Udemans had concluded that eventual emancipation of the slaves was necessary, but not as urgent as their immediate spiritual freedom.[14]

In contrast, another predicant, Johan Picardt from Coevorden, developed a specific interpretation of the legend of Ham for the Netherlands in his 1660 historical work. He characterized Netherlanders as descendants from Japheth, the youngest of Noah's three sons, and thereby superior to others. In Picardt's view, they had gained the favor with God lost by the Jews, whom he characterized as descendants of Shem, Ham's remaining brother, and as having fallen out of grace by crucifying Christ. Likewise, in his scheme all of Europe was destined to rule over Asia, Africa, and America. Picardt's ideas, as were those of others mentioned here, were consistent with the principles laid out by his contemporary Hugo Grotius. Grotius held that, while slavery was an unnatural state of existence, it could be justified in certain circumstances. The one most consequential for this discussion is the assertion that enslavement of a conquered people could be viewed as an act of compassion, since the victor had the power to take their lives instead.[15] This principle left a great deal of latitude for arguments, both religious and secular, on both sides of the debate over slavery.

The Dutch clergymen most interested in this subject were invariably those most aware of growing involvement of the Netherlands with the outside world. Especially prominent were those from Middelburg, Vlissingen, Amsterdam, and Rotterdam, the main ports involved in the slave trade. From another port city, Hoorn, sounded at least one shrill voice in opposition to the trade in the late seventeenth century. This was the predicant Jacobus Hondius, who also castigated the conduct of the planters and predicants in the colonies.[16] Even complete opposition to slavery and the slave trade, however, should not be equated with belief in equality. This distinction is often apparent in the literature on abolition, and in Enlightenment thought in general.[17]

From Legend to Life

The issue of racial equality has never been decisively clarified in the major Christian denominations, with church practices showing variation both over time and by location. While this was equally true in the Dutch experience, continuing debate was the one constant. A closer look at the work of the Dutch Reformed and Catholic churches and that of the Herrnhutter Evangelical Brotherhood offers more about how perceptions of blacks evolved historically than the more abstract debates just described. This is to be expected since it was through missionary activities in the African and American colonies that the church first came into extensive contact with blacks. Even there the church communities were initially restricted to whites. Nevertheless, constant exposure to the colored peoples was unavoidable. It is first necessary to trace the broad historical pattern of development of the missionary activities of the main churches in the regions where they most frequently confronted Blacks and then to consider what image of blacks emerged from that experience.

The Dutch Reformed Church and Missionary Work

It is important to keep in mind that while the Calvinist Dutch Reformed Church was dominant due to the circumstances surrounding the United Provinces' origins, the Catholic Church was the older and more established arm of Christianity.[18] However, those same circumstances placed Catholics under limitations in the Dutch empire, tolerated, but not totally free to promote their faith as desired. Consequently, it was not until the nineteenth century that the history of Catholic missionary work begins in the Dutch empire. The Reformed Church too was slow to undertake missionary work per se, content at first just to minister to the needs of European Christians in the Dutch colonies as well as at home. The belief in predestination fostered inherent ambivalence on this question.

Of the colonies, most attention was devoted to the East Indies. One reason for this was that the church abroad during the lifetimes of the East and West India trading companies was essentially a company church, with ministers assigned by the companies and employed by them just like other officials. They were not even allowed to communicate directly with the church at home except through the company. Since the East Indies was the region most important to the Dutch economy, it received the most attention. By the end of the eighteenth century over eight hundred predicants had been sent to East India Company areas. On the other hand, relatively few were sent to the West Indies areas. By 1800 there were only a few hundred native Christians in Suriname, the Antilles, and the Gold Coast, the areas where most contacts with blacks would occur. Moreover, these converts had not resulted from deliberate missionary work. The company apparently saw no potential for material profit from Christianizing the populations, and the planters generally opposed it.[19]

The development which contributed most to an upsurge in missionary activity from the Netherlands was the influence of pietism there beginning in the late eighteenth century. This stream of Christian thought, which was especially strong in Germany, was more ecumenical than the earlier preoccupation with separate denominations. It therefore generated greater interest in drawing non-Christians into the faith and also in cooperative interdenominational efforts. This would be reflected in the great variety of Protestant missions abroad by other denominations, such as the Lutherans, the Methodists, and the Baptists, as well as in Europe. Predestination notwithstanding, it would have been difficult for a church as much involved in everyday affairs as the Reformed Church was to ignore this harvest of souls.[20]

So distinctive was the change in mood of this period that it came to be referred to as "the New Mission." This term described an era which would last until the 1920s, when churches in the colonies would gain greater independence. Crucial developments which brought on the new stage were a loosening of the bond between church and state in the late eighteenth century in the Netherlands and the termination of the East and West India trading companies. This allowed independent organizations to take up missionary work. In fact, only the Orthodox part of the Calvinist church directly sent out missionaries in the nineteenth and twentieth centuries. Most of the work was carried on by separate organizations formed outside by members of the various denominations.[21]

In one sense this represented a case of Protestant churches taking on some of the structure the Catholic Church already had enjoyed in the form of its special orders. However, it also reflected a more modern bent toward organization and rationalization consistent with the Enlightenment worldview as well as the more ecumenical spirit inspired by pietism. The formation of the Dutch Missionary Society (*Zendelinggenootschap*) in 1797 arose from direct contacts with the London Missionary Society, one of several formed in England beginning in 1792. The Dutch Bible Society was formed in 1825, a time when interdenominational Bible societies were active in Europe as far east as Russia. The changes in Europe's relationship to the rest of the world in the twentieth century brought about corresponding changes in the approach to missionary work.

In 1905 a federation of Reformed Church groups founded the *Nederlandse Zendingsschool* (Dutch Missionary School), situated after 1917 in Oegstgeest, next to Leiden. Founding of independent churches in the Dutch colonies evolved as a way to preserve the gains in a period of rising nationalism and anticolonialism. A leading figure in this direction in the Dutch Reformed Church was the theologian Hendrik Kraemer (1888–1965), who headed the Dutch Bible Society in Java from 1925 to 1945. He was also instrumental in bringing about a shift of missionary work back to the church itself after the 1951 restructure of the Hervormde Kerk. Also addressing the mood of the times, and in some ways updating elements of the "New Mission," missionary work began to be carried out mainly in conjunction with the World Diakonat and with a stress on development aid. One final new feature was a shift in focus to Africa, Latin America, and other parts of Asia due to burgeoning nationalistic conflicts in Indonesia.[22]

Dutch Catholic Missions

The separateness of the work of the Reformed Church and that of the Catholic was underscored by the use of two different Dutch words to describe the missionary work of the respective churches: *zending* and *missie*, respectively. As one recent scholar observed, the timing of the Reformation schism was unfortunate for the interests of Christian missionary efforts, occurring as it did precisely when the New World was being discovered.[23] He further points out that due to political circumstances the Netherlands itself was viewed as a missionary field for the Catholic Church, which further retarded Dutch Catholic chances for foreign missions. However, Christianity had been brought to the Netherlands as early as the seventh century by the Irish monk Willibrord. More recently, while the Netherlands was part of the Spanish empire, Dutch Franciscan and Jesuit priests had accompanied Spanish and Portuguese explorers to the New World. An example is Captain Caspar Berse (1515–1553) from Zeeland. Thus the exposure of Dutch Catholics to the outside world was more advanced than that of Dutch Protestants, notwithstanding the relative lack of Dutch Catholic missionary activity in the seventeenth and eighteenth centuries. The Catholic Church was not allowed in the East India Company jurisdiction. About fifty missionaries went to the West during those two centuries, mainly to Suriname and Curaçao.[24]

Although a priest was allowed in Curaçao in 1699 and the Catholic Church was formally recognized in Suriname in 1785, it was not until the early nineteenth century that sustained work began to be carried on in the Americas. This was aided by the measures promoting religious freedom resulting from the French Revolution's impact. In 1817 the priests Paulus Wennekers and Ludovicus van der Horst founded the first mission. Then Jacobus Groof (1800–1852) and Petrus Donders (1809–1887) began an enterprise prominent for the next century by devoting special attention to work among the lepers. A number of the Catholic orders became active in Suriname and the Antilles in the nineteenth and twentieth centuries, including the Franciscanessen sisters of Roosendaal, the Fraters from Tilburg, the Dominicans, the Dominicanessen from Voorschoten, and others. In the second half of the century the Suriname mission was elevated to the level of vicarate. As with the Protestant churches, that in Suriname functioned highly independent of the bishop in the Netherlands by the beginning of the twentieth century. The Catholic missionaries also resembled the Protestant in their relative disregard for national identity. They did not, for example concentrate on Dutch colonies. They showed special interest in Africa in the nineteenth century.

In addition to its numerous religious orders, the Catholic missionary movement organized even further in the nineteenth century. A key early figure in this was Joachim Le Sage ten Broek (1775–1847), who stimulated interest in the Netherlands through his periodical *De Godsdienstvriend* (The Friend of Religion; 1818–1869). In 1830 a Netherlands branch of the *Genootschap tot voortplanting des Geloofs* (The Society for Propagating the Faith) of Lyon was founded. Other such societies and their respective periodicals followed, resulting in such volume that their number was a hindrance to concerted effort. This culminated in the early twentieth century in the burst of missionary activity which has been called *Het Grote Missie-uur* (The Great Missionary Time).[25] This period began with the publication of the Jesuit L. van Rijkevorsel's books *Missie en Missie-aktie* (The Mission and Missionary Action) and *Missie-aktie in Nederland* (Missionary Activities in the Netherlands), published in 1916, which called for uniting of forces. This call achieved striking results. Between that time and the Second World War even more organizations came about, but they were more coordinated, with many existing institutions joining in fund-raising and other support.

After the war more foreign missions became independent of the church in the Netherlands. The Catholic Church, just as the Protestant, had also to cope with nationalistic protests and the new twentieth-century outlook on missionary work. This brought some resentment from Catholics, who felt their mission had been doing all along what was now being termed development aid and being juxtaposed to earlier colonialist exploitation, for which the church was blamed along with other societal elements. One other element in the most recent twentieth-century developments is a move at long last toward uniting the *zending* and *missie* efforts, as evidenced by the annual joint publication of a *Missie-Zendingskalender* (Missionary Calendar) by the *Centraal Missie Commissariaat* (Central Mission Commission) and the *Nederlandse Zendingsraad* (Dutch Missionary Council).

The Herrnhutter Brotherhood

The *Evangelische Moravische Broedergemeente*(Evangelical Moravian Brotherhood), sometimes called Moravian Brethren, was an embodiment of the pietist spirit mentioned earlier. Of the Christian missionary organizations operating out of the Netherlands, this most vigorous one was not an established church. And, like the Catholic Church, its highest leadership was not in the Netherlands. German remained the official language of the society all the way into the twentieth century, even for the many Dutchmen who joined. Founded in 1722 in Herrnhut, Saxony, by Nikolaus Ludwig Count von Zinzendorf (1700–1760), the *Broedergemeente* began gradually in 1735 to send missionaries all over the world to Christianize the "heathens" of all lands. In the eighteenth century, perhaps mindful of Philip the Deacon, they would also attempt, unsuccessfully, to establish contacts with Christian Ethiopia.[26]

Its organization featured affiliates in various countries, including scattered independent, sympathetic congregations in some Dutch towns, with the most important being the formal affiliate center located at Zeist, near Utrecht. The first congregation in the Netherlands was at a settlement called 's-Heerendijk near IJsselstein, launched in 1736. Support circles were started in a number of towns. In 1737 a group including Reform Church predicants, Baptists, and merchants founded in Amsterdam a society (*Genootschap tot uitbreiding van het Evangelium onder de Heydenen* [Society for Spreading the Gospel to the Heathens]) to function as a major support group for the Herrnhutters. It was strong until 1750 and lasted until 1772. After IJsselstein was closed in 1770 all the *Broedergemeente's* activities in the Netherlands were centered in Zeist, on an estate which had been purchased for the society in 1745 by a sympathetic Amsterdam merchant named Schellinger. Missionaries, including natives from Africa and Asia, were trained at IJsselstein and at Zeist for service in Africa, the Americas, Greenland, and Tibet.

The Herrnhutters are of particular interest in the present study because they were the most eager to reach out to the native peoples in Africa, the Americas, and Asia. While the Dutch Reformed and Catholic churches—or at least their planter congregations—only very grudgingly admitted blacks into the Christian community, the Herrnhutters immediately went far beyond that to pioneering efforts at formally educating the converts. In 1793 another aid society was founded in the Netherlands. The new society, *Broeder Sociëteit ter uitbreiding van het Evangelie onder de Heidenen* (Brother Society for Spreading the Gospel Among the Heathens), maintaining close ties with the headquarters in Herrnhut, would continue to furnish financial support for more than 130 years. Its periodical, *Berichten uit de Heidenwereld* (Reports from the Heathen World), begun in 1798, was a major organ for publicity and fund-raising. In the mid-nineteenth century another strong Netherlands support agency was the *Maatschappij ter Bevordering van het Godsdienstig Onderwijs onder de Inlandsche Bevolking in de Kolonie Suriname* (Society for Religious Education Among the Native Population in the Colony of Suriname).[27]

Although the *Broeder Sociëteit* was founded initially to support the work among the Khoikhoi in South Africa and the Eskimos in Labrador, it was especially in Suriname, among the Amerindians, slaves, and free blacks, and later among emigrant Asian contract laborers, that the *Broedergemeente* made its greatest impression. It went to Curaçao and Aruba only in the twentieth century, when it followed the migration there of part of its following in Suriname. By 1928 it counted 55,000 faithful in Suriname. The price of success was very high. Of 466 brothers and sisters sent out up to 1882, 166 died in Suriname, often soon after arrival. Many others became ill and had to return home.[28] New volunteers continued to arise despite such grim statistics. That they were common to missionary work in general is shown by a similar report, published in Leiden in the late nineteenth century, about another Protestant mission. Between 1828 and 1848 the Basel Mission, a missionary training institute founded in 1815, sent 148 men and 81 women from Basel, Switzerland, to the Gold

Coast of Africa. Of these, 55 men and 24 women died there; 62 men and 36 women returned home in broken health.[29]

The Moravian Brethren were in a more delicate position in their relation to the Dutch government than the Catholic and Dutch Protestant churches, in two respects. First, they did not represent an established church or any specific denomination. Second, they inclined toward rejection of slavery. On the latter point, a condition of their being allowed into the Dutch colonies was that they not demand freedom for the slaves. They agreed and contented themselves with demands for spiritual freedom and equality.[30] For the *Broedergemeente* this was less a concession than implementation of the general guidelines on faith that had been laid out by their founder, Von Zinzendorf, and reinforced by later writings of his Dutch disciple Spangenberg. It was also consistent with pietist thought in general.

Zinzendorf had held that each missionary should be guided by the Spirit in spreading the Gospel. In the same vein, the message to the "heathen" was that they not trouble about economic or political forms, but rather should concentrate on their inner selves. Even those whose way of life already appeared to the missionaries more upright than those of the colonists were to be instructed that they were still lost without the true Christian faith. The role of the missionary was to proclaim the Gospel, to lead in worship, and to serve.[31] The key to the Herrnhutter success in Suriname appears to have been a heavy emphasis on the worship and service part of their mission. Their early entry into educational activities with the natives seems also to have enhanced their own education about the people. Especially important was their willingness to learn the local languages.

The Missionary Encounter with Blacks

The way in which these three Christian missions related to blacks reflected their own respective places in Dutch society. The Reformed Church, as the only established Dutch church, was the church of the privileged and the most reticent to accept blacks as equals in Christ. The Catholic Church, as the even older established church, was conservative and also exclusive; but, functioning as an outcast in the Dutch colonies, it was more inclined than the Calvinist to make common cause with the other outcasts, that is, the slaves and free blacks as part of the lower classes with which it was allowed to work. During the century and a half of the trading company government of the

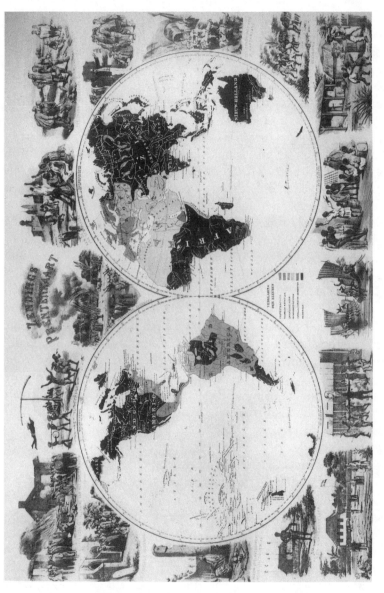

111. P. W. M. Trap, Leiden, nineteenth-century Dutch Reformed Church Missionary Calendar. Atlas van Stolk, Rotterdam. The darkest areas are "heathen," the lightest Islamic, and the others various types of Christian.

colonies another powerful determinant of the relationship between the missionaries and the peoples they proselytized was company policies. Nevertheless, examination of some of the practices employed can also give an idea of the attitudes of the missionaries toward the peoples they sought to serve.

In one sense, that of seniority, the Catholic Church set the tone. Its priests had been regular companions of explorers during the early Iberian domination in New World discoveries and likewise proclaimed and supervised the Iberian monopoly, the *asiento*, of the early slave trade. One of its provisions was that the slaves be baptized in Africa before transport. This concession to Christian decorum was apparently observed in only the most perfunctory manner if at all. At times expediency dictated massive baptisms in which large numbers of slaves would have water splashed over them simultaneously in the presence of a priest. Many arrived in America unbaptized and had to receive the sacrament from chaplains of the local sugar, cotton, and coffee plantations or gold mines. When Dutch traders eventually acquired the *asiento* in the late seventeenth century they too followed this procedure.[32] The significance of such baptism, is, of course, unclear. It is difficult to view it as any more religious than the hygienic washing of the slaves by the West India Company. The supposedly sacramental cleansing was intended to make them morally fit to be slaves of Christians, just as the washing of their bodies was to ensure a higher survival rate during transport and greater prosperity for their owners.[33] Its symbolism is surely a far cry from that of Philip the Deacon and the Ethiopian eunuch.

On the other hand, the Catholic Church, the Dutch Reformed Church, and the Herrnhutters all eventually offered baptism to slaves and free blacks, with each meaning to convey through that some degree of acceptance within the fold. Looking at another index of acceptance, the admittance of black clergy, affords a more penetrating view of the attitudes at work, but still leaves many questions unanswered. The ambivalence of the Dutch Reformed Church here can be seen in the career of the predicant Capitein. His case reveals the Reformed Church in a pioneer role, ordaining Capitein in 1742 as the first black minister of any Protestant church. Assigned to serve the European settlement in Elmina, he was treated just as any other predicant would have been in his place. Ironically, this contributed to his downfall rather than to success. A native of Elmina, Capitein arrived as predicant in 1742, having already spelled out years earlier in Leiden his approach to missionary work. In a 1736 speech, "Roeping der Heidenen" (Converting the Heathens), he had stressed use of the native language, provision of separate worship places for them, daily contact, and the development of missionary training in The United Provinces. In his writings, referring to himself as a Moor, he marveled at his good fortune in escaping slavery and his former state of unbelief.

Although he was initially well received in Elmina, Capitein's effort to get more than 17 of the 107 West India Company force involved in religious practice failed. Meetings virtually stopped. It should be noted here that this was the normal experience of all the predicants who had served there. Periods of years had sometimes passed without communion being observed, because too many of those Reformed Church adherents present were deliberately living in sin. One of Capitein's predecessors, Isaac Ketelanus, was himself dismissed for degrading conduct. Meanwhile Capitein attempted to revive a religious school for mulatto children which had been started by the Dutch in the previous century. However, even after personally translating materials which he then had printed in Holland, he could not awaken sufficient interest locally in the project.

In another realm of disappointment, the West India Company and the church would not condone his marrying an African woman, choosing instead to provide him a Dutch bride all the way from Rotterdam. The marriage too was a failure, in part because of constant financial difficulty. Although consistent with company policy, his salary was not sufficient for all that his duties required. He requested to be relieved in 1745, but was refused in Amsterdam. He was expected to supplement his income by personal business enterprises, as many predicants did in various colonies. Capitein then took up trading and began sending false, glowing reports home, while becoming completely ruined, some accounts say morally as well as physically. He died suddenly in 1747, leaving his widow heavily indebted. Opponents of inclusion of blacks into full membership in the church would later use his fate as evidence that such inclusion is folly.[34]

While the Dutch Reformed Church holds the distinction of being the first established Protestant church to ordain a black preacher, the Herrnhutter Brotherhood, as might be expected, had actually preceded the church in this and also was to ordain blacks more frequently than the two churches included here. By chance it was also at Elmina that the first representative of this Herrnhutter practice surfaced.

Christian Jacob Protten was born around 1710 near the Danish fort Christiansborg (Accra-Osu), son of a Danish soldier and an African. He was educated at the Castle School in Christiansborg. In 1722, in accord with orders by the governor, he and another African boy accompanied the Danish chaplain, Elias Svane, who was returning home after duty, to Copenhagen, where they were to study theology. They were baptized in 1727 in Copenhagen, with royalty serving as godparents. By 1728 both were enrolled in the university. Although never finishing his studies, Protten gained some mastery of Danish and German. He attracted attention through translation of a catechism into the Akan and Ga languages.

Owing in part to this reputation, in 1735 Protten met Count Zinzendorf and traveled with him to Herrnhut, where he joined the *Broedergemeente*. A year later he was sent to Guinea, sponsored by the Dutch West India Company. After arriving, in May 1737, Protten soon found himself imprisoned by the company director Des Bordes for attempting to organize the same school for mulattoes which would later frustrate Capitein. Released after Des Bordes's departure in 1740, Protten pursued other assignments for the *Broedergemeente*, including the Danish West Indies and Herrnhut, before returning to the Gold Coast in 1757, this time to Christiansborg. Similar to Capitein, his stay there also ended tragically after he accidently killed one of his students while cleaning his gun. He spent most of his final decade in Europe, partly in Herrnhut and partly in Copenhagen, before returning to Guinea in 1767, where he died in 1769.[35]

As with their missionary work in general, the Moravian Brethren produced the greatest number of black predicants in Suriname. From the late nineteenth century forward they engaged in systematic recruitment there and trained Surinamer missionaries in Herrnhut and in Zeist, which in 1927 assumed fully the work formerly done at Herrnhut. However, the early nineteenth century also produced at least two notable black predicants. The first was Johannes King (ca. 1830–1898), a Bush Negro from the Matuari tribe. This was all the more significant because Christianity had made only modest inroads into the Bush Negro communities up to that point. The only remarkable earlier success in conversions was that of the Saramakaner chief Alabi in 1771. The church's influence gained from this was completely lost with his death in 1820.[36]

King's attraction to Christianity apparently began through visions he reported experiencing in the 1850s. In 1857 he appeared at the Moravian church in Paramaribo and related his experiences to Van Calker, head of the mission there, who gave him a primer and a catechism. Although illiterate at the time, King eventually learned to read and write, becoming perhaps the earliest author from the Maroons (in Sranan). In 1861 he was formally baptized, and in the following decades he became famous throughout the Maroon tribes as a Christian preacher, winning many converts and founding a Moravian Church at his own village of Maripaston. The Herrnhutters valued his work highly, especially because of his facility with the native languages and his familiarity with the pagan religions with which Christianity was competing. His writings include an autobiographical account of part of his ministry period and a description of his many visions.[37]

Another nineteenth-century black Herrnhutter predicant was Cornelis Winst Blijd (1860–1921), who was born a slave. Educated by the Herrnhutters, he eventually became an assistant missionary and a teacher at the Moravian settlement in Paramaribo. In 1902 the *Broedergemeente* officially ordained him as the first Surinamer at the rank of deacon. In 1913, on the occasion of the fiftieth anniversary of the emancipation, the Moravians sent him on a visit to the Netherlands, Germany, and Denmark. At one ceremony in the Netherlands he spoke before Queen Wilhelmina.[38]

The Catholic Church, more restricted than the other two by Dutch law, and later in starting its missionary work in the Dutch empire, was also late in developing native priests. With the various orders of fathers, deacons, and sisters carrying out the work themselves, the Catholic effort can quite literally be described as the most paternalistic. However, while the Herrnhutters consistently showed higher regard for the indigenous cultures, and the Reformed Church showed some regard in isolated instances, the Christian missionary movement as a whole rested on the assumption that it offered the "heathens" its superior legacy. For some missionaries the stress was on civilization more than religion; but the essential attitude toward nonbelievers was the same. In this confrontation between cultures the preparation of native clergy represented an important stage in the understanding between the Christians and their new audience. On one hand it provided an improved basis for integration of Christianity into the existing cultures, where, to the present, elements of the native religions can still be seen in the Christian Churches in Suriname, the Caribbean, and South and West Africa. More significant for the present discussion, native clergy enhanced education of the Europeans through these articulate spokesmen from the "other" world who could also speak the European languages.

Often overlooked in the ominous shadow of the devastating destruction that slavery and colonial exploitation would bring about in relations between the Europeans and Africans is the sense of wonder upon the initial encounter. It is interesting to note that in the Dutch response the experience of the missionaries quickly captured the imagination of writers in general as a literary theme. At the same time, some of the most popular authors in Dutch literature were predicants who gave special attention in prose and poetry to the topics of slavery and the equality of blacks. Both these types of writing are shown in chapter four. For the remainder of the present chapter it will be useful to look at some of the written narrative accounts sent home to the Netherlands from the missionary fields, to the members of the numerous support societies in particular, but also to all who could be induced to read the periodicals of the movement. Such reports are one source through which the Dutch public could form an impression of what blacks were like.

A well-known eighteenth-century report from the field was that provided in the two books of Jan Kals mentioned earlier.[39] Born on the border of the Netherlands in Düren, Germany in 1700, Kals was raised in the Reformed Church but educated in a Jesuit school, which later influenced his approach to the ministry when he was stationed in Suriname as a predicant for the West India Company. After studying theology at Utrecht from 1722 to 1728, he took the assignment in Suriname in 1731, only to be expelled in 1733 for promoting the rights of Indians and slaves. His official post, like Capitein's for example, was to serve the white Reformed congregation only. He instead openly advocated admitting the Indians, slaves, and free blacks as well. His parish encompassed ninety plantations along the Cottica and Perica rivers. He wanted to have an "open church" and "open schools," arguing that it was also in the best interest of the planters and the company. In one of his books, published long after his expulsion but while he remained a crusader, he used the examples of the "Pious Savages" (*vroome wilden*) Trouble and Isabella as support for his arguments. Trouble had been raised to age 18 on a Jewish plantation and had picked up Christian Bible knowledge along with the children he had to care for for his Christian master who had bought him later. He astounded Kals by his knowledge of the word and meaning of the

Scriptures. He was content just to be free to talk to Kals about the faith and was afraid for his owner to find out.

Isabella was an African woman whose previous owner had allowed her to attend catechism and to join the parish Kals now led. However, she had left under ridicule by both blacks and whites. Whites had told her that blacks were the devil's children, created to serve whites. She alleged further that the white men had turned on her because she preferred living with the black father of her children over serving as their whore. Now she and her family held private worship as Christians without recognition from the church. She was instructing the others. Although freed by her master, she was technically reenslaved as a result of violating a rule that any free black who "mingled" three times with a slave became a slave. Kals was forced to leave the colony before he could follow up on his desire to recruit members such as Trouble and Isabella.[40]

Kals would have been deeply impressed at what the Herrnhutters were doing a century later in Suriname. An 1851 report to Zeist reads in part:

> A multi-year investigation in our missionary work, both here and elsewhere, has taught us that in order generally to introduce the Christian life and morality in place of the idolatry reigning among this ignorant folk, it is not enough to preach the saving gospel from time to time just to the older Negroes who grew up heathen; but it is especially necessary for upcoming youth to instruct them early, acquaint them with God's word and raise them as Christians. . . . We feel that rather than through a general dissemination of Christian knowledge and civilization, the morals can be best affected when schools are set up on many, if possible all, of the plantations in this colony. There designated, appropriately prepared, slave boys will be given elementary education in reading, singing and Bible lessons.[41]

Far beyond questioning whether or not blacks should become Christianized, the Herrnhutters debated only the strategies for accomplishing it. They became convinced that conversion and baptism of the children was the most fruitful approach. All the while they sent back glowing reports attesting to the high aptitude of blacks for biblical knowledge and education in general:

> Their comprehension improved unusually quickly. They had such a strong memory that they quickly mastered whole psalms and

songs without difficulty. One of them learned to cite the section and page on which to find noteworthy passages I had taught him from books. They write better than I . . . [42]

Viewed from the twentieth century such amazement over such an elementary level of skill and intellect might suggest disabusement from condescending preconceptions. However, it should be remembered that the basic literacy rate was not high anywhere until the twentieth century. The achievements of the Herrnhutters' pupils were quite possibly higher than many of the faithful in Holland because of the amount of concentrated effort devoted to them by the missionaries. The potential for education of the native students from Suriname, the Caribbean, and Africa was further tested and proven through education of a growing number of them in the Netherlands from the late nineteenth century onward. The first living black person seen by many Netherlanders was often a student training in one of the missionary schools in Holland.

Along with the missionary reports celebrating the great strides made in educating the converts in the tropics would invariably come others listing the constant heavy toll in missionary lives lost as a result of the climate and disease. This persistent pattern among the many religious groups over several centuries helped to establish a tradition of service and sacrifice which survives to the present day and redounds to the benefit of numerous ongoing humanitarian aid projects. One unintended consequence of this, however, is a tendency for those aided and the areas from which they come to be thought of as always in a state of dependency and inferiority.

Although the various churches also continued their missionary work within the Netherlands and other parts of Europe, the peoples of the tropics have usually been considered more helpless. Within this context the transition from slavery to freedom for blacks and from symbolic to real beings within the religious tradition did not necessarily mean full acceptance and equality. Thus the scattered images of blacks which emerge from the Dutch religious traditions defy any single, focused picture. However, as will be shown presently, when considered alongside those coming from other elements of Dutch culture which are considered here, they contribute significantly to its character.

THE BLACK PRESENCE
IN THE DUTCH WORLD

Slaves, Servants, and Free Laborers

THE RELATED DISCUSSION in chapter one explains how Dutch entry into the African slave trade, beginning in the seventeenth century and eventually accounting for their removal of around half a million Africans to the Americas, contributed most to increase the actual presence of blacks in the Dutch empire and made the single greatest impact on the subsequent image of blacks in Dutch culture. The image of blacks as a servile race eventually eclipsed all other images earlier present in Dutch society. This became all the more reinforced as the practice of slavery in the Dutch colonies led to an actual presence of hundreds of black servants and slaves in the Netherlands by the mid–eighteenth century. They initially served as house servants, as coachmen, in various roles as laborers, and in a number of military roles. Only in the twentieth century would the actual number there increase dramatically. In the meantime their status and activities both in the Netherlands and in the Dutch empire as a whole would become much more diversified. While the images before the seventeenth century were based on concepts, the later ones derived more from direct experience.

The Dutch role in the African slave trade contains much of the explanation of Dutch attitudes and practices toward blacks during these centuries. It accounts for important inconsistencies in behavior and stark contrasts between the prevailing values at home and those in the colonies. It is still not known for certain when the Dutch involvement in the slave trade first began. One apocryphal story from the period suggests that the initial European impressions of the Africans did not differ greatly from some of the fantastic, erroneous notions

Europeans had held about Black Africa in earlier centuries. The Portuguese chronicler Duarte Pacheco Reviera described a joint Flemish-Castilian voyage to Elmina in 1475 which ended in disaster when the ship wrecked on the African coast during the return trip and the crew of 35 was reportedly eaten by the natives.[1] The chronicler's almost gleeful tone makes his account suspect. The lucrative expedition was undertaken in violation of the trade monopoly granted Portugal by the Pope; such was the punishment for violators! On the other hand, the Africans' impressions of the Europeans were quite comparable. It appears that from the earliest beginnings of the European importation of African slaves, some Africans believed the Europeans took them in order to eat them.

The first sizable population of blacks in the Netherlands, broadly defined, was an outgrowth of its place in the Portuguese trading empire. Antwerp was made a major commercial and diplomatic center and Spanish and Portuguese traders and officials were the first routinely to bring colored slaves and servants of foreign races and colors into the city. Scholars in the region have tended to ignore this topic. One recent scholar has speculated that this is either because in more recent centuries it has become embarrassing or because the practice was just considered too commonplace for its time to merit comment.[2] A number of others have cited evidence from parish and city records describing the baptism and manumission of "Moorish" slaves in the sixteenth century. The city's law actually prohibited enslavement, and provided that slaves brought there had to be freed if they petitioned the authorities. However, owners were not forced to free them in the absence of such demands. Most granted freedom received it voluntarily from the master, as in wills.[3] J. Denucé, in his classic study on trade between Africa and Antwerp, estimated that of European cities its colored population in the sixteenth century was second only to Lisbon's. There were also a few in other port cities and their environs.[4]

The earliest conspicuous contingent of a black population in the northern Netherlands was the group of a hundred and thirty slaves who were brought to Zeeland in 1596.[5] Some of these came to be buried in churchyards in the Netherlands. It is not known what became of the others; but it is likely that at least some melted into the surrounding population. As the Dutch trading empire took shape and incorporated areas with large black populations, more blacks also ap-

peared in the Netherlands. A very noticeable rise in the number occurred after Suriname was taken over by the Dutch Suriname Society
in 1682. Then in the course of the eighteenth century hundreds of
slaves and freemen came with their masters or employers. Some
stayed for periods of years. Like Antwerp, Amsterdam also considered slavery illegitimate. The city also had stringent laws against violent coercion of slaves. Some managed to flee from their masters in
Amsterdam and seek other employment there or in the provinces.
However, instances of this were rare because most of those in question were in more comfortable circumstances in the service of
wealthy families than they would have been on their own. Some af-
fects of the more liberal laws in the Netherlands were also at times felt
in the colonies as well.[6]

An amusing episode surrounding the Aucaner Maroon Jeboa provides a colorful illustration. The son of Aucaner tribal chief Jakje,
Jeboa was one of several Maroons sent as "hostages" to Paramaribo in
accordance with the 1760 treaty signed between the Maroons and the
Dutch. In 1767 the church council in Paramaribo sent Jeboa to Amsterdam for training. After unsuccessful attempts by the church to
have him accepted in the city orphanage, he was placed in three different boarding houses in succession, while all the time his relationship with his hosts became increasingly less agreeable. At meals with
a family, he would demand better food. He asked for more spending
money and better clothes, and sold some to get more money. Jeboa
made disreputable friends and bought such goods as silk handker-
chiefs and a silver pocket watch. After the master with whom he had
been placed informed the church council how much it was costing to
support Jeboa it was decided to send him back to Paramaribo, where-
upon he threatened to disrupt the social order there if they did. And,
indeed, upon his return he ended up in jail on one occasion for inter-
fering with a Jewish plantation master who was beating a Negro slave
girl.[7]

The blacks did not come only to Amsterdam. There is the celebrated case of Jan Kompanie, a slave boy taken from the coast of
Guinea by Admiral De Ruiter in the early seventeenth century. After
accompanying the Admiral for a number of years and residing in Zeeland for a time, Kompanie was eventually freed and returned to Africa. There are numerous scattered references to others in rural areas
of the Netherlands. The practice of maintaining black servants in the

region around Groningen, for example, was well established by the late eighteenth century. The close connection between the colonies and the wealthy class inhabiting the castles of the Groningen lands can be seen in the history of the family of Pieter Woortman, whose father of the same name had gone to the Gold Coast as a seaman and made a fortune by rising through the ranks in the West India Company there. He served as director-general from 1767 to 1780 and provided lucrative positions for his sons and other relatives. One son, Jan, had a son named Pieter and a daughter, Johanna, by a Negro woman named Acoua. This Pieter was serving as a customs officer when he died in 1785.

The family of the predicant and educator B. Houwink, who taught Negroes in St. Maarten, has an eighteenth-century portrait of Houwink and a black boy. A black servant named Jan Christiaan was brought by his master, Jacob Appius, from Suriname in 1775 when Appius settled at his residence, Stadtwijck, in Sappemeer. Upon the master's death in 1789, Jan Christiaan was mentioned in his will. In the same neighborhood he had found other blacks already present. Maria Kock and her husband Cornelis Star Lichtenvoort, whose family owned the nearby country estate, Welgelegen, at Kleinemeer, had brought two slaves from her Curaçao plantation, Rozetak, in 1764.[8] The history of the city of Hoorn provides materials showing similar practices there. Reinier Jongemaats, a regent's son who rose to good fortune in the maritime service despite his father's bankruptcy, freed a slave named Leander van Bengalen in Hoorn, whom he had acquired abroad in 1747. Adriaan van Bredehoof in his will left his slave boy Tabo 12,000 florins with the intention that it would make it possible for him to become a merchant. Tabo soon afterward married a Dutch girl, Wolmetje Bakkers, opened a tobacco shop, and changed his name to Adriaan de Bruijn (the Brown).[9]

That some of the blacks who entered the Netherlands during this period left a permanent imprint on Dutch society is richly documented in the history of the Alons family of Groningen province. Compelling circumstantial evidence suggests that one of the two Lichtenvoort slaves from Curaçao was "Luois Aalons," the first Netherlander in the family. He lived to the age of 76 in Sappemeer, where the death report in 1831 described him as a worker. The documentation for the marriage of one of his sons gave the father's occupation as coachman.

The Black Presence in the Dutch World

The marriage and baptism book of Sappemeer for 1779 lists the marriage of a Louis Alons, described as "a Negro from Curaçao," to a village girl, Hindrikje Luitjens, who died in September 1799, the death certificate describing her as the wife of "Lowijs Allon." It is interesting to note that this would be the last ethnic reference to appear in any of the official registers on the family. A further tracing of this family's history shows how it became completely absorbed into Dutch society.

Allon was confirmed as a member in the Dutch Reformed Church in 1784 under the name "louys Allon," most probably having already been baptized earlier. The family continued in this tradition with each new generation, while the name continued to take variant forms on down to the twentieth century. The Allon first child was baptized on the same day as the marriage. Allon's second marriage, also in Sappemeer, was to Maria Harms, a rope maker from Groningen, in November 1799. She died in Sappemeer in 1824 at the age of 48. There were four children from the first marriage and three from the second. Of the first four, one was named Cornelius and one Maria, apparently after Louis's former owners. His first child, Susanna, worked as a shopkeeper/innkeeper, survived almost to the age of 80, married twice, and had six children, one of whom was named Louis.

One of her children, Luitje Alons, worked as a hat maker in Sappemeer after apparently living for some time in Friesland to learn the trade. He fathered seven children in two marriages. One, Meindert, born in 1817, died in military service. Another, Freerk, born in Sappemeer in 1822, became a writer and shopkeeper. Another, Lodewijk, became a farm worker and later a farmer. Still another, Cornelius Louis Alons, born in Sappemeer in 1833, became a house painter and married the daughter of a captain of a merchant ship. Susanna's brother Cornelius worked as a clerk in the office of the United Courts at Meppel until his death there in 1813 at age 30.[10]

A sixth-generation descendant, the Reformed Church predicant Louis Alons, in his retirement at Eelde in the same region sought to complete this genealogy by seeking more on the Antillean origins and attempting to trace it on down to the present. In the process he discovered that Cornelis Star Lichtenvoort and Maria Kock had three Negro slaves left after selling her plantation, Rozetak, in 1764 upon their marriage. Their names were Francisco, Jacob, and Thicco. In the church records in Sappemeer he also noted the marriage of a Jan Francisco and Maria Isabel Salbador, both from the West Indies, in 1782. The name of a third, Joseph Francisco, is also there. He also found that the name Alons appeared in a number of forms, and often prominently, in books tracing the old families of the Netherlands Antilles. In one instance it appears that one Alons may have been related to Petrus Bernardus van Starkenborg, a governor of Curaçao in 1818 whose family had ties with the Kock family.

Further research in local records in the Netherlands revealed an interesting entry from police documents. The original Louis Alons was once assaulted by men along the road. The report did not indicate the motivation for the attack; and no reference is made to Alons's color.[11] The experience of the Alons family suggests that in these early centuries within the Netherlands it was rather easy for blacks to melt into Dutch society once they entered. Unlike the situation in the colonies, a tinge of color did not define a person as black. This reticence to accentuate differences may stem in part from the general spirit of accommodation which became traditional in the Netherlands, but may also be due to a lingering uneasiness with the participation in the African slave trade and slavery, which remained outlawed at home. A different definition of the descendants of the early black immigrants to the Netherlands would probably show a significantly higher "black" population than is now counted.

As indicated in chapter one, the status and treatment of slaves and servants varied in different parts of the Dutch empire. They were probably best off in the Netherlands proper. One reason for this was that they were fewer and thus a novelty. More important, however, was the fact that those who were taken to the Netherlands were probably favorites, and were therefore more likely to receive privileged treatment. Their role as showpieces also ensured that they did not work nearly as hard as did their counterparts in the colonies. The Stadholder's court included black servant boys who were attired in contemporary noble costumes but with feathered turbans. Other upper-class burghers who wished to impress followed the fad. Thus, the hundreds of black figures in the paintings of the seventeenth and eighteenth centuries were describing reality, even if in some cases they were drawn in for effect by the artist without a subject present.

Separate "Equals": The Maroons of Suriname

Standing in vivid contrast to the role of Blacks as slaves in the Dutch empire was the status of the Maroons, the runaway slaves who had managed to establish independent communities in Suriname. After a century of unsuccessful, difficult campaigns aimed at defeating the rebels, the white colonists finally made peace with each of the three main groups, the Djukas (also called Aucaners), the Saramaccaners, and the Matuaris, in 1760, 1762, and 1767 respectively. As early as the 1680s their raids on European settlements had been so successful that they forced the signing of the first of a series of formal treaties between the two sides. The number of Maroons increased dramatically in 1712 when a French force invaded during the war between France and Holland. The Dutch slave masters sent their slaves and families into the bush to keep them from falling into the hands of the French. When the hostilities ended the masters were shocked into a new perception of the blacks when many refused to return to their bondage.[12] If the Europeans were truly surprised, this says much about the level of their understanding of the people they had enslaved.

The Maroons organized themselves into tribes named after local rivers or other regional features. They built their villages at the head of river rapids or other easily defensible locations and raided plantations for black women and supplies such as metal implements. By the middle of the eighteenth century they had organized into clans within their redoubts and had formulated land rights, rules of succession for leadership, ritual sites, and other attributes of disparate societies.[13] There then developed a pattern for slave revolts. The slaves on a given plantation would overpower their white masters and break out into the bush to join the Maroons. A general uprising, one which almost overthrew the Surinam colony, occurred in the neighboring Dutch colony at Berbice, in 1763. The revolt's leaders, Coffey and Accara, for a time controlled a large territory containing Dutch possessions until reinforcements arrived from Europe.

Some of the correspondence during this conflict has survived. It brings out vividly the attitudes of the leaders on both sides. A letter of J. A. Charbon, a son of one of the plantation directors, described it as a revolt of the slaves against the Christians. The same theme is echoed in a letter to Coffey from the colonial governor Hoogenheim, who expressed dismay that the slaves would strike out in such a way against righteous and divinely appointed masters. He asks why Coffey did not simply come to him and tell him what he wanted if he was unhappy. Coffey, who was illiterate, responded in broken Dutch, probably through the assistance of captured Europeans. He called himself the governor of Berbice, though offering to concede half to the Christians. He offered to allow the Dutch to keep the slaves on their ship; but the others would have to be freed. The governor declined to meet with Coffey to discuss these matters further unless Coffey would come to him. He added that he had loved the Negroes as long as they had behaved; but now he and God would have to punish them. He falsely reported that he had sent Coffey's proposal for the division of territory to Holland for consideration. When new troops arrived, the Dutch brutally suppressed the uprising and punishments included burning alive, quartering, and various other tortures (see figure 112).[14]

The Maroons were far more successful when their aims were limited to Dutch recognition of their independence in exchange for their staying out of areas inhabited by the Europeans. Johannes King, the nineteenth-century Matuari Maroon predicant, has left one of the most informative accounts of the history of this. The agreements sometimes provided for return of runaway slaves by the Maroons, for pay. In addition they were given rights for farming, hunting, and fishing on the land they roamed. Some treaties also included trade agreements. According to King, agreements with two of the main tribes were sealed with a blood oath taken by pricking fingers and mixing blood from both sides with wine and having each drink. This ceremony was repeated at three-year intervals for over a hundred years.[15]

Around 1770 the Dutch undertook to force all those Maroons not under treaties to come to terms. This resulted in a protracted war, with Dutch soldiers campaigning against the Maroon leaders Bonni, Baron, and Joli Coeur. It was at this juncture that the soldier of fortune John Stedman entered the story. His subsequent account provides information on the Maroon leaders as well as on European attitudes. He wrote that Baron had been a slave of a Swedish gentleman who taught him to read and write, took him to Europe, promised him freedom upon return, but then sold him instead. Baron

112. William Blake etching, Slave Torture in Surinam. Drawing from John Stedman, *Narrative of a Five-Years' Expedition Against the Revolted Negroes of Surinam* (London: Johnson, 1796).

113. Maroons. Photo and Print Collection, Koninklijk Instituut voor Taal-, Land- en Volkenkunde, Leiden.

had refused to work for his Jewish master in Suriname; he was flogged and then fled to the forest. Joli Coeur had rebelled to avenge his mother. Bonni was born of a runaway and was a son of the planter she had fled. Stedman first grew to admire the rebels as he hunted in the bush for two years before personally sighting a Maroon on the loose. Then he was amazed when in one battle nearly all his soldiers were hit, but none died because the rebels were firing substitute bullets such as button fragments, pebbles, and coin bits. He could not help but marvel at such resourcefulness and determination. He also found his opponents to be brilliant military tacticians.[16]

The war between the Dutch and the Maroons went on throughout the eighteenth century. The difficulty of penetrating the interior of Suriname, which obtains to this day, convinced the Dutch to concede freedom to the runaways in exchange for relative peace on the plantations. In 1738 the Maroon population was estimated to number around 6,000, an estimate perhaps inflated by the planters' fears. There were about 400 plantations with 50,000 slaves and 2,000 Whites.[17] Especially after the events in Haiti in the 1790s, the planters could consider themselves lucky to have such an arrangement. Even in Curaçao in 1795 there was a general, if relatively mild, revolt of the slaves when the masters tried to violate customary work obligations.

In accordance with the treaty, the Dutch government stationed an official called *posthouder* (postholder) with the Maroons to act as an intermediary and to ensure that treaty provisions were being observed by both sides. Another duty, until the early nineteenth century, was regulation of a pass system developed to limit the number of people traveling along the rivers. This was intended to limit the possibility of attack by the Negroes while at the same time respecting their desire to live in isolation from the colony. Enduring even after emancipation in 1863, the isolation of most of the Maroons continued into the twentieth century, although their movement between the two worlds for trade and other purposes was constant. The Saramaccaners, the largest group, numbered around 20,000 by the 1980s.

A remote array of cultures in a colony which itself was seldom on the minds of the Dutch public, the Maroon communities nevertheless played a significant role in shaping the Dutch image of blacks. For three hundred years they stood as a reminder of the resourcefulness and political and military acumen blacks could display when independent in juxtaposition to the prevalent image of dependence and servility. At the same time, their isolation did perpetuate the Dutch view of the Maroon as wild and primitive. They also represent a significant stream of the population and culture from Suriname that would suddenly enter the Netherlands proper in the late twentieth century. One wonders if the mutual suspiciousness deeply ingrained in both cultures over the centuries of stalemate between the two "worlds" might not have direct bearing on the current process of accommodation.[18]

Soldiers and Seamen

Another role blacks have played in the Dutch historical experience which departs from the servile mold is that of soldier, although it should be noted that in Dutch tradition that does not translate into respect as readily as in most societies. The heavy employment of foreigners in the Dutch military and the maritime service seems to suggest a lack of attraction to these pursuits as well as a small population upon which to draw. Regrettably for the student of history, the identification of blacks in the Dutch maritime service is nearly impossible because of the laxity of the records kept on seamen. From works of art and from other indirect sources it is apparent that the Dutch readily employed black seamen over their vast trading empire as did the other major European shippers. However, there is little evidence that permanent colonies of black sailors ever materialized in the major port cities of the Northern Netherlands as was the case in Britain, for example.

It is equally certain that blacks were employed as boatmen and dock workers in the Netherlands and of course particularly in the American colonies and African posts. Meanwhile, the practice used in hiring seamen generally involved half payment before the voyage and half at the end, with no other questions asked and no detailed records filed entailing physical descriptions of crews. Consequently, most of the history of this group must be garnered from scattered references to Negro cabin boys and a few sailors described in literature, such as those mentioned in earlier chapters here. There is as well one story concerning a possible major role played by a black slave in a crucial naval battle during the sixteenth-century wars between the Dutch and the English over sea dominance. One conjecture concerning the unexplained explosion which sunk the flagship of the fleet from Zeeland under Admiral Van Wassenaar's command in 1665 is that a vengeful slave ignited the powder whose explosion sent most of the crew to its death.[19] The actual record of black sailors remains to be uncovered.

On the other hand, the story of the black soldier is much more accessible and is one of the most fascinating episodes in the experience of blacks in Dutch history. The history of blacks in the regular Dutch army is similarly as elusive as that of the sailors because of the tendency to avoid making racial distinctions for the relatively few soldiers of African descent in the regular military forces. However, for the land forces historical circumstances dictated that blacks remain conspicuous in certain special types of units. In Dutch military forces the earliest blacks to appear in uniform were apparently musicians. Evidence of this can be seen in numerous works of art from the seventeenth century forward. They are first apparent as drummers and buglers, and later in full bands in the West Indies. Both instances represented deliberate use of blacks literally for color, decoration, and symbol, and for entertainment. This tradition was still evident in

World War II, when even the Dutch forces landing in Indonesia included a Negro band.[20]

Several hundred Surinamer marines also participated in the war in the Pacific and in the Caribbean; and some accompanied U.S. forces in the invasion of Europe against the Germans. Blacks also served as armed soldiers, at least in the colonies, from the earliest decades of the Dutch Republic. They were employed in defense of both the South and North American colonies against both native American and rival European forces. The Dutch West India Company used only a few black soldiers, as compared to hundreds in the Portuguese forces under white officers. Blacks were, of course, used even more extensively to help control the rest of the black population, slave and free. Finally, in the Dutch East Indies they came to form a significant part of the Dutch East Indian Army in the nineteenth and early twentieth century.

The Black Rangers of Suriname

As would be expected, it was in Suriname that black soldiers became the most numerous and conspicuous. The historian Silvia De Groot has provided the most comprehensive account of these developments. Supplementing the earlier relevant contributions by J. Wolbers and other scholars, she found that the first organized black units were formed by the governor to augment the beleaguered European forces which were so overwhelmingly outmanned and unsuited for tropical combat that the colony's very survival against attacks from the Maroons was in doubt. The first unit formed was called the Free Negro Corps. Comprised of freed blacks and mulattoes, it had about 150 men in 1770, commanded by officers detailed from the regular militia. Like the latter, they served only when called up in emergencies and earned pay during that time alone.

A second, quite different type of black unit, called the Black Rangers, was formed by Governor Jan Nepveu in 1772 and played a critical role in Colonel Fourgeoud's survival against the Bonni uprising, which was to tax colonial resources until 1793. The Rangers were a quasi-military corps, placed under the colony's governing Council of Policy and Justice rather than the military commandant. It was comprised of former slaves purchased from the slave market and plantations for the purpose. Their main function was to patrol and preserve the cordon established by the governor between the colony and the Maroons. The force was set at 300 slave soldiers who would be paid while in active service and were provided a small plot of land near Paramaribo to support themselves during peacetime.

Also commanded by officers recruited from the colony's militia, the Black Rangers proved to be a more stable military organization and more effective than the Free Corps, although the Rangers too were partly civilian as well as military in their legal and social status. They earned a reputation as the military elite in the colony, which facilitated recruitment of officers. One of these was the later governor Friderici. Another famous admirer of their prowess was John Stedman, who participated in the campaign under Fourgeoud and later praised the black soldiers in his famous account. Even a few Maroons were persuaded to join. Popularly known by the color of their uniform cap (at first green and later red), they gave rise to the social category their descendants are still known as: *Redi Moesoe*. The two types of black units were eventually merged, in 1803. In 1818 their name was changed to Corps Koloniale Guides and in 1834 to Compagnie Koloniale Guides. After 1840 they were known mainly as rowers at the remote outposts.[21]

A mutiny within the Black Rangers (now merged with the Free Corps) in 1805 revealed much about the place of this unique group within its historical setting. The uprising, which began on September 7, was led initially by thirty Rangers and within two months grew to include around eighty plus Bonni and Djuka Maroons who also joined or supported their raids, the most successful of which was the overrunning of the army post at Armina on the Marowijne River. A number of whites were murdered during the rebellion. It may not be an exaggeration to describe the rebellion as an identity crisis. According to Silvia De Groot, its occurrence may be closely tied to the instability and uncertainty brought by the upheaval of changing governments and clashing cultures during this phase of the Napoleonic era.

Even though the English raised salaries after they came into control of Suriname in 1799, their imposition of stricter military discipline was sufficiently abhorrent to the Black Rangers to provoke desertions and finally open rebellion. Another contributing factor may have been an increase in the number of "trusted" Maroons in the Corps. It would appear that the presence of these blacks, from free

114. Colonial Guides in Surinam. Atlas van Stolk, Rotterdam.

societies of their own making, disquieted those bought out of slavery to serve the white world just as that world offered some allurements to those who had tasted freedom but also desired some of the material advantages of European civilization. The freer lifestyle of the Rangers, featuring furloughs to visit family and hunting and fishing privileges, also conditioned them more to the expectations of freemen.

That they found freedom, even if in the bush, more appealing than a stricter regimen is attested by their revolt and flight. Remnants of the rebel force settled on an island in the Marowijne River.[22]

Blacks in the Dutch East Indian Army

It is at first glance surprising that it was in the East Indies that the Dutch made the most extensive use of black soldiers. However, it is easily understandable in the context of the interconnectedness of a maritime trading empire. For the same reason it was probably the Portuguese who first transported black Africans into the region in the modern period. However, in the early nineteenth century the Dutch found it expedient to recruit West Africans in large numbers for that area of operations. By the early twentieth century around 3,000 had traveled to East Asia in the service of the House of Orange. Toward the end of the century a few would also be brought from the West Indies. A deliberate strategy of recruiting blacks on the Gold Coast at Elmina and Kumasi for East Indies service emerged in the 1820s after the performance of European troops in the Dutch East Indies forces proved unreliable.

A comprehensive scheme for recruiting Africans was reflected as early as 1828 in a letter from a certain Major Charles Hamilton Smith to the Minister of Navy and Colonies.[23] In it he proposed building a corps of black soldiers for the East Indian Army out of incorrigible slaves, petty criminals, and free volunteers recruited in Suriname, Curaçao, St. Eustatius, and the Dutch possessions in West Africa. They would be first assembled in West Africa at Friedrichsburg for training. He emphasized throughout his letter that the handling of the men was of paramount importance for determining the success of the experiment. As evidence of the good results which might flow from good treatment he cited the experience of the British with the Maroons of Jamaica and that of the comportment of the Maroons in Suriname. His illustrations of the types of measures which might be used ranged from simple gestures of respect for customs such as dancing to provision of pensions and land plots in Java after the end of service. Anticipating accusations of slave trading, in violation of the ban which the British had been attempting to enforce since proclaiming it in 1807, he suggested calling it a form of voluntary servitude to a sovereign, a familiar practice in Europe.[24]

The government response, reflecting some of the reservations of

The Black Presence in the Dutch World

the Commissioner-General of War Prince Frederick and the Minister of the Navy and Colonies, was penned by General Van den Bosch, who had been dispatched to Paramaribo in 1828. He pointed out that the issue of slave trading could not be easily put to rest, since the profit motive would lead some of the African potentates to deliver recruits by whatever means possible. Furthermore, he believed the peculiar nature of warfare in Java, which was responsible for a rising demand for troops, was not like the search and engage and destroy missions in the West Indies; it was more like the complex political and civil warfare in Europe. He also doubted that the free blacks in the West Indies would be willing to leave their families, or that the mulattoes would be willing to fight alongside the blacks. Van den Bosch's conclusion was that the war could be better waged in Java by employment of different strategies there with the present forces. Other proposals received by the colonial ministry included one for recruitment of Negroes from North America, and another advocated establishment of a colony of blacks in Java which would become a military caste loyal to the Dutch. Probably the overriding concern of the government regarding recruitment from the West Indies was the possible adverse impact on the agricultural labor force there.

Actual recruitment began in 1831, with a plan to form a 150-man unit as a kind of pilot project. However, normal recruitment proved extremely difficult. The Africans did not want to go to a strange world across the seas. In 1831–1832 only eighteen recruits were taken from Elmina to Java.[25] Although the policy called specifically for Negroes, its first, very limited, success was with petty criminals and *tapooyers*, a group of mixed African and European blood who were given special rights within Elmina's social structure. Eventually the recruiters resorted to offering to buy conditional freedom for some slaves from the Ashanti king. This proved to be the main source of the troops eventually obtained. The slaves were normally not Ashanti, since Ashanti law prohibited sending their own away. The process became regularized only after the appointment of a special royal commission under General Jan Verveer, who arrived at the end of 1836 complete with a military brass band. After successful negotiations, he signed in 1837 a contract with Kwaku Dua, king of Ashanti, establishing a depot in his capital, Kumasi, which was 300 miles in the interior.[26]

Soon thereafter a similar one was opened on the coast at the

Dutch fortress of Elmina. In the contract the king promised 1,000 recruits within the first year, although only 51 were delivered after thirteen months. In fact the level of 1,000 was never to be reached in any year. This led the Dutch to covet what they believed to be 3,000 to 4,000 human sacrifice victims offered up annually at funeral ceremonies by the Ashanti.[27] The king was to be paid 100 guilders bounty per recruit, in armaments, according to the contract, but in reality often in precious metal. They were valued at 2.5 ounces of gold a head, to be paid preferably in old weapons, gunpowder, shot, and flint. Five healthy 17–22-year-olds were considered to be worth one rifle, fifty pounds of powder, two pounds of lead shot, and a thousand flints. Verveer also gave Kwaku Dua gold and silver with which to purchase slaves. The recruits were given physical examinations twice before acceptance, then given pay advances to purchase their freedom. Most recruits in Kumasi were Donkos, slaves taken in war. As agents at Kumasi, responsible for delivering the slaves to the coast, the Dutch employed J. P. Huydecooper until 1842, Kwasi Mijzang, who came in 1857, and P. de Heer, who served from 1859 to 1868.[28]

On cue, the British government, and some observers in the Netherlands, promptly charged the Dutch with engaging in a form of disguised slave trading. Indeed, the Dutch had officially stopped slave trading in 1814. This charge may well have had validity, although the French and the British themselves also employed former slaves in their armies. There had been some effort to attract Negro volunteers from the United States before it was decided to turn to Africa. The Dutch had the Africans enlist for a specified time. These blacks were to pay back the War Ministry through automatic deductions from their military pay and were technically classified as performing contract labor. Eight cents out of their daily pay of 33 cents would go to the government. Their contracts were for six, twelve, or eighteen years. Upon completion of twelve years of service they qualified for a pension.[29]

Normally troops destined for the Dutch East Indian Army were given preliminary orientation in the Netherlands, where Harderwijk had become the center for training colonial troops. To view the African troops in proper context, it should also be noted that the Dutch army in general was made up of mercenary outcasts from the rest of Europe. As for the East Indian Army, attempts had been made to find soldiers more effective in the tropics than the Europeans as early as the mid-eighteenth century. For example, under Governor-General Jacob Mossel there was an effort to acquire Arabs and Persians through the East India Company agencies in Persia and Hindustan. The Chinese in the East Indies region were another group earlier targeted.[30] A count in 1840 revealed that about 50 percent of the Dutch East Indian Army consisted of natives of the region. There were 879 officers, 6,090 European troops, 763 Ambonese, 1,502 Africans, and 10,760 other Asians.[31]

Military service was held in low esteem in nineteenth-century Europe in general. Little wonder that Harderwijk was called "the sinkhole of Europe," with the soldiers mocked even by Harderwijkers and soldiers as a group considered to be of low character. The soldiers were also regarded with some contempt in Indonesian society. Some effort was made in the second half of the nineteenth century to raise standards and pay and the switch to steamships from the 1870s onward improved the attractiveness of colonial service, since travel and resupply from Europe were made easier. Nevertheless, Dutch expansion into broader reaches of the East Indies coincided with a decline in the number of volunteers.[32] At the same time, chronic resistance in the Atjeh region of Indonesia during the latter part of the century made the Dutch manpower shortage more acute. This points up why desperate resort to resources such as the African troops remained a constant tendency regardless of such factors as racial attitudes. Obvious practical considerations also dictated that in this instance there was no thought of first transporting the recruits to Holland for orientation, although they were routinely brought back through the Netherlands, sometimes wintering there, on their return to Africa after service.[33]

Transport of colonial troops to the East Indies was carried out normally by commercial vessels of private firms, through the lowest bidder. For the African troops the main firm contracted was Anthony van Hoboken and Sons. Van Hoboken saw in transport of the troops an opportunity to have return cargo to the East Indies, which would otherwise have been lacking. In about twenty voyages between 1831 and 1841, using ten different ships, Van Hoboken delivered over 2,000 African troops to the East Indies. Recruitment was temporarily suspended from 1841 to 1855, after which it was stipulated that the soldier had to have been free at least two years before recruitment. To avert allegations of slaving, it was specified by the State Council for Navigation, Industry, and the Colonies that the recruits during shipment be fed just like all others and that safe water be brought from the Netherlands for them.

The contract also required observance of treaty provisions for open inspection by the British if they intercepted the ship at sea. For his part, Van Hoboken promised further that the troops would have music, dance, and recreation aboard. They were also given some weapons training. A doctor was also aboard. In 1838 the ship *De India* left Rotterdam for Guinea with a midwife, because the recruits were also allowed to take their wives and children, although apparently few did. In transit the troops were in a section partitioned off from European passengers bound for the East Indies. However, the recruits were given the choice of eating either a European diet or their own customary foods such as rice, corn, yams, and dried fish.[34]

The available information on the survival rate of recruits transported suggests that the conditions of the contract were probably met. Based on one count of 2,283 troops delivered by February 1842, there was an average death rate of one in sixteen. Considering the hardships of ocean passage in general of the time, with monotonous food, water shortage, and sickness, it would seem that the recruits fared at least as well as did normal passengers. However, the process was not altogether peaceful or smooth. Some early recruits, for example, discovered that they had been tricked when promised access to the higher ranks. In an incident in 1838 related to broken promises by the Dutch in recruitment, a punitive expedition had to be dispatched from the Netherlands to put down an uprising on the Gold Coast led by the chief of Ahanta, Aadu Bonsu, who was enraged by tactless actions by Governor Tonneboeijer. The latter was killed and his forces routed when he marched on Ahanta with an army of 250. There is also evidence of friction aboard ships between the recruits and crewmen.[35]

Within the East Indies the actual employment of the African troops appears to have been largely successful from the Dutch perspective. Arriving with what was obviously very limited military training, these soldiers did perform with at the very least as high a degree of loyalty and reliability as their European comrades displayed. Although initially fighting in units separate from the others, they were also Europeanized in the process of achieving military uniformity. Many became Christians. They were routinely given Dutch names, probably as early as the sea voyage, and probably primarily to simplify the task of their European commanders. Thus the Africans landed in the East Indies with such names as Klaas Zuurzak, Willem Lijm, Hendrik Slemp, Karel Glas, Kwassie, Piet Geel, and Joost Vondel, Jacob Big, Frits Hoed, Hein IJs, Janus Kars, Johannis Luns, and Piet Klink.

Nevertheless, military records later show the survival of such African and slave names as Abraba, Korocomi, Akonkwassie, Orestes, Azor, and Coffie. The soldiers also quickly found themselves called Europeans as a group. The term most often used to describe them, *Wolanda Itam*, or *Blanda Itam* ("Black Hollanders"), is from an Indonesian language. In Javanese they were called *Londo Ireng*, which had the same meaning.[36] One important, lingering distinction, however, was that the Africans continued to receive lower pay than did the Europeans and Ambonese, the largest East Indian component. This inequality continued even after emancipation of all slaves in the Dutch empire removed even a shadow of a justification based upon the original nature of the recruitment. In fact, even in the conditions for retirement the Africans had to serve many more years than did the Europeans, and slightly more than the Ambonese, in order to gain comparable benefits.[37]

Toward the end of the century they also came to be legally classified as Europeans within Dutch East Indian society. Also like the European colonial soldiers, the Africans were allowed to take a local wife. These partners, called in the local language *njai*, constituted a camp labor force as well as companionship. The *njai* and children were camp followers even on some campaigns, cooking, cleaning gear, and otherwise supporting the soldiers. August Van Pers, in the accompanying notes to his 1850 portrait of an African soldier, his *njai*, and child, observed that the black soldiers were the envy of the army in the pride they took in their personal appearance and that of their families. He also noted that the local women were not put off by the Africans' color since they too were of a darker hue. A number of sources note that the most striking physical feature from the point of view of the East Indian natives was the size in stature of the soldiers, since most of the natives were much shorter than the Africans or the Europeans.[38]

By all accounts, the *Blanda Itam*, reminiscent of the Black Rangers of Suriname, did not submit easily to military discipline. Some memoirs of European officers also reflect an element of cultural shock and racial prejudice in the relations between Europeans and Africans. One major recounted that first both the Africans and the Europeans had to become accustomed to the other's peculiar smell! For the officers it was also important to learn some of the African jargon which the men used. He further remarked that his approach was to think of the recruits as needing to be trained, just as one would train monkeys or dogs. The first stage was to raise them to the level of men, and then to that of soldiers.[39]

Serious resumption of discussion in military circles in the early 1880s about the desirability of recruiting black troops from the Americas provides further insight into the perception of the black soldiers. Appraising the suitability of the Africans for various military functions, one observer wrote:

> As for their physical strength, the Africans—especially those in the garrison artillery—should be better paid than the natives. That the *Africans* were not popular in the artillery and therefore speedily only assigned to the infantry must be attributed to their low intelligence. They were, however, *African*, half-savage, Negroes. That on the contrary the American, the more civilized, *English-*, *French-*, or *Dutch*-speaking Negroes are intelligent enough for the artillery weapons is apparent, we think, in the thirty or so Negroes known as "Americans," for the most part former sailors, who were to be found among the artillery of General De Neve, the Commander-in-chief. I have in mind Hunt, Matthews, Connell, Wilson, Wright, et al. If they are intelligent enough for the artillery, they can also be very well used if necessary to replace the natives in the miners and sappers corps. Whether the *American* Negro is competent for the cavalry and would be successful on our horses we do not know.[40]

The writer argued that the American Negroes were more capable overall because they were more civilized, that is, had been exposed longer to European culture. He proposed mounting a trial force of some several hundred American blacks and distributing them in the different branches of service in order to test his hypothesis. Should there be objections from the United States government to recruiting there, he proposed that the Dutch government nevertheless recruit in its own West Indies and Suriname. As a parting suggestion he added that it would help if the Dutch uniforms were made more colorful, because this was an important attraction for blacks.[41]

The Black Presence in the Dutch World

An infantry captain, S. de la Parra, who had served for ten years in the West Indies, and who also felt the West Indian blacks were more intelligent than the African, contributed still more details to the discussion. Carrying the racial theory even further, he saw potential for the mulattoes to aspire to become officers in the East Indian Army. First he countered arguments that the recruitment from the West Indies would siphon off a badly needed labor force from Suriname, which was already looking to import Chinese and Bengali contract laborers. Noting that the navy was already freely recruiting in Suriname and the Antilles, he pointed out that those targeted in both instances were from the part of the black population which had been free prior to the emancipation, while it was the former slaves who were deemed suitable for the sugar, coffee, and cacao plantations. He had been further assured by reports from naval officers that black sailors recruited in Suriname were quite intelligent and competent, and that black soldiers used there also enjoyed a good reputation among the field officers who watched them in action, although perhaps not among the high command further removed. He also speculated that the negative image was fostered simply by the anxiety over the prospect of the Dutch West Indian forces becoming largely black, given the government's desire to economize and the comparative cheapness of the black soldiers.

De la Parra further recalled some of his own firsthand observation of mistreatment of the black soldiers, which led them to have a negative attitude about military service. They were physically abused in drills, were segregated from the Europeans, and were constantly called "*Neger.*" He also noted that one reason the navy was more attractive in the West Indies was that the sailors received better rations than did the soldiers. On the other hand, although he had no knowledge of the blacks in the United States, he argued adamantly against those from the English colony of Barbados, whom he judged to be "lazy, quarrelsome, arrogant, and recalcitrant in the highest degree."[42] Ten years later there appeared an item in response to De la Parra, then a lieutenant colonel, which quoted the colonial minister to the effect that in 1887 the governors in Suriname and Curaçao had been urged to recruit blacks and coloreds locally, but for the West Indian Army, and had experienced good results with those soldiers.[43]

Most reports indicate that black soldiers performed well and courageously in combat. Between the onset of recruitment and 1844, it is estimated that one in sixteen who came died in the East.[44] They were especially conspicuous at the Battle of Djagaraga on Bali in 1849, where over five hundred of them supported the 7th Company's victory. In 1850 forty-one Africans were decorated with bronze or silver medals bearing the words "for courage and fidelity," the highest awards for valor designated for them at the time. Newspaper notes in the *Overveluwsche Weekblad* (Veluwe Weekly) and the *Harderwijker Courant* (Harderwijk News) from the mid-nineteenth century to the early twentieth made frequent references to African soldiers from the East Indies in the Netherlands, some en route back to Africa. An 1898 article describes one Tobey, who had finally realized his long-standing dream of seeing the Dutch Queen in person, albeit on the street. Some recruits took extremely well to military life; many signed up for multiple contracts, and after the Africans became integrated into the regular companies in the late nineteenth century, some sons followed fathers' footsteps into army careers.[45]

The most famous decorated hero was Jan Kooi, a corporal born in Elmina (figure 115). The August 5, 1882 *Overveluwsche Weekblad* reported his arrival in the Netherlands from the Celebes. Then aged 33, he was the first of the *Blanda Itam* to be decorated with the vaunted *Militaire Willemsorde*, 4th Class. On January 31, 1878, he had saved the life of his commander, Captain Bloom, by killing two Atyehers while himself suffering ten bullet wounds under enemy fire in the process. On July 25 of the same year he had earned a reward of 100 florins for saving the life of his lieutenant Bijleveld by killing a heavily armed Atyeher. Then on April 26, 1879, he had further distinguished himself when he and two other Africans, Corporal Blik and Fuselier Jaap, beat off an enemy attack on a convoy of 25 Europeans and 65 chain gang laborers. The article noted that Kooi spoke perfect Dutch, but also spoke most warmly about his family and homeland. In the September 9, 1882, issue of the same paper, the book dealer J. Wedding advertised portraits and biographical sketches of Kooi along with city scapes of Harderwijk. However, Kooi's fame did not carry over to subsequent generations and few in the twentieth century ever heard of him, despite the portrait of him, executed by J. C. Leich in the late nineteenth century, now in the Museum Bronbeek in Arnhem.

Meanwhile, since 1890 there had also been a serious effort to obtain recruits from the "Pepper Coast" of Liberia. Such recruitment

115. J. C. Leich, Jan Kooi. Museum Bronbeek, Arnhem.

was in clear violation of international agreements, again flirted with the slave trade issue, and was strongly opposed by a Liberian government incapable of actually preventing it. [46] In January 1891, 187 Africans landed in the East Indies, including a woman and child. The group refused a standard three-year contract and eventually was given a contract for one year. Most members apparently returned home, disgruntled, at that time. An officer assigned to the recruits later assessed the reasons for the failure of this experiment in terms which provide further insight into the experience of the Africans in the East Indies.

He concluded that first of all it was a mistake for them to sign for only one year. This could have been avoided by having them bring their families with them. Although they were encouraged to live with native women, this was hampered by language difficulties and by the fact that the native women were not eager to join them since their army pay was so low. This officer observed further that it would have been better if these recruits had been given Dutch names, rather than the English ones they had reflecting their colonial origins. Given the short duration of their stay, it would also have helped if Malay had been the official language used with them rather than Dutch, since Malay was easier for them to learn and more useful in the surrounding society.[47]

An accurate count of *Blanda Itam* who settled in the East Indies is difficult to ascertain. It is certain that the vast majority of the few thousand who were brought during the course of the century returned to Africa, often by way of the Netherlands, with a few settling there. It is worth noting in passing that this global odyssey also washed new ripples of color back to the shores of Africa. Some have speculated that it was the returning *Blanda Itam* who brought the batik method for decorating textiles to Africa from Asia. One definite related development which did occur was the formation of a small settlement of returnees called Javaberg in Fort Coenraadsburg.[48] Only about seven hundred new recruits were transported to the East Indies between 1855, when recruitment was resumed after the suspension, and 1872, when the Dutch West African possessions were transferred to England in exchange for a free hand for the Netherlands in Sumatra. One scholar has estimated that by 1892 only fifty-four of the recruits from the Gold Coast remained in the East Indian Army; in 1899 thirty, and in 1915 none. There was, however, an indefinite number of civilians remaining. A number of memoirs mention fondly a certain black police inspector in Batavia in the early twentieth century. Dubbed "Snowwhite," he patrolled astride a large Harley motorcycle and clad in a white uniform.[49]

Most of the African population in the East Indies eventually became mixed with different elements of the local population, including the Dutch and Eurasian. Nevertheless, many of their descendants retained distinctively African physical traits. One reason for this is that a conspicuous community of black Africans settled in central Java, in the villages of Semarang, Salatiga, and Poerwaredjo, where to this day there are roads called Africa Way. Here the Dutch government had provided small land plots for retiring soldiers. The Indonesian government respected this arrangement sufficiently to compensate the Indo-Africans for their homes when they were forced to emigrate along with all others classified as Dutch following Indonesian independence in 1949. During that war too the *Blanda Itam* remained loyal to the Netherlands, fighting against and then imprisoned by the Japanese, and then by the nationalist Indonesians. Some, including Gert van Riessen, who later settled in Maastricht, survived the sinking of the freighter *Junyo Maru*, in which many prisoners of war died while being transported to work sites by the Japanese.[50]

Nearly all of the *Blanda Itam* sided with the Dutch because, in the words of a patriotic hymn echoed by one Indo-African applicant for passage to the Netherlands interviewed by the scholar W. Coolhaas, "omdat Neerlands bloed ons door de aderen vloeit, van vreemde smetten vrij" (pure Dutch blood flows through our veins). It should be noted that a shipment of Surinamer volunteers, including blacks, also sailed to the East Indies to fight alongside Australian and Dutch troops against the Japanese and later against the Indonesians during the independence struggle. Some seventy-five families descendant from the *Blanda Itam* settled in the Netherlands, where they still periodically hold reunions which attract a few hundred people.[51]

Intellectuals

Among the most curious features of the status of blacks in the Dutch world were the scope and variety of roles accepted for blacks by the dominant society. Hence, the eighteenth century, which saw Dutch involvement in African slavery still in sway, could also produce the predicant J. E. Capitein through the University of Leiden. The significance of this for the Dutch religious tradition has been treated in chapter five. This strange career, full of contradictions, merits further discussion here as evidence of early acceptance in Dutch society of the notion that blacks may have useful minds as well as strong bodies. Capitein was the most spectacular early example of a black student in the Netherlands, a group whose number would not be really significant until the late twentieth century. His high visibility, in addition to contributing to the religious debate concerning the nature of blacks, also demonstrated conclusively his ability to master European languages and rhetorical skills. His example was all the more welcomed because he trumpeted so well the popular chorus of the time condoning slavery. He concluded his closely reasoned, "political-theological" research paper in defense of slavery as follows:

> From all the preceding, although I in no way accept all the words of these learned writers, I conclude, however, going to the heart of the matter (as I see it) with sufficient certitude, that *slavery . . . is in no way antagonistic to Christian freedom*. Whence it thus follows that there is no impediment to spreading the gospel in the Christian colonies, where to this day slavery is in usage. For in this way a very friendly and God pleasing domain can and must be established between the masters and slaves in an improved religious instruction.[52]

As was discussed in chapter five, the West India Company's commitment of resources for Capitein to serve the European congregation to which he had been sent to minister was grossly inadequate. Not surprisingly, support of Capitein's efforts at Christianizing Africans was even less substantial. The lack of support for his efforts at sustaining a school for colored children was especially disappointing. There was, likewise, little interest shown in his sermons and religious commentaries beyond his views on slavery, although these were considered to be of sufficient interest to be published.[53] Nevertheless, judging by tributes written to him by witnesses, his delivery of these sermons in the Netherlands made a memorable impression.

> He impressed upon your mind
> How the Supreme wisdom comes to teach us,
> The true *wealth and honors*,
> Which is something to be highly esteemed,
> Never shall the Muiderberg [church] forget,
> Nor the Hague this wondrous work,
> It shall also in Amstel's Ouderkerk
> Never be forgotten.

The Black Presence in the Dutch World

The heavenly language the congregation heard
From this miraculous African Moor.

Joan Boursse[54]

In order to view Capitein in proper perspective, it should be noted that, although unusual, his status as a black intellectual in Europe was not unique for his time. Just as his career on the Gold Coast begs comparison with that of Christian Protten, a comparison of his experience in Europe with that of Anthony William Amo is irresistible. Born on the Gold Coast around 1700, Amo also arrived in Holland as a boy. The West India Company brought him to Amsterdam when he was about ten years old and presented him to the Duke of Wolfenbüttel. He was baptized in Wolfenbüttel in 1707 and given the names Anton and Wilhelm in honor of the reigning duke and his son. A grant from the duke allowed him to be educated to a point where he was able to enter the universities at Halle in 1727 and Wittenberg in 1730, where he became skilled in Latin, Greek, Hebrew, French, German, and Dutch and concentrated on philosophy. In 1729 he held a public disputation on the subject *"De iure Maurorum in Europa"* (Concerning the Law of the Moors in Europe).

In 1730 he gained the degree of Master of Arts in Philosophy at Halle. In 1734 he was awarded the doctorate degree from the University of Wittenberg with a dissertation *"De humanae mantis apatheia"* (On Apathy in the Human Mind). In his philosophical work he was a rationalist, and devoted special attention to mathematical and medical knowledge in the context of Enlightenment thought. He became a lecturer at the University of Halle and later at the University of Jena. By some accounts, the court at Berlin awarded him the title of Counsellor of State. However, due to his declining fortunes in Europe, possibly related to loss of favor from his patron and affiliation with intellectual circles also out of favor, Amo returned to obscurity in the Gold Coast around the 1750s.[55]

Another eighteenth-century black personality who enjoyed fleeting fame among the Dutch public was Granman Quassie, who lived in Suriname most of his life, but twice visited the Netherlands. Whether born on the coast of Guinea and transported to Suriname as a child, as one version on his origins goes, or actually born in Suriname, he first gained status as an intermediary between the Dutch and the Maroons in Suriname. The Saramaka tribe called him Kwa-simukamba. In 1730 Jan van Sandick, a member of the Policy Council at Paramaribo, awarded him a gold breastplate with the inscription "Quassie, faithful to the Whites." Governor Mauricius bought him in 1744 and used him both as a scout and as emissary to the Maroons. The governor also had him teach his own youngest son the Sranan, Carib, and Arawak languages.

In 1755 Quassie was given his freedom as a reward for his military services in particular. He also became a renowned herbalist and healer, the discoverer of a popular bitter stock which controlled fever, and which was therefore later named Quassi-bitter by Linnaeus in his honor. In Suriname some Europeans, as well as blacks and Indians, believed that he had miraculous powers. In fact when accompanying Dutch forces into battle against the Maroons he would sell charms promising invincibility to the black troops of the Free Corps and Black Rangers placed under his command for the occasion. In 1776 he was received at court in The Hague by William V and awarded a medal for his service to the Dutch authorities in Suriname. Other gifts included a gold-laced coat and hat with white feather, a large gold medal, and a gold-headed cane and silver gilt hanger. It was in this costume that he was captured in the John Stedman portrait that served as the basis for the famous engraving of him in his eighties by William Blake, later published in Stedman's book on Suriname (figure 116).[56]

Anthropologist Richard Price, in comparing the Maroon oral tradition regarding Quassie to the rest of the historical record, has convincingly depicted him as the consummate double agent and opportunist, as well as a shrewd, though not very successful, businessman. Even better than the careers of Capitein and Amo, Quassie's details the complexities of the paths confronting the African attempting to walk on the higher levels in the European world in the eighteenth century. Throughout his long life Quassie actually lived more between the two worlds than as part of either. The respect of his fellow blacks was tinged with envy, fear, and contempt for betrayal; while respect from the whites was accompanied by fear and ridicule. As Price also suggests, his situation may thus be instructive for understanding the subsequent evolution of racial attitudes and relations in Suriname, and perhaps in a broader context in the Dutch experi-

116. William Blake, *Granman Quassie*. From John Stedman, *Narrative of a Five-Years' Expedition* (London: Johnson, 1796).

ence as well.[57] Although he drew some satire as a public figure, his epitaphs suggest that the most lasting impression he left was one of amazement. The poet P. F. Roos wrote:

> Here lies an old man, who in the course of his life
> Gave much evidence of good and *evil* to the country.
> His magic continues to evoke wonder!
> If this folk wishes adequately to praise his craft,
> It should name him Apollo instead of Quassie.

H. Schouten was even less restrained:

> Here rests a wonder of our age
> In herbs, and healing so adept,
> That no matter how the faculty [academic] screams,
> They never shall dim this light.
> He has already healed himself from the brink of death,
> And aided the suffering.
> Let this man's name among us for centuries glitter,
> Widely renowned through the healing *Quassie Bitters*.[58]

The nineteenth century also featured at least one black from Africa who earned distinction for intellectual achievements in the Netherlands and then cast his lot with the Dutch empire. This was Aquasie Boachi, son of King Kwaku Dua of the kingdom of Ashanti. His dispatch to the Netherlands at the age of ten was closely tied to the Dutch recruitment of soldiers in his homeland, although the exact relationship between the two is uncertain. One version has it that he and his cousin Kwame Poku, who accompanied him, were sent as gifts from the Ashantehene to King William II as a show of good faith in connection with the recruitment agreement. A less generous description views the two boys as hostages; while still another finds Kwaku Dua simply taking advantage of the new relationship to have some of his family educated in the West.

Under the sponsorship of the Colonial Ministry, the two boys arrived in the Netherlands in 1837. After a brief stay in The Hague, they moved to a boarding school in Delft, where they began a typical middle-class education for the time, complete with courses in French, German, history, geography, science, and religion. They moved in the highest social circles, befriended by Crown Prince William III and other notables. They cut a striking picture out and about in their straw hats, clasping silken umbrellas with hands clad in evening gloves. Nevertheless, Kwame Poku was to suffer a tragic fate from his sojourn. Apparently either unnerved by life abroad, or distraught by the cool reception he received after he returned to Elmina in 1847, in 1850 he committed suicide.[59]

Aquasie Boachi, on the other hand, excelled as a student and, riding the scientific current of the era, pursued training as a mining engineer and enjoyed a long career in the Dutch service. He became a Christian and began his advanced studies at the newly founded Mining Academy in Delft beginning in 1843. Then in 1848 he attended the Mining Academy in Freiberg, Saxony, studying with the geologist Bernhard von Cotta. One investigator has speculated that the Dutch government supported him in his ambitions with the hope that he would return to the Gold Coast and conduct gold mining operations for them. However, he decided not to return to Africa. Instead, after obtaining his diploma in Delft in 1849, he gained appointment in 1850 as a mining engineer in the government service in the East Indies, where he was to spend the rest of his career.

His dislike for the climate in the Netherlands was probably the main reason Boachi did not attempt to remain there. While his engineering career was a notable achievement in itself, it was scarred by bitterness and by his complaints against racial discrimination and systematic limitation of his level of achievement, which he carried all the way to his boyhood friend, and now king, William III. While Boachi was unable to gain satisfaction concerning his complaints within the service, the king at least ensured that upon Boachi's resignation he was provided lease of an estate in Madioen near Ponorogo. Boachi unsuccessfully attempted to establish a plantation there, and then later in Preanger and Buitenzorg, with the same result. In these endeavors too his race may have played a role, since it may have hampered his success in dealing through the Europeans and Eurasians and in exercising authority over the local populations. At the same time, his status as a member of the foreign ruling class must also have been significant here. He spent the final years of his life in Bantar Peteh near Buitenzorg, where he died on July 9, 1904 at the age of 77.[60]

On the brighter side of Aquasie's career, he apparently had a full family life, with more than one wife and at least four children and two grandchildren. His son Aquasie and daughter Quamina appear with him on a handsome photograph executed by the photographer P. Hermann from Buitenzorg around 1898 (fig. 117). There is, incidentally,

117. Prince Aquasie Boachi with his son Aquasie and daughter Quamina. Photograph by P. Hermann, from Buitenzorg around 1898. From cover of *Ghana Nieuwsbrief* no. 20, April 1986.

also one letter of 1853 from his father Kwaku Dua to the Dutch governor at Elmina requesting that Aquasie be allowed to visit home. There is no other evidence of Boachi's thought about Africa. This question is all the more interesting since his relationship to the *Blanda Itam*, with whom he must have come in contact, is unknown. Did he, because of class status, consider himself to be above identifying with this group of cultural kinsmen who similarly suffered from discrimination in their distant Asian home? He continued to enjoy the respect of some in higher circles, including Governor-General O. van Rees, himself a former engineer. Also the government had provided him a pension of 500 florin for life, an amount above that of a captain's. Boachi's professional achievements included technical studies, for instance one on coal in Bantam. He was for years a corresponding member of the Society of Civil Engineers in Delft, and in 1900 he received much public recognition for his fifty years of residence in Java.[61]

The history of Suriname in the nineteenth century also affords a number of examples of highly trained black professionals whose careers defied the boundaries within which the roles of blacks were considered to be confined. One was Adolf Frederik Gravenberch (see figure 118). Born in Suriname in 1811 of two slave parents, he was placed by his master as an informal assistant to a plantation physician, A. Steglich, who taught him many medical skills. Upon Steglich's death his master allowed Gravenberch to work in the hospital directed by Dr. George Cornelis Berch Gravenhorst, a leading surgeon and authority on the treatment of leprosy and elephantiasis. Here he acquired even more medical knowledge. Then in 1847, when he was thirty-six, Gravenhorst, a known critic of slavery, bought Adolf Frederik's freedom and made him an assistant surgeon. It was in honor of his benefactor that he came to take the name Gravenberch. After Gravenhorst's permanent departure for the Netherlands, Gravenberch set out to pursue a medical career on his own. Toward that end he petitioned King William III to practice medicine. The latter responded with a royal appointment of Gravenberch as a municipal surgeon in the colony of Suriname.

Gravenberch thereupon set up a hospital in Paramaribo and developed a large practice, including all classes of the city and patients drawn in from the plantations as well. Some he treated without charge. He also had a successful marriage, with children. He lived in the district of Boven-Commewijn and bought other houses and plantations such as Osembo on the Para River, Libanon in the Saramacca district, and La Jaloussie in the Commewijn. However, he lost most of his fortune with the fall in sugar prices and the emancipation. His plight was compounded when in 1875, after the officials had allowed him all this time to extend his practice into the districts, they now

118. Dr. Adolf Frederik Gravenberch, Parimaribo City Healer,
1811–1906. From Fred. Oudschans Dentz, "Eenige bladzijden uit het
leven van Dr. George Cornelis Berch Gravenhorst." *Nederlands
Tijdschrift voor Geneeskunde* 86 (6 June 1942).

brought charges against him for crossing the restrictive boundaries.
However, with the help of his lawyer, Colaço Belmonte, he was ex-
onerated; and his request legally to practice in the districts was
granted. Thousands of well-wishers joined in the silver jubilee celebration of his career as a surgeon in 1880 and he went on to celebrate
the golden jubilee in 1905. In 1879 he had moved his residence to

Paramaribo, where he remained until his death in November 1906 at the age of 95.[62]

A testimony to the impact of Gravenberch's career on black Surinamers is the inspiration it brought his first biographer, the black Baptist minister Carl P. Rier:

> He was a man of the people, for the people! He was a genius, widely loved, honored, and respected. The mention of his name will evoke friendly and thankful memories in many people. He was born to be what he was and called to do what he did. He was a star in the Ethiopian sky amidst the azure of Suriname, to cast the first light in dark places.[63]

Rier (1863–1917) deserves special mention here in his own right, as an early articulate champion of Surinamer rights and black pride. Born in Paramaribo of Moravian parents, he initially followed in his father's footsteps as a carpenter after limited secondary schooling. It was while working as a plantation foreman in British Guiana that he first joined a church of the American Baptist Convention. In 1905, after years of assisting in establishing a Baptist church in Paramaribo, he went to the United States to be formally ordained a minister. For the final thirteen years of his life he was a tireless advocate of black emancipation and unity. Already in 1903, at a packed commemoration of the emancipation attended by the governor he stated:

> . . . Once slavery is abolished, every aspect of the institution must be buried. Although freedom came here forty years ago, many still do not know what freedom means or how to use freedom. . . . Moses wanted a general emancipation, with rights for all. In short, he wanted a new life. We are of the humble opinion that we need a general emancipation—a personal, civil, and legal emancipation: personal in terms of people among themselves, civil in terms of equal rights, and legal in terms of a fair execution of those rights. We need a change of life, in thinking, in acting, in speaking, in clothing, in our use of language, in our customs, in our education, in our values, in our religion, and in our attitude to work. . . . How can we reach freedom when we are so divided among ourselves? If we want to reach a general emancipation, then the school, the church, the family, and the state each has to make a larger contribution than it has up to now.[64]

Sounding at times like his North American contemporary Booker T. Washington, and like him addressing both the white and the black audience, Rier placed much emphasis on the work ethic. One of his main proposals centered on the need for black Surinamers to engage in agriculture, which both the history of the colony and urbanization had conditioned them to avoid:

> We need to know and should never forget that Suriname is an exceptionally rich land. We have discussed it often. Would it not be silly and thoughtless of us to watch passively while strangers take away our bread? Every nation that came ashore here has, through industriousness, thrift, and a sense of duty, taken a large part of our treasure home, while we, children of the same race, sit here cursing each other. I have seen myself how much a farmer who has a practical and theoretical education can accomplish. In the U.S.A. 75 percent of the population (black and white) lives directly from agriculture. . . .
>
> Our people of all classes have an aversion to agriculture because during slavery and after the Emancipation no one showed them the value of agriculture, because their masters and their offspring seldom if ever gave them examples, and because strangers who came as farmers have turned their backs on agriculture—with the exception of the colonized Dutch farmers. Agriculture was always considered by these masters as something humiliating (we still hear: "Let the Negroes plant bananas; they are born for the shovel and the pick-ax; they have no needs"). Further our people dislike agriculture because of the unhappy experiences on the large farms. After emancipation, people assumed that they would find a reasonable living there, but they were treated badly. Is it a small wonder that those inspired by the spirit of freedom would not work for nothing? This is where the dogmatic statement originates: "The Negro is lazy." Also our people disliked agriculture because before the mother country decided to resort to immigration she did not provide us with an agricultural school. Finally, agriculture is disliked because although it was known that Suriname was suitable for agriculture, the government never promoted agriculture for the small farmer. . . . Only . . . through colonization, through construction of roads and railroads, through immigration of Chinese, British-Indians, Javanese, and through strong financial support for the large farmer—the capitalist farmer—who should not be placed above the small farmer. [65]

It should be noted that there were other free blacks in nineteenth-century Suriname who would qualify as middle or upper class but would not be detected as black in the historical record due to either their particular status or the definition of color used. An example of the former was the mulatto wife of the U.S. Consul at Paramaribo in 1861. She was said to own a plantation and slaves which he thus also gained. During the same period, when the American Civil War Confederate ship CSS *Sumter* refueled at Paramaribo the successful bidder for a coal supply was a quadroon who considered himself white and seemed to sympathize with the Confederate cause.[66]

Just as Boachi's and Gravenberch's achievements as formally educated scientists reflected the degree to which blacks were participants in the modern historical currents shaping new occupations, Rier can be seen as an example of black intellectuals in the Dutch empire prominent in articulating some of the new systems of thought which arose in Europe in the nineteenth century. He was a precursor of later full-blown black nationalists. Two stalwart continuators in this tradition are the socialist and nationalist thinkers Otto Huiswood and Anton de Kom. Huiswood, the grandson of a slave, was born in 1893 in Suriname (figure 119). In 1912, following a pattern that would be characteristic for many West Indian and South American black intellectuals in the twentieth century, he moved to the United States. There he was working as a trader in tropical products, and later as a printer in Harlem, when he became involved with American socialist and Negro organizations.

Huiswood's earliest known affiliation was with a group surrounding *The Messenger*, a monthly established by A. Philip Randolph and Chandler Owen which ran from 1917 to 1928. Originally socialist in orientation, it sought to spread radical socialist thought among American Negroes in support of the Russian Revolution. However, this group's leaders rejected the communist insistence on stressing class struggle rather than racism in addressing the plight of blacks.[67] Also associated with *The Messenger* were Cyril Briggs and Richard B. Moore, who in 1919 founded a nationalist organization called the African Blood Brotherhood. Huiswood for a time also was part of this organization, which advocated establishment of an independent Negro nation in the western or northwestern United States, South America, the Caribbean, or Africa.[68] Huiswood accompanied these more radical members of the African Blood Brotherhood when they left the *Messenger* group and joined the new American Communist Party which was just in the process of organizing.

119. Otto Huiswood. From *Famiri* vol. 2, no. 10, 1978. Koninklijk
Instituut voor Taal-, Land- en Volkenkunde, Leiden.

By 1920 Huiswood was reputed to be the first black member of the Communist Party USA, although no proof has yet surfaced to support the persistent rumor that he participated in its founding. In 1922 he was a member of the American delegation to the Fourth Congress of the Communist International (Comintern). While there he was elected an honorary member of the Moscow city council and had a rare audience with Lenin, who was already mortally ill. Huiswood was elected to the American Party's central committee and later to the executive committee of the Communist International. In 1927 he studied at the Lenin School in Moscow, one of the political institutions founded to train elite communist leaders. At the meeting of the Sixth Comintern Congress in 1928 he was one of the several black delegates who helped shape the official policy on nationalism, which urged creation of independent black soviet republics in the southern United States ("Self-determination in the Black Belt") and in southern Africa.[69]

This policy stressed, however, that the "Negro question" had to be viewed primarily as a class question related to colonialism and not as a race question. This policy was adopted in spite of the fact that only one black delegate, Harry Haywood (Haywood Hall) of the United States, agreed with this main thrust. Two years later Huiswood openly challenged this position in an article entitled "World Aspects of the Negro Question."

> Our approach to the Negro question has not only been largely sectional rather than international, but our concept and interpretation of the Negro question was narrow and incorrect. The old Social Democratic notion that the Negro question is only a class question, prevailed with us for a considerable time. We are only now beginning to realize that the Negro question is not only a class question but also a race question. We are beginning to understand that the Negro masses are not only subjected to the ordinary forms of exploitation as other workers, but that they are also the victims of a brutal caste system which holds them as an inferior servile class; that lynching, segregation, peonage, etc., are some of the means utilized to keep them the underdog in capitalist society—social outcasts. In order to maintain its policy of repression, violence and exploitation of the Negro, the bourgeoisie creates a false racial ideology among the whites and fosters contempt and hatred for the Negro. The idea of "superior" and "inferior" races is the theoretical

justification for their policy of super-exploitation of the Negro race.

The situation of the Negro masses varies in different countries and therefore requires investigation and analysis. . . . It is essential that we distinguish the situation of the Negro masses in the colonies—Africa and the West Indies; the semi-colonies—Haiti and Liberia, who suffer from colonial exploitation, from that of the Negro in America, a racial minority, subjected to racial persecution and exploitation. We must take into consideration the national-colonial character of the Negro question in Africa and the West Indies and the racial character of this question in the United States.[70]

Although Huiswood based most of his detailed discussion of the West Indies on the islands, and focused the statistics he presented only on Jamaica as a representative example, he also mentioned the Guianas as showing similar characteristics. Thus he also was referring to his native Dutch Guiana when he wrote:

The natives of these islands are the victims of a most vicious colonial policy and are subjected to pre-capitalist forms of exploitation. The great mass of pauperized peasants live under the most primitive and poverty-stricken conditions. In most of these islands a semi-slave condition exists on the huge banana and sugar plantations, largely owned and controlled by big foreign corporations and absentee landlords. Working long hours under a broiling sun, housed in company-owned shacks, the mass of agricultural workers are paid a miserable pittance for their toil. . . . There are in most of these Islands a growing city proletariat. These workers, divorced from the land, are forced to live in crowded, unsanitary shacks. Receiving small pay (one to two dollars per day) they can only procure the barest necessities of life.[71]

Huiswood became a veritable authority on conditions in the Caribbean region because he was assigned by the Comintern to be the primary organizer there. His knowledge, of Jamaica for example, was enhanced through visits during which he delivered lectures at public meetings.

Another important post with the Comintern followed in 1934 when he became the editor of *The Negro Worker*, the organ of the International Trade Union Committee of Negro Workers. In this he succeeded the Trinidadian George Padmore, who was expelled from the Communist Party for failing to toe the party line.[72] This monthly had been based in Hamburg; but flight from the Nazis prompted moves to Copenhagen and and then to Paris from 1936 to 1938. Huiswood and his British-Guianese wife, H. A. Dumont, traveled through the European cities with uncertainty concerning the welcome from nervous local authorities. In 1935 they were in the Netherlands. In 1938 he moved back to New York. Then in 1941 he finally returned to Suriname when advised to move to a warmer climate for health reasons.

Upon Huiswood's arrival in Paramaribo in January, however, the authorities arrested him without charges and detained him for twenty-two months in an internment camp whose mixed population of Nazis, Jewish refugees, and anti-fascists reflected the political uncertainty common to a number of European colonies during the war. The government was apparently apprehensive because of his reputation as a radical communist. After the war he and his wife moved finally to the Netherlands. There he took a job with the PTT national communications company, and was a leader in the Surinamer community. Serving for years as president of the nationalistic association *Ons Suriname* (Our Suriname), he transformed it from a social society into a Surinamer advocacy organization. In collaboration with two other likeminded groups, *Wie Eegie Sanie* (Our Own Things) and the *Surinaamse Studenten Vereniging*(The Surinamer Students Union), *Ons Suriname* promoted cultural pride and spoke out against colonialism and racial discrimination in various parts of the world, including the Dutch empire.[73]

The career of Huiswood's more famous contemporary Anton de Kom illustrates even more clearly the extent to which blacks within the Dutch empire had come to articulate the same sort of penetrating critique of empire as did native intellectuals in many other parts of the world during the same period. It shows some of the contradictions contained in Western societies for non-European intellectuals: the limitations bridling their aspirations, and their counterattack using reformist and revolutionary doctrines originating in those very Western societies. De Kom (Cornelis Gerard Anton de Kom) was born in 1898 in Paramaribo, where he also gained a formal education, acquiring a working knowledge of English, French, German, Sranan, and Papiamento in addition to Dutch.[74] After working four years as an office worker in Paramaribo, in 1920 he moved to Amsterdam. He

Blacks in the Dutch World

there volunteered for four years service in the cavalry, a fact that is sometimes omitted in later biographical sketches, which usually stress his militancy of a different order. He next acquired a certificate as an accountant and worked briefly at a bank.

In 1926 De Kom married Petronella Catherina Borsboom, a Dutch woman. They were to have four children. He was for a number of years a traveling salesman marketing tobacco and coffee for the firm of Reussen and Smulders in The Hague. This ended in 1931 when he was fired, in part because of his growing political activities. During these years De Kom was intensively involved in formulating a comprehensive approach for opposing colonialism; that approach was socialistic in orientation and envisioned a concerted effort by all the diverse ethnic groups of Suriname and also supported the aspirations of nationalists in the Dutch East Indies and elsewhere. In addition to becoming a public speaker for the cause at meetings and on the radio, he published many articles in communist and other radical periodicals, worked on related novels, collected Anansi stories, and wrote poetry and a film script.[75]

At the same time De Kom must have been working on his book *Wij slaven uit Suriname* (We Slaves of Suriname), which he published with difficulty only in 1934. A ringing hymn to his homeland, this first history of Suriname by one of its African offspring begins its description of the country as follows:

> . . . rich in enormous forests, . . . rich in broad rivers, . . . rich in natural treasures, in gold and bauxite, in rubber, sugar, bananas and coffee . . . poor in men, poorer in humanity. *Sranang*—our fatherland, *Suriname* as the Dutchmen call it. The Netherlands' twelfth and richest, no, the Netherlands' poorest province.[76]

This book was to have a tremendous inspirational impact on the subsequent development of nationalism in the Dutch empire. In the concluding chapter, "*Weerzien en Afscheid*" (Reunion and Parting), he wrote: "*Sranang*, my fatherland, I have seen you again, and your beauty was just as I had dreamed, longing, tossing in my bed in Holland." Here in alternating poetic and polemical musings he recounts the dramatic developments which occurred during 1933 when he went to Suriname to visit his dying mother. There, as in Holland, his reputation as a radical continued to plague all his further endeavors. It had in 1929 hindered his effort to work in Curaçao in the petroleum industry and in 1930 an application for government support for his return to Suriname to become a farmer. In both instances, of course, the government was probably quite correct in thinking that his true intention was to agitate and organize the workers in these colonies. His editorship at the time of the periodical *Links Richten* (Left Directives) was certainly credible evidence. Nevertheless, he was still somewhat surprised at the reception he met upon his return to Paramaribo in January 1933.

On February 3 he was arrested, and on May 10 released only after promising to curtail his political agitation. He was then forced to depart with his wife and children for the Netherlands. In explaining that action to the government, Governor Rutgers explained that De Kom's presence posed a much greater threat to order in Suriname than it would in the Netherlands.[77] This turn of events occurred because De Kom had arrived championing organization of the workers and unity of all ethnic groups in a setting where the colonial elite lived in luxury while the majority of the people were suffering economic hardship, with low agricultural wages, with the urban population housed in slumlike conditions, and with poor opportunities for education or health care for all. There had already been disturbances and demonstrations over these conditions before De Kom's arrival. Hundreds greeted his arrival at the docks. The garrison was put on alert amid rumors that De Kom was planning to provoke a communist uprising. His movements were followed by secret agents.

Meanwhile, he set about attending meetings with hundreds of Maroons, Hindustani, Creoles, Javanese, and Indians. He set up an information bureau to deal with the many complaints from far and wide which now came to him as if by magnetic attraction. Attracting hundreds of complainants some days, this may have been what sealed his fate in the eyes of the authorities, although they arrested him under no specific charges. This action brought masses of Hindustani and Javanese farmers to the city to join the Creoles there in demanding his release. The newspaper *De Banier* of February 4 reported that over four thousand marched to the prosecutor's office on that day and were confronted by a detachment of police with fixed bayonets. In a later gathering the police unexpectedly opened fire, killing two and wounding twenty-two demonstrators. The governor's solution to the crisis was to release De Kom and place him on the boat to Holland.

With this even more conspicuous reputation preceding him back to the Netherlands, he was no longer able to find his usual employment there. Now he became fully engaged in radical work, supported in part by the Communist Party, although it is not clear that he ever actually joined it. There is some evidence that he briefly met Huiswood during this period. During the Second World War, De Kom joined the resistance; fascism was clearly a more urgent threat to all that he stood for than was colonialism. In August 1944 he was arrested by the Nazis, and he eventually died in the concentration camp Neuengamme in April 1945.

As illustrations of black intellectuals, Huiswood and De Kom followed quite similar dissident paths. Examples of others with different perspectives and alternative tactics have been presented in chapter four on literature. One other particularly insightful twentieth-century observer who deserves mention here, one who worked within the establishment to advance his views, was the sociologist R. A. J. van Lier, a Surinamer of African and Jewish descent who came to Holland early in this century, and whose book *Frontier Society* is a classic study on Suriname. During his years as a professor he also carried out national and international cultural assignments for the Dutch and Suriname governments at home and abroad. Toward the end of his life he recalled the peculiarities of his status:

> As I reminisce over my school class . . . full of Negroes, Chinese, every type was there. I found it delightful. You didn't think about that difference. It was there. . . . I have had the privilege of being born on the edge of groups and civilizations. I proceed upon the assumption that an intellectual is marginal by definition. If he is not he is not an intellectual, for his intellect places him on the edge and outside the group. And I was *born there*—between civilizations. What a privilege![78]

Van Lier, who died in 1987 in the Netherlands, was born in Paramaribo in 1914 and moved to the Netherlands at the age of fourteen. He recalled that in the decades before the Second World War there was actually reverse discrimination toward colored peoples in the Netherlands. Although he encountered offensive stereotypes in the minds of some of his teachers, he did not find them a hindrance. Studying history, sociology, and anthropology in Leiden, he became attracted to the "Chicago School" of study emphasizing ethnic diversity, but discovered that study in ethnic categories did not even exist in Dutch universities. Therefore, he also studied at the Sorbonne in 1937 and in Chicago for a year after the war. In 1947 he also spent eight months of study in Suriname and the Caribbean.

In his resulting classic study, which was to earn him a chair in sociology at the University of Leiden, he advanced a new, more realistic interpretation of colonization than the then standard Marxist emphasis on class struggle. He instead saw a better explanation for society in terms of pluralism, with society divided mainly along ethnic lines, with even the classes defined primarily by color, and with the ethnic groups playing a major role in perpetuating the whole. In other words, he championed complexity over the type of simplicity offered by the Marxist interpretations. He reminded one interviewer that even within the Hindustani community there was the saying: "Never trust a darker Brahman."[79]

In Van Lier's view it was only with the rapid influx of immigrants in the 1970s that real racial discrimination arrived in the Netherlands. Here again, however, he rejected the primacy of color in the relationships, viewing economic and other ethnic traits as more decisive. Thus he saw the Surinamers of African descent adapting more easily than the other Surinamer ethnic groups because the blacks have more fully adopted Western civilization. At the same time, Van Lier proposed a different approach to the concept of discrimination, which he feels has been distorted by young radicals. He stated:

> I assume that everyone discriminates, including myself. Discrimination has something to do with one's own identity. . . . Outward traits can play a role in this, but the problem is not the race. The problem is: how does one cope with the unfamiliar? Race is an external distinction that accentuates strangeness. . . . It is treated just as sexuality was in earlier times: it is taboo, it does not exist, it is something for an interior room which is not to be taken outside. But since it cannot be discussed it can lead to infection and sickness.[80]

Regardless of how one might view Van Lier's specific interpretations, his formulation, in his life and work, of the penetrating questions concerning race relations in the Dutch world which had evolved by his time is telling testimony that the questions can no longer be avoided.

At the End of Empire

The distinctive character of the Dutch world as a trading empire had faded after the demise of the East and West India trading companies at the end of the eighteenth century. Meanwhile, the loss of her possessions in northern Brazil and North America to colonial rivals in the seventeenth century and of the Cape Colony and West African possessions to the British in the nineteenth paralleled the relative decline in stature of the Netherlands as a world power. The critique of the Dutch role in the world by Huiswood and De Kom foreshadowed the urgent discussion of these issues, which would reach its full dimensions in the Netherlands only in the second half of the twentieth century. However, they echoed a chorus of like voices throughout the world which accompanied the disintegration of all the European empires as the century progressed.

In the twentieth century the subject peoples would pass out of the control of the European powers into their own, rather than simply falling to other European domination as before. By mid-century the Dutch East Indies would take this path; a quarter of a century later Suriname would follow; and the Netherlands Antilles, amid discussions of independence, has become more a part of the Kingdom of the Netherlands. The empire is, therefore, all but over. However, it left a permanent mark on the makeup of Dutch society, one which the Dutch themselves were slow to grasp. In a way the popular mood might be symbolized by the worlds fairs held throughout the Western world in the late nineteenth century, with Amsterdam hosting one in 1883. The representatives of the Suriname population (including eleven blacks) transported with great effort for the fair could be placed on display in their "proper" place along with all the other exhibits celebrating the achievements of Western industry and progress.[81] The onlooking crowds did not yet realize that these dark guests were part of Dutch society. This would not become fully manifest until most of the other vestiges of empire were gone, but representatives of its various peoples remained.

For present purposes the most important change which the ending of empire brought was a massive shift in the distribution of the black population, especially from the colonies to the "mother country." The most dramatic shift, of course, was that which came after

1970, with more than 225,000 emigrants from Suriname and the Netherlands Antilles moving to the Netherlands. However, a pronounced shift on a much more modest scale had begun in the late nineteenth century, so that by the middle of the twentieth century the new arrivals numbered several thousand. This new level of frequent contacts and in a new setting has had a profound mutual impact on perceptions and relations between blacks and whites in Dutch society. In the historical evolution of the perception of blacks by the Europeans it was even more important than the transition from the period when most knowledge about blacks shaping Dutch perceptions was vicarious to when contacts first increased, mainly abroad.

Now there was even greater pressure on the Dutch to think of blacks as equals. Most of this early movement was by colonial elites, the local colored populations who had inherited the mantle of leadership after most Europeans had gone, especially from Suriname when the agricultural economy proved unprofitable. The remaining ruling and administrative class of Jews and mulattoes customarily sent their children abroad for education, for the Surinamers usually to the Netherlands, although the Antilleans often went abroad in the Caribbean or the American continents. The students often remained in the Netherlands after their studies, marrying lighter-complexioned mates and becoming doctors, lawyers, or teachers. For some their assimilation of European culture and values was so complete that they thought of Holland as true home, a virtual promised land. However, many others going there felt like a people in diaspora, but longing for their native American or Indonesian shores, not the African clime of their ancestors. Hence, in the twentieth century, black Surinamers, Antilleans, and the few Indonesians felt some of the same kind of ambivalence, in the crease between two cultures, that the Maroons had experienced for centuries in Suriname.

After emancipation the number of blacks in the higher circles in the colonies increased. The tremendous economic boom brought by the introduction of oil refineries in Curaçao and other islands in the 1920s made the trip to Holland more affordable for Antilleans. However, it was only after the Second World War that Antilleans systematically replaced Dutchmen in the highest posts, that is, those necessitating formal advanced education.[82] Such students were the single largest category of blacks going to the Netherlands in the late nineteenth and early twentieth centuries from the Dutch American colonies. Others came in connection with the firms they worked for. Some remained to pursue careers there. The colored elite often found better treatment from Europeans in the Netherlands than at home. The character of their relations in Europe appeared to be based mainly on their economic and social status, not on their race per se.

As we arrive now back to the present, touched upon briefly in chapter one, it can be seen how various elements of the past covered in the previous chapters contributed to the current situation. Recent scholarship shows that stereotypical images represented in the majority population's everyday language are shaped by the society's total historical legacy and tend to reinforce prejudice against minorities.[83] It is therefore not surprising that with the heavy migration of the 1970s racial discrimination became pronounced and persistent within the Netherlands, as the declining economy, rising unemployment, and increased strain on limited space and resources fostered in the minorities a growing demand for employment, education, health, welfare, politics, and social services, and in the majority increasing prejudice and discrimination.

While the evidence belies a popular perception that the minority presence is responsible for the unemployment, housing shortage, deficiencies in education, and other problems such as rising crime rates, the belief persists that the minorities are being given preferential treatment detrimental to the rest of society. Thus for the Dutch the same process of modernization which created empire with its wealth has in its further course ended the empire and attenuated both the physical and social boundaries which had separated its component parts, leaving the Dutch to grapple with a dilemma they earlier thought existed only in other societies. Now a way must be found to make the resultant society whole. Yet, these words of Rudolf van Lier remind us that in the tradition of Dutch pluralism this must somehow be achieved while still respecting distinctions:

> . . . what makes a community? What holds people together? Why does life involve discrimination? Because value formation and a striving toward values is part of human nature. Man cannot live without drawing boundaries.[84]

CONVERGING IMAGES IN
A CHANGING WORLD

I am an invisible man. No, I am not a spook . . . I am a man of substance, of flesh and bone, fiber and liquids—and I might even be said to possess a mind. I am invisible, understand, simply because people refuse to see me. Like the bodiless heads you see sometimes in circus sideshows, it is as though I have been surrounded by mirrors of hard, distorting glass. When they approach me they see only my surroundings, themselves, or figments of their imagination—indeed, everything and anything except me.

from Ralph Ellison, *Invisible Man*

In Historical Perspective

THE IMAGE of Blacks which emerges from the Dutch historical experience is centuries old, multifaceted, and at times paradoxical. It was embedded in Dutch folklore, art, literature, and the religious traditions from the very beginnings of the Netherlands, and thus long preceded an actual significant presence of Blacks in Dutch society. This is one key to understanding the nature of color prejudice. The inimitable, enduring figure of Zwarte Piet may be the best representation of all of the composite image of blacks which has come down through the centuries. He is based in a Christian religious tradition going all the way back to the Classical period of Western civilization. Yet he also draws upon pagan elements from local folklore and evolves with changing times and technologies. As further acknowledgment of a changing world, he is a "Moor." Thus his pairing with Sinterklaas symbolizes the meeting of East and West as the civilized world expands just as it does good and evil. The significance of the Moors' heads in heraldry and the Gaper in Dutch folkways can be viewed in the same light. In his variant poses as slave, servant, authority figure, teacher, and clown, Zwarte Piet also suggests the variety of roles played by blacks in the Dutch world. Finally, in his role as a bogeyman he embodies an ambivalence which is apparent in the attitude of the Dutch toward blacks down through the centuries.

Incorporation of imagery concerning blacks into commerce, place names, proverbs, music, literature, and the visual arts attests the depth of the impression they made in Dutch culture and accounts for the persistence of related themes even in the absence of black people. The Smoking Moor was another especially potent symbol. In addition to bearing all the exotic connotations of the concept of the Moor, it stood for almighty commerce, the force so central to the Dutch achievement. At the same time it associated this narcotic which was at once alluring and suspect, some thought sinful, with blacks. Once again ambivalence is underscored.

In music this constant tension between attraction and repulsion is apparent in the almost unconscious acceptance, at least in the American colonies, of African influence in Latin American music at the same time that the music of the Africans in its purest forms was viewed with contempt and often feared for the spontaneity and freedom of spirit it celebrated. Meanwhile in the Netherlands the popularity of the songs related to the Sinterklaas tradition and, at least in earlier centuries, of jingles such as "Moriaantje zoo zwart als roet" (Little Moor as black as soot) and "Tien kleine Negertjes" (Ten Little Niggers) shows a certain pleasure in singing about blacks mixed with a tendency to demean blacks. The bakers and confectioners showed that they grasped fully the multisensual expression of these ambivalent tendencies by providing such favorites as the *moorkop* (Moor's head) pastry and the *neger zoen* (Negro's kiss).

It was of course in the visual arts and literature where the most graphic and voluminous expression of the image of blacks occurred. The Dutch artists, although like their counterparts in all societies never completely time-bound nor strictly limited to one cultural perspective, nevertheless left a telling assortment of pieces reflecting these same crosscurrents of thought and developments related to blacks. Both religious and secular allegorical themes further illustrate the oscillation between positive and negative highlighted here and run the gamut from true-to-life to caricature. The usually elegant black king in the Adoration of the Magi coexists with the Ethiopian in the "baptism" theme whose character and depiction connote a certain inferiority. Meanwhile allegories such as Bosch's *Garden of Earthly De-*

lights and the various depictions of blacks as symbols of the elements of nature or parts of the world once again play on the theme of sensuality and the association of blacks with primordial urges which are tantalizing, forbidden, but perhaps inexorable.

Then with the actual arrival of a noticeable black population in the Netherlands in the seventeenth and eighteenth centuries the art began to show them as real people, but continued also to project in them some of the old symbolism. For example, in their depiction as servants, an accurate reflection of the role most occupied in Holland, there was frequently accentuation of their exotic origins through their costumes or by food or animals shown in their charge. Some of the genre portraits also often used debasement of the black figures to emphasize the grandeur of the Dutch commercial or military achievements. There also continued an artistic play on the color black, either simply for balance in composition or in allusion to the various traditional, sinister meanings of the color.

An intriguing question concerning genre paintings with respect to the depiction of blacks concerns the extent to which they were realistic or historically accurate. It is an established fact that in some instances artists simply painted in black figures as props. However, in other instances, such as the examples given of the servant in Helst's *Company of Captain Roelof Bicker* and the bugler in Troost's painting of Stadholder William IV, blacks are clearly captured from life by the artist's eye and brush, only to be ignored by many viewers later surveying the work. This quality of "invisibility" of blacks leaves open the possibility that blacks actually present were unconsciously omitted by the artist in some scenes depicted. This point of course alludes to the elusive question of who or what was considered to be worthy of portrayal, just as their omission from commentary suggests that some of those featured were deemed insufficiently important to mention.[1]

To the extent that blacks were visible in Dutch society, it appears that it was not as they really were but rather as the popular opinion of them wished them to be. This highly significant imprecision mandates caution in any approach to art as literal history. Further evidence of this is presented in instances where the art was specifically intended to chronicle history. The Eeckhout portrait of the Congolese emissary to Johan Maurits in European garb intended as gifts for his king from Maurits is one striking example of how misleading a very realistic portrait can be. The Blake engraving of Granman Quassie in a similarly foreign costume he probably wore only once, if ever, is another. In this context, however, it can be seen that the art does provide important material for the history of perceptions and the history of ideas.

Dutch entry into the African slave trade and slavery and the development of the Dutch empire brought blacks fully into Dutch history for the first time. This also brought a merging of the images from imagination, those from the Western tradition in general, with those from immediate reality. Whereas before a general characterization of negative or positive might describe most attitudes, now more specific vital questions were raised about the place and character of blacks. Moreover, society was becoming more articulate, with the institutionalization of education, the development of literature for all ages, and the advent of mass media. Now art and literature became indistinguishable in some respects, as each contained some of the other. The *volksprenten* and engravings and illustrations for all sorts of books are examples of this. Thus the general public was presented verbal and graphic pictures of blacks from real as well as imaginary travel accounts, literary stories, and scientific studies. They followed as well actual relations between the Dutch and blacks in developments such as Christian missionary work, the abolitionist movement, the emancipation of the slaves, and the eventual severance of the colonies.

The evolution of the image of blacks in Dutch literature was often merely literary expression of the very same feature expressed in folklore and art. In the Arthurian tale *Morien*, which found its way into the Netherlands in the fourteenth century, we once again find a black figure tottering between the role of angel and devil, hero and villain, noble and clown. Bredero and Visscher in their play on sexual stereotypes for blacks touch upon symbolism which some associated even with the quasi-sacred Zwarte Piet and which is more openly suggested in allegorical pieces such as Bosch's *Earthly Delights* and many others. The applicability of the term "noble savage" to some Dutch literary figures captures succinctly the type of pervasive ambivalence under discussion here. When represented by a black protagonist, as in the case of Elisabeth Maria Post's Reinhart, it is another reminder that the society in question is engaged in an unresolved effort to determine how to regard the outsider. One of the main differences between the image of blacks projected in literature and that in art is that literature could be more clearly didactic. Hence in both *belles-lettres* and other literature can be found examples of writings meant to explain the nature of blacks and to instruct behavior accordingly. This is true of all forms, including scientific reference books, novels, short stories, periodical literature, and all sorts of children's literature.

The fact that literature was more articulate and specific than folklore or art does not, however, mean a diminution of the contradictions in characterization of blacks. In fact it simply means more numerous and more explicit variations, with some still highly negative and some positive, as has been shown in the previous chapters. This became especially pronounced in the debates concerning abolition, writings surrounding the emancipation, and twentieth-century writings concerning the separation of the remaining colonies. The rise of black nationalism in particular pushed some of the same issues involved in the discussions about abolition and emancipation to new levels. These interpretations gained a new dimension as peoples of black African descent themselves joined the discussion as access to education widened and with the advent of black professional writers and black periodicals. However, despite the new depth and variety of interpretations, and literature's asset of affording a real exchange and ongoing modification of interpretations when desired, there remains the contrasting images in the literary tradition as in the rest of Dutch culture. On this subject the continuing popularity of caricatured black stereotypes alongside scholarly treatises by black professors in Dutch bookstores speaks volumes.

In many respects the Dutch religious tradition presents the most serious test on the nature of the image of blacks, because it touches on the theme of the very humanity of blacks in the most vital sense for the majority of the public. Here again it might be said that the Dutch have it both ways, in this instance because of the toleration of diverse religious beliefs, in other words, their lowercase catholicism. It was in fact the Moravian Brotherhood, a non-Dutch, evangelical movement, which established the most positive record with reference to blacks in the Dutch empire. However, its very presence, with a major base in the Netherlands and others in the colonies, in itself evinced an unusual level of tolerance by the Dutch compared to their contemporary societies. Furthermore, in all the other denominations there were at least some exceptionally progressive groups or individuals in this regard.

Notwithstanding the aloofness of the Dutch Reformed Church, it also contained a streak of humility, as is revealed by the following two favorite biblical passages drawn from the Old and New Testaments. From a prayer of King David in I Chronicles 29:15 comes "For we are strangers before thee, and sojourners, as were all our fathers: our days on the earth are as a shadow, and there is none abiding." From Ephesians 2:19: "Now therefore ye are no more strangers and foreigners, but fellow-citizens with the saints, and of the household of God." If applied to all peoples this could be a formula for harmony between all groups in a plural society. In short, the image of blacks in the Dutch religious traditions is just as ambiguous as it is in the folklore, art, and literature, which often drew upon religious themes.

Although never able to resolve the questions concerning the place of Blacks in the world order, the Christian churches have been drawn to continual engagement with the issue by the dual pressure of inherent contradictions within their faith and the course of history. The universality of Christianity impels Christians to confront the question of whether all of mankind is to be included as well as the further question of defining humanity. The global nature of modern world history, with the world largely dominated by the Christian West, has left no alternative to interaction between all peoples and cultures. Yet an often dominant strain of exclusivism in both Calvinism and Catholicism has more often increased than decreased the distance between them and those of differing culture and religion. While the related thesis of Frank Tannenbaum suggesting that there was better treatment of slaves and freer societies under Catholicism than under Protestantism is valuable for analysis of the Dutch world and continues to enjoy some scholarly support, its validity is far from certain. It is safest to say that the difference between the European societies is only one of degree; for all of them asserted racial superiority. Recent studies of the former Spanish and Portuguese possessions show that subtle but powerful vestiges of this still survive, if sometimes beneath the surface.[2] In the Dutch empire the difference where Catholicism was strong, as in Curaçao, could be explained more in terms of the distinctive economy there than in terms of religion.

For the Dutch Reformed Church it is not possible to determine conclusively whether attitudes viewing blacks as inferior stem from racial bias or from the fact that black societies in the modern world have been under the domination of whites, therefore in Calvinist terms less successful, outside God's favor, and inferior. The same would of course apply to individuals in the Dutch world. The hope for brotherhood symbolized in the early period by the Adoration of the Magi and the Baptism of the Ethiopian themes was tried sorely in the Middle Passage and under the slavers' whips. On the other hand, a black slave might well find more compassion in traditional Christianity than in bourgeois humanism, which held little sympathy for the meek and lowly, favoring rather those who prevailed in competitive struggle.

The interplay between religion and commerce which many students of Dutch history have treated brought many compromises. It is probably in this context that the church's acquiescence to the slave trade and racism can be understood. The Hamitic legend, which became more popular in the late modern period, was indeed a more appropriate symbol for that period for all its inaccuracy in other respects. Yet, it is not clear that a consensus has ever been reached to discard the idea of equality before God. The discussion of definitions in chapter one shows that over the centuries opinions continued to vary concerning the nature of blacks. The same was true within the religions.

But what of the impact made by the growing presence of blacks in the Netherlands, and their functioning on ever higher levels there and in the former colonies? The examples presented here in chapter six, including some interesting figures unknown to the general public, only begin to suggest the character of the picture which might be drawn of blacks of note if a more thorough survey were conducted. This picture is certain to unfold in the near future as an increasing number of blacks begin to study their role in Dutch history. Should not this reality, which was certainly known to participants and observers even if not chronicled, at least by the twentieth century have made a decisive impact, indeed blotting out many of the stereotypes and obsolete imagery of the past? Perhaps so; but in fact positive examples have had as little power to dominate in the modern period as they did to survive in the early modern. Viewing this in its broader historical context, it should be noted that the patterns outlined here for the Dutch world closely resemble those in many other modern societies. Of the other European colonial powers, England and France are conspicuous in sharing some of the same difficulties with racial bias as the Netherlands. The question as to why such attitudes can persist in a world which glorifies reason and empiricism goes to the very heart of the present study. It is now time to sum up what the Dutch experience contributes toward an answer.

Color Prejudice and Modernization

From the Dutch experience it would appear that a key to conceptualizing the problem in an instructive way is to acknowledge a relationship between the nature of modern color prejudice and developments related to the process of modernization. The most compelling reason for linking color prejudice to the general process of modernization, in addition to the fact that it appears so universal, is that it seems to defy any real logic or teleology. The trends in folklore, art, literature, and religion examined here were definitely influenced by longstanding biases; but they seem to be determined even more by current world developments. In no case is there a straight-line development over centuries, either from positive to negative or the reverse. Linking modern color prejudice to the process of modernization does not, however, preclude the existence of color bias before the modern period, which might well have existed on other bases. Before addressing specific ways in which the process of modernization influenced the evolution of racial bias in the Dutch world, it will be useful to review the possible origins of color prejudice encountered in the present study, to see to what extent they can be traced to earlier times.

The most ancient and persistent basis of color bias, which the Dutch share with most world cultures, is the association of blackness with evil. The social consequences of this can be seen in the color spectrum and hierarchy which developed in the Dutch empire, which may be usefully viewed as part of what Harry Hoetink describes as the "somatic norm." Another widely known basis of prejudice, in the Netherlands as in the Christian world in general, is the Hamitic legend. However, although this too is of ancient origin, it appears not to have been revived in Europe until the eighteenth and nineteenth centuries, and then mainly as a justification of enslavement of Africans. The association of blacks with slavery was the other main origin of bias specifically related to color that surfaced in the Dutch empire. The depth of the impact of this is the subject of some disagreement among scholars.[3] Closely related to this was the fostering of various stereotypes aimed at restricting Blacks to certain functions and to suit psychological needs of the slave masters. These stereotypes lived on after emancipation and, indeed, were in some instances reinforced to serve as a social control device in the absence of formal slavery.

For all the importance of these three sources of color prejudice—that is, the association of blackness with evil, the Hamitic legend, and the association of blacks with slavery—in Dutch history they are overshadowed by a number of biases not directly related to color but which may often be associated with or confused with color bias. One is religious affiliation. The Calvinist concepts of the *vreemdelingen* and *bijwooners* (strangers and sojourners), used to describe all those not in the faith, can easily be taken personally by the outsider. He may not be aware of the deeply rooted tradition in this aristocratic, bourgeois democracy which in the formative period of the country led individual Dutchmen to perceive themselves as superior to others, even other Dutchmen from a different polder or city. The same psychology operating on the global plane also instilled a group bonding in the collective enterprise of commercial exploitation of the wider world.

Class affiliation is another basis of bias. This point may appear contradictory when addressed to Dutch society, given what Simon Schama has described as its "potbellied" social structure at the height of its empire, and in view of what some other visiting Europeans observed among the Dutch as a lack of refinement and an absence of respect for pomp and status.[4] It would seem that such a society might be predisposed to more tolerance of others looked down upon in these respects. In reality a categorical statement on this is not possible. While it is true that proper class was of less significance in the Netherlands than in other contemporary European societies, class was more strictly observed in the colonies, where the most contact with blacks occurred. The sociologist W. F. Wertheim recalled that when he worked at the Department of Justice in Batavia in the 1930s there were four types of toilets, three for various ranks of Europeans and the other for the indigenous peoples.[5]

And in the twentieth century class allegiance has been found by some to be stronger than national allegiance.[6] But it was precisely the observance of class lines which in some instances accounted for more favorable status for blacks. Thus, some might be subject to class discrimination, which might be mistaken for racial discrimination, in the Netherlands or in the colonies. At the same time, those actually in the favored status, such as the *Blanda Itam* in the East Indies or the *tapooyers* in West Africa, owed their elevation to the class systems. Likewise, the favored treatment of black servants of notables in earlier centuries and the happy experience of black artists visiting or immigrating in the early twentieth derived from their perceived position in society.

Another form of exclusive group affiliation in Dutch society which may easily be misread by outsiders is that represented by the unique system referred to as "pillarization." This system of social blocs centered on religion, class, culture, and ideologies by the nineteenth and twentieth centuries became more important than class in determining one's world outlook. The "pillar" definition came to encompass all major social affiliations: church, school, political party, trade union, professional societies, recreational organizations, communications media, libraries, and hospitals. Friendships, marriages, housing, and employment could be traced along the same lines.[7] It can be seen how the development of such complex blocs can be viewed as an embodiment of the traditional Dutch pluralism and toleration. It also underscores the relative isolation of someone in Dutch society who would not be part of one of the "pillars." Schama points out that in Dutch society the group most roundly scourged were the Gypsies, not because of any physical characteristics but because of their rootlessness.[8] A glance at the structure of the "pillars" alone suffices to show how alien such an existence is to Dutch traditions. An outsider then, of whatever ilk, must find a way "inside" the established institutions in the society before full acceptance can be possible.

Yet another important source of biased discrimination may be covered by the term nationalism used in its broadest sense. Nationalism in its narrow definition based on the concept of the nation-state has not found much resonance in Dutch culture. The respect for particularism has been too strong. This is one reason that fascism, the consummate nationalistic and racist ideological response to modernization, never made much headway in the Netherlands, notwithstanding sympathy expressed by some small groups and individuals.[9] One of the most essential elements in determining "national" status throughout the Dutch empire was the Dutch language. Together with religion, this was the primary determinant of "Dutchness," and command of the language was definitely one possible means toward greater acceptance. One obvious reason is that it provided greater opportunity for economic improvement, which in turn meant higher social status. Considering the extent to which the Netherlands historically is comprised of immigrants, mainly from other parts of Europe, it is not surprising that language and religion would be so important in shaping national identity.

There is another closely related factor which should also be mentioned here: kinship. Especially in view of the extreme particularism in Dutch society, the family has played an enormous role in shaping concepts about belonging. The strength of family ties accounts for the difficulty of implementing the government's efforts to restrict the entry into the Netherlands of Asian family members of Dutch colonials from East Asia and later the ready acceptance of mulatto offspring from the West Indies for education in the Netherlands.[10]

One final attitude which is harder to verify and which often features in racial discrimination without really being racial is that stemming from fear of competition between groups. W. F. Wertheim has proposed this as the central issue in the current racial situation in the Netherlands. He argues further that it is precisely when groups which were formerly oppressed begin to become emancipated, that is, to gain civil and social equality, that the problem is likely to become acute. For it is at this point that the formerly dominant group begins to sense a threat. If such an occurrence coincides with a time of scarcity of basic living needs, as was the case of the Netherlands of the 1970s and the early 1980s, friction seems inescapable.[11] Such a situation can immediately become racial, of course, because of the ease of identifying the newcomers by conspicuous physical traits and cultural practices. Historically similar "racial" situations developed in a number of societies immediately after the emancipation of African slaves in settings where they were viewed as competitors for jobs or land desired by whites.

In weighing the three specific ideas about color from history and legend which are often used to explain color prejudice against the several other discriminatory social attitudes and practices not based specifically on color, it would at first seem that the latter are far more significant than blatant color bias in the Dutch experience. In an increasingly secular world, few now can even define the Hamitic legend, although some notion of it still persists. However, the vague associations of blackness and evil and of blacks with slavery have retained more lasting attraction. These three taken together have had an influence far out of proportion to their objective significance. In a sense they represent the proverbial "two strikes against" for blacks which is often invoked in discussions on race relations.

The reason that history does not wipe this slate clean is that this would require some type of historical force equivalent to the controversial late twentieth-century United States concept of "affirmative action," since the damaging negative notions are already embedded. But the impersonal forces of history do not play favorites. Indeed, the forces of modern history have moved rather to nurture these negative notions. An appreciation of their peculiar character and relative significance in Dutch society requires that they be viewed against the background of the much larger related phenomena represented by religion, nationalism, "pillarization," and the competition syndrome just described. The negative images concerning blackness have been convenient, erstwhile dormant, devices which have been raised sporadically to suit other, much broader purposes than the promotion of racism per se.

This is where modernization enters the picture in full focus. Promotion of color prejudice has proven a very compliant handmaiden for certain major developments in the modern world. In the Dutch experience, race and color became pragmatic, useful devices for defining a desired massive, cheap labor force in the division of labor which developed in modern capitalism. In his study of race, the state, and capitalist development, Stanley Greenberg states that race became a basis for broad group identity and ideology only from the mid-nineteenth century.[12] However, for all practical purposes the Dutch were applying it much earlier in the East Indies as well as in the Americas. That the black seamen, soldiers, and freemen of various sorts did not emerge more visibly in history, and thereby give a more balanced image, was at least in part because entrenched bias caused them to be undervalued. However, it is probably also true that they received attention just equal to others involved. Given their smaller number they would have needed to be given special attention to be noted. The consequence of such equal treatment for the image of blacks was disproportionately great because of the already existing power of the negative established images which needed to be offset.

Racial bias did not lose force after emancipation. It served in the Dutch colonies as elsewhere as a convenient replacement for the traditional definition of a desired exploited class. Slavery and serfdom, which had served this purpose in the traditional societies and had now broken down in the face of modernization, because of its late arrival and bourgeois character had never really existed in the Netherlands. Some observers have noted that the very fact that the emancipation was granted by the king and not brought about by force led the former slaves as well as the general public to a feel that freedom was a gift and not a right. This notion could only serve to reinforce the many stereotypes about inferiority which would continue. The surviving thought system proved sufficiently entrenched to keep the racial barriers in place and in some instances to implant new ones.

William Julius Wilson, in his recent study on the status of blacks in the United States, asserts that industrial society provides a more favorable environment than preindustrial for race and color to lose significance, since pragmatic demands of the market dominate and all groups become more diversified. However, one interesting aspect of the Dutch case is that the creation of some of their racial societies followed rather than preceded the development of a capitalist economy. Does this mean they should have been harder to create and less durable? Robert Rydell, in his colorful study on imperialist thought at the turn of the century, shows that more was at work than the objective market forces. Racism dignified by science could divert the eyes of the white masses from the general class exploitation in progress, which was directed at them as well as their black brethren, by making them feel superior to the other, more conspicuous group.[13]

One reason that the image of blacks in the modern world has been so ambiguous is that almighty science, inherently reflecting society but achieving almost sacred authority, has played a duplicitous role. For example, with one hand it brings the power to break off the shackles of ignorance; but with the other it crowns false ideologies as well as sound ones. In addition to science's legitimization of racism, it also brought technologies which could produce and disseminate on a limitless scale the stereotypes related to color and servility. It brought unprecedented literacy, but this also meant that more could be indoctrinated with falsehoods just as easily as with truths. The new secular ideologies too brought little relief. Even the most humanitarian in theory showed racist sides in practice. That the question here is not purely one of race and color is evident in the fact that blacks in the Dutch world often also accepted the dominant color biases, and to this day show little sense of common identity. The very fact that over a third of the population of Suriname moved to the Netherlands in the 1970s shows the extent to which the issues involved are basic human issues and are not only racial. Apart from any theories, economic factors may be the most decisive of all.

Meanwhile, although canonizing negative stereotypes of blacks, European civilization has not hesitated to appropriate cultural elements such as music from blacks, thus acknowledging the worth and universality of these elements, but often disassociating them from blacks as much as possible. Just as in earlier centuries it was acceptable for white males to mate black women and adopt their children, in the twentieth the Europeans could take African-rooted music and eventually give it white cloaking such as in the evolution of jazz and rhythm and blues.[14] This too is a reflection of the impact of industrialization, as mass culture has become just another part of big business. Such market forces drive blacks themselves to sacrifice unique and authentic elements from their African heritage for profit. While blacks in Dutch society are gradually becoming involved at all levels, this study has shown that the most prominent images which continue to be projected are the older ones, found on product labels rather than on boards of directors. The sixteenth-century canvases on which blacks are handsomely displayed in fine art may still be viewed in museums; but blacks will be found more often on twentieth-century trademarks for fine produce.

The character of Dutch society as consciously pluralistic probably influenced the nature of the colonial societies and the attitude toward color, although it is difficult to determine to what degree. Use of such a broad spectrum of colors as occurred in the Dutch experience must have in a sense made color more "neutral," allowing for less pejorative attitudes. It would seem that this would give the Netherlands an advantage in addressing the current situation. Indeed, reflecting this distinctive tradition, those studying the problem, such as Lijphart and Pierre van den Berghe, show a preference for using the terms "pluralism" and "ethnicism," rather than "racism" in discussing it.

One scholar, Chris Mullard, sees these as possible new shields for racism. He views the attempt to focus attention on individual rather than group rights and concerns as a sleight of hand for the benefit of conscience-stricken liberals and minorities, an attempt to move away from a class analysis, just as the fairs did earlier for the general public. However, as Greenberg points out, the neglect of the individual and specific incidents is often also a fault in Marxism, the temple of class analysis. Besides, revolutionary change is one other aspect of modernization which has not offered much direct benefit for blacks, as they have most often been exploited to help others profit from the revolutionary change. Times of great upheaval favor those who already have power or easiest access to it. Thus the French Revolution was more favored than the Haitian; and the skilled and educated, that is, the most "modernized" Surinamese and Antilleans have fared better than the vast majority. Mullard is also concerned that European ethnic problems not be seen as part of a universal phenomenon, lest that be used as an excuse to ignore the demands of the oppressed. However, this seems extreme. What would seem preferable would be both to admit the universality and still to demand attention to the specifics of the local situation.[15] The relationship of the Dutch with peoples of black African descent around the globe and across the centuries suggests that what is generally thought of as race and color prejudice is essentially not really about race and color per se.

As intimated earlier, it seems more plausible that what has really occurred historically is that racial differences and skin color have been used to cloak all sorts of devilment in human affairs. The reinforcement of the marginality of blacks by modernization postulated in the introductory chapter can be seen by considering their place in the major secular doctrines which have arisen in response to modernization. Capitalism favors those with capital and encourages competition while sanctioning virtually all ways of eliminating competitors. Liberalism favors those with property and access to power. Nationalism tends to stress national and ethnic differences and at times fuels racism. This scenario is unfavorable for any not already in a dominant position.

Returning to my earlier reference to Frank Snowden's thesis in his *Before Color Prejudice*, I would further speculate that similar attitudes and practices probably also existed in the ancient world, but in more subtle ways which allowed Snowden to conclude there was no color prejudice. The growing political and economic dominance of Europe in the modern period since the fifteenth century represented a type of interaction between continents and world cultures that was not possible in earlier times, neither in character nor in scope. The Greco-Roman world Snowden treats was ruled by a cosmopolitan culture that could not be easily separated into East and West or North and

South. The basic arguments in Martin Bernal's *Black Athena*, asserting that the denial of African origins of Western civilization is a result of scholarship dating only from the eighteenth century, are a compelling reminder of how cosmopolitan that culture was.[16] Bernal's finding that a biased re-creation of ancient history took place just in the modern period also speaks to the issue at hand. The many examples of racial harmony at the individual level even in racist societies suggests that there is a pervasive understanding that racial and color characteristics are not in themselves qualitative distinctions. However, when in the modern world the continent of Europe managed to gain material domination over Asia, Africa, and the Americas—aided greatly by navigational tools, gunpowder, and other vital resources borrowed from East Asia, Africa, and the Middle East—the Europeans could not resist the temptation to buttress their hold on power with the myth of racial superiority.

The Dutch experience in this regard shows that a considerable variation is possible even within the same cultural framework and the same time period, and that bias becomes manifest when and where it becomes convenient or expedient. The reason that this finding is significant is that it suggests that a solution to this problem lies less with the question of race and color than with the nature of discrimination. Discrimination, that is, the making of choices and evaluation, is necessary in human affairs, on both the individual and the collective level. However, misguided discrimination allows racial and color prejudice to flourish. The point here is that it might be better to replace the usual focus on issues of race and color with an emphasis on education about discrimination, which results in many types of harmful bias besides the racial.

Consistent with this approach, racial and color bias would then be addressed by better education or by removing the conditions which motivate prejudicial discrimination. The findings here also point up the critical role of the various forms of communication, especially in an era of mass media. On the question of exactly how racial imagery is communicated, the evidence examined here provides only inconclusive guidance. For example, in addressing the problem of racial imagery, should greater emphasis be placed on the power of words, on pictures and other visual symbols, or on the realms of thought and the imagination? The sojourns here into Dutch folklore, art, literature, and religion make it clear that all of these types of communication must be kept in mind and that they are all closely inter-twined.

It is tempting to hope that, as a solution to the current situation, Dutch society could become color-blind. However, an irony in the role of race and color has been that victimized groups have suffered during periods of "color-blindness" because conditions created in the other periods require a color-consciousness if injustice is to be corrected. It may be that the Netherlands can anticipate a surge resembling the "New Negro," or Harlem Renaissance, movement in the United States in the 1920s and 1930s which sought deliberately to supplant the old, limiting stereotypes. Old Amsterdam might take a cue from one of its former New Amsterdams. The tardy recognition of a color-consciousness long present but earlier denied has produced the paradox in which a society not free of racism must remain race-conscious for a while in order to end race-consciousness. It is perhaps fitting that one contradiction, color prejudice in the modern world, must be rooted out by another.

NOTES

All translations into English throughout the text are mine, except where otherwise noted.

Introduction

1. Thea Beckman, *Het wonder van Frieswijck* (Amsterdam: Stichting Collectieve Propaganda van het Nederlandse Boek ter gelegenheid van de Kinderboekenweek, 1991). For examples of the discussion, see Henry Dors, "Geschenk kinderboekenweek affront voor alle kinderen," *De Volkskrant*, 7 October 1991, and Ruud Kamphoven, "De mensen discrimineren, niet het boekje," *Brabants Dagblad*, 12 October 1991.

2. A Dutch scholar who has conspicuously advanced this approach is the historian Dik van Arkel. See, for example, his "Historisch racisme—onderzoek; Achtergronden, benaderingen, problemen," *Tijdschrift voor Sociale Geschiedenis* 10 (1984): 438–62.

3. A tour de force which for decades has moved along some of the same lines is the multi-volume work *The Image of the Black in Western Art*, published by the Menil Foundation under the general editorship of Ladislas Bugner. Incidentally, this series includes considerable evidence of racial prejudice before the modern era. For example, see Jean Devisse, *The Image of the Black in Western Art*, II, *From the Early Christian Era to the "Age of Discovery,"* Chap. 1, "From the Demonic Threat to the Incarnation of Sainthood" (Cambridge: Harvard University Press, 1979), pp. 17–47.

4. Frank M. Snowden, Jr., *Before Color Prejudice: The Ancient View of Blacks* (Cambridge: Harvard University Press, 1983), p. 108.

5. Winthrop D. Jordan, *White Over Black: American Attitudes Towards the Negro, 1550–1812* (Chapel Hill: University of North Carolina Press, 1968). George M. Fredrickson, *The Black Image in the White Mind: The Debate on Afro-American Character and Destiny, 1817–1914* (New York: Harper & Row, 1971). Fredrickson, *White Supremacy: A Comparative Study in American and South African History* (New York: Oxford University Press, 1981). James Walvin, *Black and White: The Negro and English Society 1555–1945* (London: Allen Lane, 1973). Hans Werner Debrunner, *Presence and Prestige: Africans in Europe* (Basel: Basler Afrika Bibliographien, 1979), p. 406.

294
Notes to Pages xix–6

6. Simon Schama, *The Embarrassment of Riches: An Interpretation of Dutch Culture in the Golden Age* (New York: Alfred A. Knopf, 1987).

Chapter One: The Dutch World

1. Adam Westermann, *Groot christelijke Zee-Vaert In XXVI Predicatien, In maniere van een Zee-Postille; In welken een Schipper/Koopman/Oorlogsvolk/ Zee-ende Reysende-man/geleert wort/ende ook andere kan leeren/hoe men in de vreese Godes Godtsaligh en voorspoedigh in zijne Reyse/gelijk ook een negelijk Mensche in tijde van Onweder/Dom . . . [damaged] men/harde Winden/hooge Vloeden/en . . . [damaged] lende periculen/ook de henlige Dagen des dood na de gedane Reyse ende ontkominge de noot . . . [damaged] den ende dragen sal.* (Amsterdam: [widow of] Gysbert de Groot, 1692), p. A4.
2. See also William Z. Shetter, *The Netherlands in Perspective: The Organizations of Society and Environment* (Leiden: Martinus Nijhoff, 1987), pp. 275–86.
3. For discussion about this attitude in eighteenth-century Europe in general, see Martin Bernal, *Black Athena: The Afroasiatic Roots of Classical Civilization* (New Brunswick: Rutgers University Press, 1987), p. 28.
4. The Europeans at first thought of a very broad region as "India." Columbus, for example, thought he had landed in Asia and had thus found a new route to "India." (Hence, the natives in the newly discovered lands were called "Indians.") The term "India" in the Dutch East and West India trading companies accurately reflects the usage of that time and is found in most historical records and books by specialists. Although early documents often refer to "Dutch East India" or "Dutch West India," these geographic areas have become more commonly known as the East Indies and the West Indies. While we here retain the original titles of the trading companies, we apply current terminology to geographical areas.
5. Pieter Emmer, "The History of the Dutch Slave Trade, A Bibliographical Survey," *Journal of Economic History* 32 (June-December 1972): 728; Cornelis Goslinga, *The Dutch in the Caribbean and on the Wild Coast 1580–1680* (Gainsville: University of Florida Press, 1971), p. 340.
6. J. M. van der Linde, *Heren, Slaven, Broeders: Momenten uit de Geschiedenis der Slavernij* (Nijkerk: [Seminarie der Unitas fratrum—Evangelische Broedergemeente te Zeist] G. F. Callenbach, 1963), pp. 52–70.
7. Philip D. Curtin, "The Slave Trade and the Atlantic Basin: Intercontinental Perspectives," in Nathan Huggins, ed., *Key Issues in the Afro-American Experience* (New York: Harcourt Brace, 1971), p. 76; and Curtin, *Cross-Cultural Trade in World History* (Cambridge: Cambridge University Press, 1984), p. 119.
8. Charles R. Boxer, *The Dutch Seaborne Empire: 1600–1800* (New York: Alfred A. Knopf, 1970), p. 12.
9. Nigel Worden, *Slavery in Dutch South Africa* (Cambridge: Cambridge University Press, 1985) pp. 8–9.
10. Emmer, "The History of the Dutch Slave Trade," p. 732; Johannes Menne Postma, *The Dutch in the Atlantic Slave Trade, 1600–1815* (New York: Cambridge University Press, 1990).

11. William Bosman, *A New and Accurate Description of the Coast of Guinea: Divided into the Gold, the Slave, and the Ivory Coasts*, John Ralph Willis, ed. (New York: Barnes & Noble, 1967), p. xviii.

12. Goslinga, *The Dutch in the Caribbean and on the Wild Coast*, pp. 353–66; Emmer, "The History of the Dutch Slave Trade," pp. 738–41.

13. Jan Lucassen and Rinus Penninx, *Nieuwkomers: Immigranten en hun nakomelingen in Nederland 1550–1985* (Amsterdam: Meulenhoff Informatief, 1985).

14. Simon Schama, *The Embarrassment of Riches: An Interpretation of Dutch Culture in the Golden Age* (New York: Alfred A. Knopf, 1987), p. 594.

15. Bert McDowell, "The Dutch Touch," *National Geographic* 4 (October 1986): 501–02. See also Gert Oostindie, "Caribbean Migration to the Netherlands: A Journey to Disappointment?" in Malcolm Cross and Han Entzinger, eds., *Lost Illusions: Caribbean Minorities in Britain and the Netherlands* (London: Routledge, 1988), pp. 62–67.

16. The term "Hindustani" as used in Suriname describes the descendants of contract workers who came there from British India between 1873 and 1918, regardless of religion or exact regional origins in India.

17. Arend Lijphart, *The Politics of Accommodation: Pluralism and Democracy in the Netherlands* (Berkeley: University of California Press, 1968), p. 202.

18. Lijphart, *The Politics of Accommodation*, p. 102.

19. Lijphart, *The Politics of Accommodation*, p. 79; Schama, *The Embarrassment of Riches*, pp. 51–58.

20. Lijphart, *The Politics of Accommodation*, pp. 87–88.

21. The brevity of the presentation on this subject can be justified on the basis of the rich and growing literature on this topic. Examples are Philomena Essed, *Alledaags Racisme* (Amsterdam: Sara, 1984); Frank Bovenkerk, *Emigratie uit Suriname* (Amsterdam: University of Amsterdam, 1975); Malcolm Cross and Han Entzinger, eds., *Lost Illusions: Caribbean Minorities in Britain and the Netherlands* (London: Routledge, 1988); J. M. M. van Amersfoort, *Immigratie en minderheidsvorming* (Alphen aan den Rijn: Sampson, 1974); Fred Budike, *Surinamers naar Nederland* (Amsterdam: Instituut Voortgezet Agogisch Beroepsonderwijs, 1982); and Joan Ferrier, *De Surinamers* (Muiderberg: Dick Coutinho, 1985).

22. Jean Taylor, *The Social World of Batavia: European and Eurasian in Dutch Asia* (Madison: University of Wisconsin Press, 1983), pp. 14–16.

23. Taylor, *The Social World of Batavia*, p. 168.

24. Taylor, *The Social World of Batavia*, pp. 6, 18, 46–47.

25. Boxer, *The Dutch Seaborne Empire*, pp. 269–72.

26. Worden, *Slavery in Dutch South Africa*, p. 4.

27. Shula Marks, " 'Thievish and Not to Be Trusted': Racial Stereotypes in South Africa in Historical Perspective," *History Today* 31 (August 1981): 15–21.

28. Pierre van de Berghe, *Race and Racism: A Comparative Perspective* (New York: John Wiley & Sons, 1967) pp. 18, 96–98. Richard Elphick, *Kraal and Castle: Khoikhoi and the Founding of White South Africa* (New Haven: Yale University Press, 1977), pp. 86–181.

29. Worden, *Slavery in Dutch South Africa*, pp. 11, 16. For more detail on

the Khoikhoi see the two works of Isaac Schapera, *The Khoisan Peoples of South Africa: Bushmen and Hottentots* (New York: The Humanities Press, 1951); I. Schapera, ed., *The Early Cape Hottentots Described in the Writings of Olfert Dapper (1688), Willem Ten Rhyne (1686) and Johannes Guielmus de Grevenbroek (1695)* (Capetown: The Van Riebeeck Society, 1933).

30. Elphick, *Kraal and Castle*, pp. 107, 201–03.

31. Worden, *Slavery in Dutch South Africa*, pp. 52–57.

32. Worden, *Slavery in Dutch South Africa*, pp. 144–47.

33. Rene Baesjou, ed., *An Asante Embassy on the Gold Coast: The Mission of Akyempon Yaw to Elmina 1869–1872* (Leiden: Afrika Studie Centrum, 1979), pp. 18–21.

34. Baesjou, *An Asante Embassy on the Gold Coast*, pp. 46–52.

35. Emmer, "The History of the Dutch Slave Trade," p. 731. Albert Helman, *Avonturen aan de Wilde Kust: De geschiedenis van Suriname met Zijn buurlanden* (Alphen aan den Rijn: A. W. Sijthoff, 1982), pp. 86–87.

36. Goslinga, *The Dutch in the Caribbean and on the Wild Coast*, pp. 343–45. P. J. Winter, *De Westindische Compagnie ter Kamer Stad en Land* (The Hague: Martinus Nijhoff, 1978), pp. 115–33.

37. Ernst van den Boogaart, "Infernal Allies; the Dutch West India Company and the Tarairiu 1631–1654," in Ernst van den Boogaart, ed., *Johan Maurits van Nassau-Siegen, 1604–1679. A Humanist Prince in Europe and Brazil* (The Hague: The Government Publishing Office, 1979), pp. 519–38. Charles Boxer, *The Dutch in Brazil 1624–1654* (Oxford: Oxford University Press, 1954).

38. Ernst van den Boogaart, "De Nederlandse expansie in het Atlantisch gebied 1590–1674," *Algemene Geschiedenis der Nederlanden* (Haarlem: Fibula van Dishoek, 1980), v. 7, p. 225. Emmer, "History of the Dutch Slave Trade," pp. 731–32.

39. Van den Boogaart, "De Nederlandse expansie in het Atlantisch gebied," pp. 228–30.

40. Oliver Rink, *Holland on the Hudson: An Economic and Social History of Dutch New York* (Ithaca: Cornell University Press, 1986), pp. 18, 48–53. *The Birth of New York: Nieuw Amsterdam 1624–1664* (Catalog for Exhibition at The New York Historical Society, October–December 1982; Amsterdam Historisch Museum, February–March 1983).

41. Ernst van den Boogaart, "The Netherlands and New Netherland, 1624–1664," in *The Birth of New York: Nieuw Amsterdam 1624–1664*, pp. 9–10.

42. David Cohen, "How Dutch Were the Dutch of New Netherland?" *New York History* 62 (1981): 51.

43. Van den Boogaart, "New Amsterdam," *The Birth of New York: Nieuw Amsterdam 1624–1664*, p. 20. Joyce D. Goodfriend, "Black Families in New Netherland," Proceedings of the Sixth Annual Rensselaerswyck Seminar, Blacks in New Netherland and Colonial New York, *Journal of the Afro-American Historical and Genealogical Society* 5 (Fall–Winter 1984): 94–97.

44. Helman, *Avonturen aan de Wilde Kust*, pp. 92, 132.

45. Harry Hoetink, "Race Relations in Curaçao and Suriname," in Laura Foner and Eugene Genovese, eds., *Slavery in the New World* (Englewood Cliffs,

New Jersey: Prentice-Hall, 1969), p. 180. J. Voorhoeve and Ursy Lichtveld, *Creole Drum: An Anthology of Creole Literature in Suriname* (New Haven: Yale University Press, 1975), pp. 2–5.

46. Rudolf van Lier, *Samenleving in een Grensgebied: Een Sociaal-Historische Studie van de Maatschappij in Suriname* (Amsterdam: Emmering, 1977 [originally in The Hague: Martinus Nijhoff, 1949]), also published in English under the title *Frontier Society*.

47. Gert Oostindie, *Roosenburg en Mon Bijou: Twee Surinaamse plantages, 1720–1870* (Dordrecht: Foris Publications, 1989), pp. 1–8.

48. Gert Oostindie, "Kondreman in Bakrakondre," in Gert Oostindie and Emy Maduro, *In het Land van de Overheerser*, Deel II, *Antilleanen en Surinamers in Nederland, 1634/1667–1954* (Dordrecht: Foris Publications, 1986), p. 9.

49. Goslinga, *The Dutch in the Caribbean and on the Wild Coast*, p. 354. Van den Boogaart, "De Nederlandse expansie in het Atlantisch gebied," p. 245.

50. Hoetink, "Race Relations in Curaçao and Suriname," pp. 185–86.

51. Mac Margolis, "Brazil's Blacks Look Anew at Issue of Race," *The Washington Post*, 13 May 1988, pp. A25–26.

52. It is not possible here to treat the broader history of the emergence and development of the Dutch language. Guidance for study in depth of this can be found in B.C. Donaldson, *Dutch: A Linguistic History of Holland and Belgium* (Leiden: Nijhoff, 1983); L. van den Branden, *Het streven naar verheerlijking, zuivering en opbouw van het Nederlands in de 16e eeuw* (Gent: Koninklijke Vlaamse Academie voor Taal- en Letterkunde, 1956); D. M. Bakker and G. R. W. Dibbets, eds., *Geschiedenis van de Nederlandse taalkunde* (Den Bosch: Malmberg, 1977); Lode van den Branden, Elly Cockx-Indestege, and Frans Sillis, *Bio-Bibliografie van Cornelis Kiliaan* (Nieuwkoop: B. de Graaf, 1978); and Leon Voet, *The Golden Compasses: A History and Evaluation of the Printing and Publishing Activities of the Officina Plantiniana at Antwerp*, v. I, *Christophe Plantin and the Moretuses: Their Lives and Their World* (Amsterdam: Vangendt & Co., 1969–1972).

53. N. E. Osselton, *The Dumb Linguists: A Study of the Earliest English and Dutch Dictionaries* (Leiden: The University Press, 1973), p. 109.

54. *Dictionaire Francoys-Flamenc*, s.v. (Antwerp: Jean Waesberghe, 1579).

55. Hendrick Hexham, comp., *Het Groot Woordenboeck: Gestelt in't Nederduytsch, ende in't Engelsch* (Rotterdam: Arnovt Leers, 1648 and 1658), s.v.

56. Matthias Kramern, ed., and M. Noel Chomel, comp., *Het Nieuw Neder-Hoog-Duitsch en Hoog-Neder-Duitsch Woordenboek (oder Neues holländisch-deutsches und deutsch-hollandisches Wörterbuch), vervattende veele middelen om zijn goed te Vermeerderen, en zijne gezondheid te behouden . . .* (Leiden: Joh. le Mair/ Leeuwarden: J. A. de Chalmot, 1777), s.v.

57. Harry Hoetink, *Caribbean Race Relations; A Study of Two Variants* (Oxford: Oxford University Press, 1967), pp. 120, 146–51, 166–75; and *Slavery and Race Relations in the Americas: An Inquiry into Their Nature and Nexus* (New York: Harper, 1973) pp. 196–200.

58. Egbert Buys, comp., *Nieuw en Volkomen Woordenboek van Konsten en Weetenschappen: De Takken der Nuttige . . . Kennis . . .* (Amsterdam: S. J. Baalde,

1775), s.v. "Neger." In this dictionary another meaning for "Neger" was a certain large fish encountered in the West Indies which had a black head. It was also called *Diable de Mer* (Sea Devil) and some varieties were said to be deadly poisonous.

59. *Algemeen Huishoudelijk-, Natuur-, Zedekundig- en Konst- Woordenboek* (Leiden: Joh. le Mair, 1778), s.v.

60. P. Weiland, *Nederduitsch Taalkundig Woordenboek* (Amsterdam: Johannes Allart, 1804), s.v.

61. Gt. Nieuwenhuis, *Algemeen Woordenboek van Kunsten en Wetenschappen, voor den Beschaafden Stand en ten Behoeve des Gezelligen Levens* (Zutphen: H. C. A. Thieme, 1825), s.v.

62. P. G. Witsen Geysbeek, comp., *Algemeen Noodwendig Woordenboek der Zamenleving, behelzende beknopt en Zakelijk Al het Wetenswaardige uit de Geschiedenis en ieder Vak van Menschelijke Kennis, De Juiste Beteekenis der Kunstbenamingen, in alle Wetenschappen, Beroepen en Handwerken; Opgave der Uitvindingen en Ontdekkingen, Plaatselijke en Historische Bijzonderheden, Zeden, Gewoonten en Gebruiken van Alle Volken der Aarde, Vermaarde Mannen en Vrouwen uit Alle Natien* . . . (Amsterdam: Gebroeders Diederichs, ca. 1845), s.v.

63. Jacob Grimm and Wilhelm Grimm, *Deutsches Wörterbuch* (Leipzig: S. Hirzel, 1889), s.v.

64. *Sijthoff's Woordenboek voor Kennis en Kunst, naar de Nieuwste Bronnen Bewerkt* (Leiden: A. W. Sijthoff, 1893), s.v.

65. James A. H. Murray, ed., *A New English Dictionary on Historical Principles* (Oxford: Clarendon Press, 1908), s.v.

66. A. Kluyver and A. Lodewyck, eds., *Woordenboek der Nederlandsche Taal* (The Hague and Leiden: Martinus Nijhoff, A. W. Sijthoff, 1913), s.v.

67. *De Katholieke Encyclopaedie* (Amsterdam: Joost v.d. Vondel, 1937), s.v.

68. J. Heinsius, ed., *Woordenboek der Nederlandsche Taal* (The Hague and Leiden: Martinus Nijhoff, A. W. Sijthoff, 1916, 1941), s.v. Rosemary Brana-Shute, "The Manumission of Slaves in Suriname, 1760–1828" (Ph.D. Dissertation, University of Florida, Gainsville, 1985), pp. 226–30.

Chapter Two: Folklore as Racial Gospel

1. The direct ties are not certain. Adriaan D. De Groot, *Saint Nicholas: A Psychoanalytic Study of His History and Myth* (The Hague: Mouton, 1965), p. 12 [original edition, *Sint Nicolaas Patroon van liefde: Een psychologische studie over de Nicolaus-figuur en zijn verering in vroeger eeuwen en nu* (Amsterdam: N. V. Noord-Hollandsche Uitgevers, 1949]. Charles W. Jones, *Saint Nicholas of Myra, Bari, and Manhattan: Biography of a Legend* (Chicago: University of Chicago Press, 1978) p. 344.

2. C. Catharina van de Graft, "Sinterklaas, goedheilig man . . . ," *Haagsch Maandblad* 4 (1927): 627–28.

3. This work, which has been titled "Saint Nicholas" by art historians, is in a private collection in Switzerland—copy at Schweizerisches Institut für Kunstwissenschaft.

4. Karl Meisen, *Nikolauskult und Nikolausbrauch im Abendlande* (Düsseldorf: Schwann, 1931/1981), pp. 504–26. De Groot, *Saint Nicholas*, p. 43. "Maske, Maskereien," *Handwörterbuch des Deutschen Aberglaubens* (Berlin/Leipzig: Walter De Gruyter & Co., 1932/1933), p. 1841. Jan de Schuyter, *Sint Niklaas in de Legende en in de Volksgebruiken* (Antwerp: "Boekuil" -en "Karveel," 1944), pp. 21–28.

5. A. Hallema, "Hoe men vroeger met kinderen Sinterklaas vierde," *Het Kind. Veertiendaags blad van ouders en opvoeders* 39 (1938): 466–67.

6. A. A. Verplanke, "Het verhaal van de Sinterklazen op Ameland," *Neerlands Volksleven* 26 (1977): 196–211.

7. K. D. Koning, "Sint-Nicolaas Historie," *Historia* (November 1940). P. J. Meertens, "St. Nicolaas in de volkskunst," *Historia* 7 (December 1941): 228–33. *Verbodt/Tegens het verkoopen ende stellen van de kramen/op NieuweJaers/ drie Koningen en St. Klaes Avonden*, Plakkaat Bks. 221/16 and 223/61, Koninklijk Bibliotheek, The Hague.

8. Jan de Schuyter, *De beteekenis van Sint Niklaas* (Zoutleeuw: Ch. Peeters, 1942?), pp. 16–19. Van de Graft, "Sinterklaas, goedheilig man . . . ," p. 631. "Het Sint-Nicolaasfeest," *Katholieke Illustratie*, v. 12, no. 21, 1878/79.

9. Meisen, *Nikolauskult und Nikolausbrauch im Abendlande*, pp. 416–26. Franz Weineck, *Der knecht Ruprecht und seine genossen* (Guben: Lübben i.d.L., 1898). Marcellyn Dewulf, "Sinterklaas, de schutspatroon van de stad Sint-Niklaas," in *Annalen van de Oudheidkundige Kring van het Land van Waals* 73 (1970). J. Rasch, "De Zwarte personage op 5 December en 5 Januari," *Eigen Volk [Algemeen folkloristisch en dialectisch maandschrift voor Groot-Nederland]* 6(1934): 52.

10. See, for example, *Vragenlijsten 2 (1937), Central Bureau voor Nederlandsche Volkskunde Commissie der Koninklijke Akademie van Wetenschappen*. In this survey some 1,500 responded out of 3,000 targeted.

11. De Groot, *Saint Nicholas*, pp. 130–31, 179.

12. Jones, *Saint Nicholas*, pp. 310–11.

13. Frank Bovenkerk and Loes Ruland, "De schoorsteenvegers," *Intermediair* 51, 21 December 1984, p. 35. Lodewijk Brunt, "Is Sinterklaas racistisch?" *Vrij Nederland*, December 22, 1984, p. 54.

14. Rahina Hassankhan, *Al is hij zo zwart als roet!* . . . (Warray, 1988), pp. 49–56.

15. *Nederlandsche Heraldiek*, Album I, *Provincie- en Gemeentewapens*, drawings by S. G. van der Laars, Gemeente-archief, Leiden.

16. Jean Devisse and Michel Mollat, *The Image of the Black in Western Art*, II, *From the Early Christian Era to the "Age of Discovery,"* Chap. 2, "Africans in the Christian Ordinance of the World (Fourteenth to the Sixteenth Century)" (Cambridge: Harvard University Press, 1979), pp. 7–58. Another scholar who has given special attention to this topic is Hans Werner Debrunner, "Drei Mohren im Jura; Überlegungen zum Wappen von Cornol," *Nachrichten* [Basler Afrika Bibliographien] 5 (September 1981): 61–65.

17. Frans Laas van Burmania, *Adelÿk wapen boeck. Begonnen in den Jare 1748 en Geÿndigt Anno 1755*, Eerste Deel. (Library, Centraal Bureau voor Genealogie, The Hague). Such families included are Fourmenois, Grombach, Herweij,

Lannoij, Van der Meer, Nitzen, Roorda, and Steernzee. Some families or branches use differing versions, but all including the Moor's head.

18. J. B. Rietstap, *Wapenboek van den Nederlandschen Adel met Genealogische en Heraldische Aanteekeningen*, 2 vols. (Groningen: J. R. Wolters, 1883).

19. Examples may be seen at the National Coaches Museum "Nienoord" at Leek, near Groningen.

20. Edouard J. C. Boutmy, "Bijdrage tot de genealogie van het geslacht Boutmy-Boutmy de Katzmann en aanverwante families," *Nederlandsch Genootschaap* . . . (1974): pp. 8–34.

21. Other Dutch families with Moors' heads in their arms include Calkoen, Coenen, Van der Does, Van Loon, Van Omphal, Paspoort, Ruysch, Van der des Willebois, Mirbach, Pot, Tuchers, De Wys, Van Walchren, Changuion, De Balbian van Doorn, Van Ewych, Ver Huell, Jantzon van Erffrenten, Testart, Van Lilaar, Brouerius van Nidek, Van Ossenberch, Kops, Swarts, Le Maire, Rover, Vand der Meret, Schorer, Paravicini di Capelli, Fourmenois, Van Suerendael, Van de Kop, Ioes, Hudde, and Von Löben Sels.

22. H. W. Alings, "De Gaper als Uithangteken [II]," *Ons Amsterdam*, 1962, DI.14, pp. 162–69. A number of old Gapers may be found in the Nederlands Historisch Medisch Pharmaceutisch Museum in Amsterdam.

23. D. E. H. de Boer and A. M. Luyendijk-Eishout, "Tien eeuwen Leiden, Leidenaars en hun ziekten," *Hutspot, haring en wittebrood* (Zwolle: Waanders, 1981–1982), p. 279. Examples with European characteristics appear in Lies Boiten, Jan van den Broek, Jenne Meinema, Catrien Santing, and Harm van der Veen, eds., "Tien eeuwen Groningen, de Groningers en hun armen en zieken," *Ach lieve tijd* (Zwolle: Waanders, 1985), p. 91.

24. "Vraag en antwoord," *Eigen Volk* [Algemeen folkloristisch en dialectisch maandschrift voor Groot Nederland] 7 (1935): 133.

25. J. van Lennep and J. ter Gouw, *De uithangteekens in verband met Geschiedenis en volksleven Beschouwd* (Amsterdam: Gebroeders Kraay, 1868), s.v. "Apothekers, Chemisten en Drogisten"; "Menschenbeeldjes, Mooren of Morianen." "Gapers geeuwen op een Haarlemse zolder," *Neerlands Volksleven* 5 (Winter 1954–1955): 79–80. J. H. Kruizinga, "Gapers: symbolen van het oude ambacht," *De Speelwagen* [Populair Tijdschrift in het bijzonder gewijd aan de historische schoonheid, folklore en geschiedenis in Noord-Holland boven het Ij]8 (1953): 40–42.

26. Alinga, "De Gaper als Uithangteken [II]," pp. 162–63.

27. Simon Schama, *The Embarrassment of Riches: An Interpretation of Dutch Culture in the Golden Age* (New York: Alfred A. Knopf, 1987), pp. 193–95.

28. J. van Lennep and J. ter Gouw, *De uithangteekens in verband met Geschiedenis en volksleven Beschouwd*, s.v. "Menschenbeeldjes."

29. An excellent example may be found at the Groninger Museum. See photo in "Tien eeuwen Groningen, de Groningers en hun handel," *Ach lieve tijd*, p. 111.

30. Floris Prims and Michel Verbeeck, *Antwerpsch Straatnamenboek; Lijst van al de straatnamen, oude en nieuwe met hun beteekenis, reden, oorsprong en veranderingen* (Antwerp: Boekhandel der "Bijdragen," 1926), pp. 208–09.

31. Augustin Thys, *Historiek der straten en openbare plaatsen van Antwerpen* (Antwerp: C. de Vries-Brouwers, 1973; first published by H. and L. Kennes, 1893), pp. 84–85.

32. P. Biesta, *Pieterburen [;] Geschiedenis van kerk, kerspel en borg* (Assen: Van Gorcum & Co. NV, 1939), pp. 30–31.

33. Robert Rentenaar, *Vernoemingsnamen; Een onderzoek naar de rol van de vernoeming in de nederlandse toponymie* (Amsterdam: P. J. Meertens-Instituut, 1985), pp. 57–58.

34. Rentenaar, *Vernoemingsnamen*, pp. 59–69.

35. P. J. van Winter, *Der Westindische Compagnie ter kamer stad en lande* (The Hague: Martinus Nijhoff, 1978), pp. 115–33. Jan van den Broek et al., "Tien eeuwen Groningen," pp. 103–22.

36. J. J. A. Gouverneur, *Fabel- en versjesboek* (Groningen: J. B. Wolters, 1890; first edition, 1849), pp. 30–31.

37. *Volkskunde-Atlas voor Nederland en Vlaams-Belgie; Commentaar* (Antwerp: N. V. Standaard Boekhandel, 1965), pp. 108–09.

38. *Volkskunde-Atlas voor Nederland en Vlaams-Belgie*, pp. 114, 120–22.

39. F. P. and A. P. Penard, "Surinaamsch bijgeloof," *Bijdragen tot de Taal-, Land- en Volkenkunde van Ned.- Indië* 67 (1913): 157–83. A. Helman, "Volkswijsheid en orale literatuur," in Helman, ed., *Cultureel mozaïek van Suriname* (Zutphen: Walburg Pers, 1977), pp. 95–107.

40. From "Lubbert Gerritsz," in J. van Lennep, *Zeemansliedjes* (Leiden: A. W. Sijthoff, 1852), pp. 26–27. For a fuller picture of the content of Dutch sea shanties see C. A. Davids, *Wat lijdt den zeeman al verdriet: Het Nederlandse zeemanslied in de zeiltijd (1600–1900)* (The Hague: Martinus Nijhoff, 1980); and *Matroosen Vreught, Vol van de Nieuwste end Hedendaaghsche liedekens, Aldermeest gebruyckelijck onder de Zee-varende Luyden* (Amsterdam: Casparus Loots-Man, 1696).

41. In the collection of the Music Department, P. J. Meertens-Instituut, Amsterdam.

42. An 1894 version from North Brabant. In Music Department, P. J. Meertens-Instituut, Amsterdam.

43. A ditty from 1891–1892. Meertens-Instituut.

44. Collected in 1894. Meertens-Instituut.

45. From North Holland, 1894. Meertens-Instituut.

46. A version from Friesland, 1935. Meertens-Instituut.

47. Iona and Peter Opie, eds., *The Oxford Dictionary of Nursery Rhymes* (Oxford: Clarendon Press, 1951, pp. 327–29.

48. Dario Saavedra, "Suriname's muziek en zang," *Weekblad voor Muziek*, Number 12, 20 March 1909. G. P. C. Breugel, *Dagverhaal van eene reis naar Paramaribo* (Amsterdam: Sulpke, 1842), pp. 51, 62–63. A. Blom, *Verhandeling over den landbouw* (Amsterdam: Smit, 1787), pp. 330, 388.

49. A. W. Nieuwenhuis, "De zending en de beschaving in Indië," *Tropisch Nederland* 11 (1930): 409.

50. L. C. van Panhuys, *Les chansons et la musique de la Guyane Néerlandaise* (Paris: Societe de Americanistes de Paris, N.S. IX), pp. 27–39.

51. Will G. Gilbert, *Een en ander over de negroide muziek van Suriname* (Amsterdam: Koninklijke Vereeniging "Koloniaal Instituut," 1940), pp. 3–5.
52. René Vervuurt, *Muziekleven in Suriname* (n.p., c. 1960), pp. 91–92. R. M. F. Abbenhuis, "Nog eens: folklore in Suriname," *West-Indische Gids* 17 (1935/36): 369–73.
53. R. A. van Lier, *Bonuman. Een Studie van zeven religieuze specialisten in Suriname* (Leiden: Instituut voor Culturele Antropologie, Sociologie der Niet-Westerse Volken, 1983), p. 19.
54. H. van Cappelle, "Van slavenhandel naar Boschneger," *Tropisch Nederland* 11 (1930): 393.
55. Albert von Sack, *Reize naar Surinamen, verblijf aldaar,* . . . (Haarlem: Bohn, 1821), pp. 152–53. Ch. Douglas, *Een blik in het verleden van Suriname* (Paramaribo: Oliviera, 1930), pp. 84–85.
56. Von Sack, *Reize naar Suriname,* pp. 102, 112.
57. H. C. Focke, "De Surinaamsche negermuzijk," *Bijdragen tot de bevordering van de kennis den Nederlandsch West-Indisie Kolonien* 2 (1858): 93–107.
58. W. R. van Hoëvell, *Slaven en vrijen onder de Nederlandsche wet* (Amsterdam: K. H. Schadd, 1864), pp. 86–88. A. J. Riko, *Ons rijk Suriname* (Rotterdam: Nijgh en Van Ditmar, 1883), pp. 104–05.
59. Van Hoëvell, *Slaven en vrijen onder de Nederlandsche wet,* pp. 53–58.
60. Institute of Archeology and Anthropology of the Netherlands Antilles.
61. P. J. Benoit, *Reis door Suriname* (Zutphen: Walburg Press, 1980; from *Voyage à Suriname: Description des Possessions Neerlandaises dan La Guyane* [Brussels: Société des Beaux-arts, 1839]), pp. 36–37. A. M. Coster, *De Boschnegers in de kolonie Suriname* (n.p.: n.d.), pp. 26–36.
62. Von Sack, *Reize naar Surinamen,* pp. 91–92.
63. G. Burkhardt, ed., *Die Mission der Brudergemeine in* . . . (Leipzig: Jansa, 1898), pp. 30–31. H. van Cappelle, *Surinaamsche Negervertellingen* (The Hague: n. p., 1904), pp. 326–27. C. van Coll, "Gegevens over land en volk van Suriname," *Bijdragen tot de Taal-, Land- en Volkenkunde van Nederlandsch-Indië* 55 (1903): 570–72. H. B. van Lummel, *Van Suriname en de Boschnegers* (Rotterdam: n.p., 1901), pp. 21–29.
64. H. C. Focke, *De Surinaamsche negermuzijk,* pp. 106–08. Focke, *Verhaal van een togtje naar de landstreek Para* (n.p.: n.p., 1830), pp. 227–37.
65. Leonard de Vries, *Humoristisch album van den 19den eeuw* (Laren: Skarabee, 1973), pp. 43, 54.

Chapter Three: Art as History

1. Peter M. Daly, *Emblem Theory: Recent German Contributions to the Characterization of the Emblem Genre* (Nendlen/Liechtenstein: KTO Press, 1979), pp. 11–12.
2. Eddy de Jongh, *Zinne-en-minnebeelden in de schilderkunst van de 17de eeuw* (Amsterdam: Nederlandse Stichting Openbaar Kunstbezit, 1967).
3. Jacob Cats, *Proteus, ofte minne-beelden verandert in Sinne-beelden* (Rotterdam, 1627).
4. Caesar Ripa, *Iconologia: Or Moral Emblems* (London: P. Tempest, 1709;

the Dutch edition was published 1764–1767). Otto van Veen, *Emblemata sive symbola a principus, viris eeclesiasticis [sic] ac militaribus, alijsque vsurpanda* (Brussels: H. Antonii, 1624).

5. Ripa, *Iconologia*, p. 53. For a present-day compilation which includes this, in a briefer and more neutral form, and other such symbols see James Hall, *Dictionary of Subjects & Symbols in Art* (New York: Harper and Row, 1974).

6. See Linda A. Stone-Ferrier, *Dutch Prints of Daily Life* (Lawrence: University of Kansas Press, 1983), pp. 4–25.

7. Jean Devisse and Michel Mollat, *The Image of the Black in Western Art*, II, *From the Early Christian Era to the "Age of Discovery,"* Chap. 2, "Africans in the Christian Ordinance of the World (Fourteenth to the Sixteenth Century)," (Cambridge: Harvard University Press, 1979), pp. 22–58.

8. Devisse and Mollat, *The Image of the Black in Western Art*, II, 2, pp. 136–37.

9. Devisse and Mollat, *The Image of the Black in Western Art*, II, 2, pp. 108, 138–39. Max J. Friedländer, *Early Netherlandish Painting*, v. IV, Hugo van der Goes (Brussels: La Connaissance, 1969), plates 11 and 12. Peter Mark, *Africans in European Eyes: The Portrayal of Black Africans in Fourteenth and Fifteenth Century Europe* (Syracuse: Maxwell School of Citizenship and Public Affairs, 1974), pp. 22–53. Alain Locke, *The Negro in Art* (Chicago: Afro-American Press, 1969; originally published in 1940), pp. 207–08.

10. Devisse and Mollat, *The Image of the Black in Western Art*, II, 2, p. 178.

11. Jean Devisse, *The Image of the Black in Western Art*, II, Chap. 1, "From the Demonic threat to the Incarnation of Sainthood" (Cambridge: Harvard University Press, 1979), pp. 55, 143–44.

12. Werner Daum, *Die Königin von Saba: Kunst, Legende und Archäologie zwischen Morgenland und Abendland* (Stuttgart/Zürich: Belser Verlag, 1988).

13. Devisse and Mollat, *The Image of the Black in Western Art*, II, pp. 236–42.

14. Museum de Lakenhal, Leiden.

15. J. Denucé, *Afrika in de XVI^dc eeuw en de handel van Antwerpen* (Antwerp: De Sikkel, 1937). A. C. de C. M. Saunders, *A Social History of Black Slaves and Freedmen in Portugal 1441–1555* (London: Cambridge University Press, 1982). R. Buve, "Surinaamse slaven en vrije negers in Amsterdam gedurende de achttiende eeuw," *Bijdragen tot de Taal-, Land- en Volkenkunde* 119 (1963): 8–17.

16. A. Staring, *De Hollanders thuis: Gezelschapstukken uit drie eeuwen* (The Hague: Martinus Nijhoff, 1956), pp. 32–44. William Z. Shetter, *The Netherlands in Perspective*, p. 204.

17. Staring, *De Hollanders thuis*, pp. 42–44. An instructive study of the depiction of Blacks in English art of the time is David Dabydeen, *Hogarth's Blacks: Images of Blacks in Eighteenth Century English Art* (Surrey: Dangaroo Press, 1985).

18. Hall, *Dictionary of Subjects & Symbols in Art*, s.v. A 1685 portrait of an unidentified man by Weenix includes one of the same dogs and the Negro, which suggests that either both were actual members of the family or both were just fictional props.

19. Staring, *De Hollanders thuis*, illustration XVI and p. 92.

20. Staring, *De Hollanders thuis*, illustration XXI and p. 108.

21. A handsome guard in Hendrick Gerritsz Pot's "Officieren van de Haarlemse Schutterij" (Officers of the Haarlem Militia) at Haarlem's Frans Hals Museum has extremely curly hair, but is not clearly of African descent.

22. This is puzzling, however, since no available sources indicate that there were black soldiers in the Dutch army at that time. A strap across his shoulder and chest, possibly for support of an instrument, suggests that he too may be a musician.

23. See, for example, Pieter Wouwerman's "Hawking Party."

24. This work is part of the collection of the Pushkin Museum of Fine Arts, Moscow.

25. *Zo wijd de wereld strekt*, Catalog of an exhibit celebrating the tricentennary of Johan Maurits's death, 21 December 1979–1 March 1980 (The Hague: Koninklijk Kabinet van Schilderijen), pp. 66, 136–37, 145–46, 210, 212, and 270.

26. *Zo wijd de wereld strekt*, pp. 66, 95–100.

27. E. Hardouin, *Java, tooneelen uit het leven, karakterschetsen en kleederdrachten van Java's bewoners; in afbeeldingen van de natuur geteekend* (The Hague: K. Fuhri, 1855). A. van Pers, *Oost-Indische typen*. Verzameling van groote gelithografieerde platen in kleurdruk. Naar de natuur geteekend door A. van Pers. Met een verklarenden tekst in 't Hollandsch en Frensch [door A. van Pers en J. C. Hageman J. Czn] (The Hague, 1856).

28. Examples can be found in Gert Oostindie, "Kondreman in Bakrakondre," in Gert Oostindie and Emy Maduro, *In het land van de overheerser*, Deel II, *Antilleanen en Surinamers in Nederland, 1634/1667–1954* (Dordrecht: Foris Publications, 1986), pp. 4 and 106.

29. "Nederlandse schilders in Suriname," *Trouw*, 19 January 1982. Johan Wesselink, *De Schilder Theo Goedvriend* (Wageningen: Gebr. Zomer & Keuning, 1854). J. Ploeger, "Theodorus Franciscus Goedvriend (1879–1969)," *S.-Afr. Tydskr. Kult.-Kunsgesk.* 1 (1987): 8–13.

30. For examples of the works of these and others see Emile Meijer, *Farawe: Acht kunstenaars van Surinaamse oorsprong* (Heusden: Aldus Publishers, 1985).

31. The Maritime Museum at Antwerp preserves a handsome example of this.

32. This sculpture forms a part of the permanent exhibit of the Rijksmuseum in Amsterdam.

33. Simon Schama, *The Embarrassment of Riches* (New York: Alfred A. Knopf, 1987), pp. 223–25.

34. *Oude Luister van het Groningerland* (Exhibit Catalog, Groningen Museum voor Stad en Land, Groningen, 22 January–5 March, 1961), p. 142. Photo Collection, Gemeentearchief Groningen.

35. H. F. Wijnman, ed., *Historische gids van Amsterdam* (Amsterdam: Allert de Lange, 1971), pp. 132, 156. *Twintigste jaarboek van het genootschap Amstelodamum* (Amsterdam: Ten Brink & De Vries, 1923), p. 30. Gemeentearchief Amsteldijk, Amsterdam.

36. H. M. J. Tromp and B. Zijlstra, *Kasteel Amerongen* (Zutphen: Walburg Pers), pp. 33–54.

37. G. R. Kruissink, *Scheepssier: Een nostalgische terugblik op de kleurige tooi van oude schepen* (Baarn: Hollandia, 1977), pp. 101, 105.

38. The collection, originally called "Negrophilia," was developed by Felix de Rooy and Norman de Palm in their company Cosmic Illusions. The collection was staged as a major exhibit at the Tropics Museum in Amsterdam from December 1989 to August 1990 and was subsequently also shown abroad. A book was written to introduce it: Jan Nederveen Pieterse, *Wit over zwart: beelden van Afrika en zwarten in de sesterse populaire cultuur* (Amsterdam: Koninklijk Instituut voor de Tropen, 1990).

39. Fl. Josephus, *Hooghberoemde Joodsche historien ende boecken* (Amsterdam: Stam, 1659).

40. *Leven van Sint Nicolaas*, a children's print from the first half of the nineteenth century, Atlas van Stolk Collection, Catalog No. 5069^{IV}. See also No. 5848^{V} Emile H. van Heurck and G. J. Boekenoogen, *Histoire de l'imagerie populaire flamande et de ses rapports avec les imageries etrangeres* (Brussels: G. van Oest & Co, 1910), pp. 196, 413.

41. *Nederlandsche Spreekwoorden/in voorstellingen* (Amsterdam: Hendrik van Munster en Zoon), Atlas van Stolk Collection, 5840. *Verschillende Volken Uit Afrika* (Gorinchem: J. Noorduyn) Atlas van Stolk Collection, 5043 (a).

42. A. Bahr, "Knecht Ruprecht in Kamerun," *Münchener Bilderbogen*, Nr. 1039, Buch 1891/92.

43. *Marius Castoulade chez Ménélick* / Marius Castolade bij Ménélick (Turnhout: Brepols & Dierckx zoon, Nr. 249).

44. Other sixteenth-century examples may be found in the classic historical account of trade ties between Antwerp and Africa by J. Denucé: *Afrika in de XVI^{de} eeuw en de handel van Antwerpen*, pp. 49, 55, 63, 69. Numerous other examples may be found in the collection of the Stadsarchiev in Antwerp.

45. Olfert Dapper, *Nauwkeurige Beschrijvinge de Afrikaensche Gewesten* (Amsterdam: Jacob van Meurs, 1676). Willem Bosman, *A New and Accurate Description of the Coast of Guinea: Divided into the Gold, the Slave, and the Ivory Coasts* (New York: Barnes & Noble, 1967; originally published in London, 1705). Paul Depondt, "De eerste Africanist aller tijden," *De Volkskrant*, 17 August 1990.

46. *Groot Prenten-Boek*, of het vermaak der jonkheid; bestaande in over de vier honderd zoorten van afbeeldingen en figuuren; als menschen, beesten, vogelen, visschen, scheepen, enz. (Amsterdam: B. Koene, 1823), Atlas van Stolk Collection, No. 3069.

47. "Prenten als bron voor het decoreren van kaarten," in J. F. Heijbroek and Marijn Schapelhomman, eds., *Kunst in kaart* [Catalog for an exhibit of the same name at the Amsterdam Historical Museum, 24 June–10 September 1989] (Utrecht: HES, 1989), p. 19.

48. Van Heurck and Boekenoogen, *Histoire de l'imagerie populaire flamande*, pp. 101, 513.

49. C. J. Visscher, *Toonneel des Wereldts Ondeckende de Ongestuymigheden en Ydelheden in woorden ende wercken deser verdorvene Eeuwe* (Weesp: Albert E. van

Panhuysen, 1658), pp. 34–35. The accompanying rhymes are presented here in chapter four.

50. *Uncle Tom's Cabin. Schetsen door Ch. Rochussen* (Amsterdam: M. H. Binger & Zonen), Atlas van Stolk Collection, Cat. No. 7064. *Uncle Tom's Almanak 1854*, a lithograph based on drawings by H. W. Last (Amsterdam: J. M. E. Meyer), Atlas van Stolk Collection. *Emancipatie* (The Hague: D. Molenkamp, 1863), Atlas van Stolk Collection. *Gedenkplaat op het vijfentwintig jarig jubileum van Koning Willem III* (Amsterdam: Tresling & Co.), Atlas van Stolk Collection, F.M. 7484.

51. Thomas Bray Series, Atlas van Stolk Collection, period 1800–1850.

52. P. J. Benoit, *Voyage à Suriname / Reis door Suriname* (Zutphen: Walburg Press, 1980).

53. G. P. H. Zimmermann, "De Surinaamsche Inboorlingen op de Tentoonstelling," *Eigen Haard Geillustreerd Volkstijdschrift* (1883), p. 414. Gert Oostindie, *In het Land . . .* , pp. 20–25.

54. Walter M. Gibson, *The Prison of Weltevreden; And a Glance at the East Indian Archipelago* (London: Sampson Low, Son and Co., 1856), pp. 297–99, 384.

55. H. J. Schimmel, "Een Deugniet," *Elsevier's Geillustreerd Maandschrift* 2 (July–December 1891): 56–97. Illustrations of Jan Companie appear on pp. 69 and 72.

56. Examples may be seen in Leonard De Vries and Ilonka van Amstel, *Het Prentenboek van Tante Pau en het mooiste en leukste uit andere oude prentenboeken* (Amsterdam: De Bezige Bij, 1974); and Martin Ebon and Marijke van Raephorst, *Sint-Nicolaas: leven en legende* (Weesp: Heureka, 1983). A sampling of these lithographs may be found at the Atlas van Stolk Collection, for instance lithographs by P. van Geldorp under the period 1900–1950. This genre is discussed in more depth in chapter four.

57. The Cosmic Illusions "Negrophilia" collection in Amsterdam.

58. The largest and most comprehensive photo collection related to present themes is that of the Tropics Museum in Amsterdam. See, for example, the Bonaparte photographs presented in Oostindie, "Kondreman in Bakrakondre," pp. 21–25.

59. See, for example, Thomas Cripps, *Slow Fade to Black: The Negro in American Film, 1900–1942* (London: Oxford University Press, 1977), pp. 8–40 and 115–49.

Chapter Four: Dutch Literature's Dark Faces

1. Jessie L. Weston, trans., *Arthurian Romances Unrepresented in Malory's Morte D'Arthur*, v. 5, *Morien* (New York: AMS Press, 1970; originally published in London: D. Nutt, 1901), pp. 29–31. I am indebted to Anneke Prins for first bringing this work to my attention. See also D. Metzitzki, *The Matter of Araby in Medieval England* (New Haven: Yale University Press, 1977).

2. G. A. Bredero, *Moortje/waar in hy Terentii Eunuchum heeft nae-ghevolght. En is ghespeelt op de Oude Amstelredamsche Kamer anno M.DC.XV* (Am-

sterdam: Cornelis Lodewijcksz. vander Plasse, 1617). *Moortje* also has a poem on *Zwarte Piet*.

3. A. N. Paasman, *Reinhart: Nederlandse literatuur en slavernij ten tijde van de Verlichting* (Leiden: Martinus Nijhoff, 1984.), p. 116.

4. J. Lennep and J. ter Gouw, *De Uithangteekens in verband met Geschiedenis*, s.vv. "Mooren" and "Morianen."

5. *Tonneel des wereldts. Ontdeckende de Ongestuymigheden en Ydelheden in woorden ende wercken deser verdorvene eeuwe*, C. F. Visscher, engraver (Weesp: Albert Elias van Panhuysen, 1658), pp. 34–35.

6. Aphra Behn, *The Novels of Mrs. Aphra Behn*, Introduction by E. A. Baker (Westport Conn.: Greenwood Press, 1969).

7. U. M. Lichtveld and J. Voorhoeve, *Suriname: Spiegel der vaderlandse kooplieden* (The Hague: Martinus Nijhoff, 1980; first published in 1958 in Zwolle), p. 253. A. N. Paasman, "Wat bezielde de literaraire kolonisten? Het beeld van de Westindische kolonist in de literatuur 1670–1830," *OSO, Tijdschrift Voor Surinaamse Taalkunde, Leterkunde en Geschiedenis* 1 (December 1982): 52–54. See also Paasman, *Reinhart*.

8. Paasman, "Wat bezielde de literaraire kolonisten?" p. 47.

9. Paasman, *Reinhart*, pp. 145–46.

10. Paasman, *Reinhart*, pp. 109–10.

11. Paasman, *Reinhart*, p. 144.

12. Lichtveld and Voorhoeve, *Suriname: Spiegel der vaderlandse kooplieden*, pp. 210–11.

13. P. F. Roos, *Eerstellingen van Surinaamsch mengelpoëzy* (Amsterdam: Hendrik Gartman, 1783–1789), pp. 56–57. Paasman, *Reinhart*, pp. 155–56. J. M. van der Linde, *Jan Willem Kals: Leraar der hervormden; Advocaat van Indiaan en Neger* (Kampen: J. H. Kok, 1987), p. 97. One scholar has found reference to this by Freemasons in the mid-eighteenth century who in defending themselves against Calvinist ministers accused the latter of hypocrisy for excluding them from the church while admitting those with ties to the slave trade. See Margaret Jacob, *Living the Enlightenment: Freemasonry and Politics in Eighteenth Century Europe* (New York: Oxford University Press, 1991), p. 79.

14. Rob Nieuwenhuys, *Oost-Indische Spiegel: Wat nederlandse schrijvers en dichters over Indonesië hebben geschreven, vanaf de eerste jaren der compagnie tot op heden* (Amsterdam: E. M. Querido, 1978), pp. 68–72.

15. Paasman, "Wat bezielde de literaraire kolonisten?" pp. 54–55.

16. P. C. Emmer, "Anti-Slavery and the Dutch: Abolition without Reform," in *Anti-Slavery, Religion, and Reform*, Christine Bolt and Seymour Drescher, eds. (Kent, Eng.: Dawson & Sons, 1980), pp. 81–89.

17. Hildebrand, *Camera Obscura* (Utrecht: Veen, 1981; originally published 1839), p. 167.

18. "Nog een lied om bevrijding," *Dichtwerken van Nicolaas Beets* (Amsterdam: W. H. Kirberger, 1876), v. 3, p. 159.

19. From "Hulde aan Mevrouw Harriet Beecher-Stowe, Schrifster der negerhut," *Gedichten van Bernard ter Haar* (Arnhem: D. A. Thieme, 1866), p. 59.

20. Multatuli, *Max Havelaar* (Amsterdam: G. A. van Oorschot, 1986; originally published by Van Lennep, Amsterdam, 1860), p. 65.

21. Jan van Luxemburg, "Zwarte slaven bij Couperus," *Tijdschrift over nederlandie letterkunde* 8 (July/August, 1991): 210–16. Guus Kuijer, *De redder van Afrika: Roman* (Amsterdam: Arbeiderspers, 1989).

22. V. A. February, *Mind Your Color: The 'Coloured' Stereotype in South African Literature* (London: Kegan Paul, 1981), pp. 1–25.

23. Hilda van Neck Yoder, "Suriname's Cultural Memory: Of Crown and Knife," *CLA Journal* 24 (December 1980): 178–88.

24. *Letterkundige uitspanningen van het Genootschap de Surinaamsche Lettervrinden*, Tweede bundel (Paramaribo: 1786), p. 22. J. Voorhoeve and Ursy M. Lichtveld, *Creole Drum: An Anthology of Creole Literature in Surinam* (New Haven: Yale University Press, 1975), pp. vii, 7.

25. Emy Maduro, "Nos a bai Ulanda," in Gert Oostindie and Emy Maduro, *In het land van de overheerser* Deel II, *Antilleanen en Surinamers in Nederland, 1634/1667–1954* (Dordrecht: Foris Publications, 1986) p. 222.

26. Hilda van Neck-Yoder, "Words and Deeds in Cola Debrot's 'De vervolgden,' " *The New West-Indian Guide* (1986): 41–54.

27. Cees Zoon, "Heraut van de Caribische culturele revolutie," *De Volkskrant*, 10 June 1988, p. 7. See also Brian Weinstein, *The Civic Tongue: Political Consequences of Language Choices* (New York: Longman, 1983).

28. Marion Peters, "Van enfant sauvage tot 'hopsinjeur'," *NRC Handelsblad*, 12 April 1990, p. 19.

29. These prints appear in chapter three on art. Olfert Dapper, *Nauwkeurige Beschrijvinge de Afrikaensche Gewesten*, pp. 122–23.

30. Pott, *Naar wilder horizon; Kaleidoscoop op ons beeld van de buitenwereld* (The Hague: Mouton, 1962), pp. 44–50. One other work which featured highly realistic depiction of Africans was P. Kolbe, *Nauwkeurige en uitvoerige Beschryving van de Kaap de Goede Hope* (Amsterdam: Balthazar Lakeman, 1727).

31. Willem Bosman, *A New and Accurate Description of the Coast of Guinea Divided into the Gold, the Slave, and the Ivory Coasts*, John Ralph Willis, ed. (New York: Barnes & Noble, 1967), pp. 117.

32. J. D. Herlein, *Beschryvinge van de volksplantinge Zuriname* (Leeuwarden: Injema, 1718). Philip Fermin, *An Historical and Political View of the Present and Ancient State of the Colony of Suriname in South America* (London: W. Nicoll, 1781; the French edition was published in 1778).

33. J. W. Focquenbroch, *Africaensche Thalia* (Amsterdam: Jan ten Hoorn, 1678).

34. François Le Vaillant, *Travels from the Cape of Good Hope into the Interior Parts of Africa*, 2 vols., E. Helme, trans. (London: Johnson Reprint Corporation, 1972; originally published in London, 1790), p. 252. Hugh Honour, *The New Golden Land: European Images of America from the Discoveries to the Present Time* (London: Allen Land, 1976), p. 81. P. H. Pott, "De Nederlander en de vreemde medemens in de 18de eeuw, beeldvorming en beeldvastlegging" (Society Publication of Utrecht Werkgroep 18de Eeuw), p. 19. The content of this paper is incorporated into Pott, *Naar wijder horizon*.

35. Anton van Leeuwenhoek, *The Collected Letters of Antoni van Leeuwenhoek*, v. IV (Amsterdam: Swets & Zeitlinger, Ltd., 1952), pp. 249–51.
36. G. S. Rousseau, "Le Cat and the Physiology of Negroes," in H. Pagliaro, *Racism in the Eighteenth Century* (Cleveland: Press of Case Western Reserve, 1973), pp. 369–86.
37. A. Blom, *Verhandeling over den landbouw in de colonie Suriname* (Amsterdam: Smit, 1787), p. 337.
38. Bert Paasman, "Mens of dier? Beeldvorming over negers in de tijd voor de rassentheoriën," in *Vreemd Gespuis* (Amsterdam: Anne Frank Stichting, 1987), p. 99.
39. Miriam Meijer, "Camper, Petrus," forthcoming in the *International Biographical Dictionary of Anthropologists* (Library-Anthropology Resource Group, University of Chicago).
40. A penetrating analysis of this is Stephen Jay Gould, *The Mismeasure of Man* (New York: W. W. Norton, 1981), pp. 108–12.
41. Petrus Camper, "Redevoering over den oorsprong en de kleur der zwarten," *De Rhapsodist* 2 (1772): 373–94. See Robert Visser, "Die Rezeption der Anthropologie Petrus Campers (1770–1850)," in Gunter Mann et al., eds., *Die Natur des Menschen: Probleme der Physischen Anthropologie und Rassenkunde* (1750–1850) (Stuttgart: Gustav Fischer Verlag, 1990).
42. *Catalogus van Tentoonstelling ter herdenking van den 150sten sterfdag van Petrus Camper 1722–1789* (Groningen: J. B. Wolters, 1939).
43. Visser, "Die Rezeption," pp. 332–35.
44. Nelly S. Hoyt and Thomas Cassirer, trans., *Encyclopedia Selections* (Indianapolis: The Bobbs-Merrill Company, 1976), pp. 260–67.
45. William Cohen, *The French Encounter with Africans: White Response to Blacks 1530–1880* (Bloomington: Indiana University Press, 1980), p. 14.
46. Cohen, *The French Encounter with Africans*, p. 85.
47. *Oostindie and Maduro, In het land van de Overheerser*, pp. 64, 77–85, 211.
48. See examples in Leonard de Vries and Ilonka van Amstel, *Het Prentenboek van Tante Pau en het mooiste en leukste uit andere oude prentenboeken* (Amsterdam: De Bezige Bij, 1974).
49. J. Schenkman, *Sint Nikolaas en zijn Knecht* (Amsterdam: J. Vlieger, 1850), passim.
50. P. J. Andriessen, *Sinterklaas Kinder Feesten* (Amsterdam: Jan Leendertz, 1871).
51. H. J. Tiemersma, *Sint Nikolaas* (Groningen: Jacobs, 1895).
52. F. H. van Leent, *De ware Geschiedenis van Piet de Smeerpoes en andere verhalen* (Amsterdam: Van Holkema en Warendorf, 1896), pp. 16–19. See also *Het Prentenboek van Tante Pau*, pp. 11–13. On the Nicholas legend see Charles Jones, *Saint Nicholas of Myra, Bari and Manhattan*, pp. 78, 248.
53. "Hoe dat ik in een neger veranderde" (Zeeuws-Vlaanderen), in Tjaard W. R. de Haan, *Nederlandse Volks Sprookjes* (Utrecht/Antwerp: Het Spectrum, 1978), pp. 165–67.
54. Iona and Peter Opie, eds., *The Oxford Dictionary of Nursery Rhymes*, pp. 327–28.

55. P. Louwerse, "Van twee zwartjes," *Voor de kinderkamer. Rijmpjes en vertelseltjes voor het kleine volkje* ('s Gravenhage: Johan Ykema, 1891), pp. K13–K16.

56. Har Brock, "Het Sjimmie-Syndroom: De neger in het beeldverhaal," in *Vreemd Gespuis* (Amsterdam: Anne Frank Stichting, 1987), pp. 152–56.

57. Piet Broos, *Vacantie in Klapperdorp: Nieuwe avonturen van de drie pikzwarte nikkertjes Piempampoentje, Pompernikkel en Piepeling* (Amsterdam: H. Meulenhoff, 1949). A number of similar Broos books followed.

58. *Egypte hertekend* (Leuven: Peeters, 1989).

59. Roline Redmond, *Zwarte mensen in kinderboeken* (The Hague: Nederlands Bibliotheek en Lektuur Centrum, 1980).

60. Harry van den Berg and Peter Reinsch, *Racisme in schoolboeken: het gladde ijs van het westers gelijk* (Amsterdam: SUA, 1983).

61. "De Zwarte Man," *De Moeder de Gans der negentiende eeuw: vertellingen voor de welopgevoede jeugd* (Amsterdam: B.C. Weddepohl, c. 1850), pp. 9–19.

62. "De getrouwe neger," *Philopaedion, Tijdschrift voor de Jeugd*, February 1826, pp. 63–66.

63. "Afrikaanen en Amerikaanen," *Weekblad voor Kinderen*, II, 52, 1799, pp. 409–16.

64. "De Kaffers," *Philopaedion, Tijdschrift voor de Jeugd*, February 1826, pp. 40–45.

65. "Suriname," *Hollands Penning Magazijn voor de Jeugd*, 1840, p. 154.

66. "De Negerslaven in Suriname," *Hollands Penning Magazijn voor de Jeugd*, 1843, p. 127; 1844, pp. 127–28.

Chapter Five: In the Eyes of God: Blacks and Dutch Religious Traditions

1. Simon Schama, *The Embarrassment of Riches: An Interpretation of Dutch Culture in the Golden Age* (New York: Alfred A. Knopf, 1987), p. 58.

2. David Brion Davis, *Slavery and Human Progress* (New York: Oxford University Press, 1984), p. 134.

3. See comparable discussion in the introduction to H. Shelton Smith, *In His Image, But . . .* (Durham: Duke University Press, 1972).

4. Hans Werner Debrunner, *Presence and Prestige: Africans in Europe* (Basel: Basler Afrika Bibliographien, 1979), pp. 21–23.

5. Frank M. Snowden, Jr., *Before Color Prejudice: The Ancient View of Blacks* (Cambridge: Harvard University Press, 1983), p. 7.

6. Davis, *Slavery and Human Progress*, p. 37.

7. Schama, *Embarrassment of Riches*, p. 379.

8. *The New English Bible*, Acts 8:36. J. M. van der Linde, *Jan Willem Kals 1700–1781; Leraar der hervormden advocaat van indiaan en neger* (Kampen: J. H. Kok, 1987), p. 52. Jan Kals, *Neerlands Hooft-en Wortel-Sonde, het Versuym van de Bekeering der Heidenen*, and *Nuttige en Noodige Bekeeringe der Heidenen* (Leeuwarden: Pieter Koumans, 1756).

9. This portrait has already been presented here in the brief mention of Capitein in chapter three.

10. J. E. J. Capitein, *Staatkundig-Godgeleerd Onderzoekschrift over De Slaverny, als niet strydig tegen de Christelyke Vryheid* (Leiden and Amsterdam: Philippus Bonk and Gerrit de Groot, 1742). Van der Linde, *Heren, Slaven, Broeders* (Nijkerk: Callenbach, 1963), p. 80. Paasman, *Reinhart* (Leiden: Martinus Nijhoff, 1984), pp. 100–104. G. Udemans, *'t Geestelyk roer van 't coopmans schip, dat is: trouw bericht/hoe dat een coopman, en coopvaerder, hem selven dragen moet in syne handelinge/in pays, ende in oorloge, voor Godt, ende de menschen, te water ende te lande, insonderheyt onder de heydenen in Oost- ende West-Indien [. . .]. Den derden druk/verbetert ende vermeerdert by den autheur* (Dordrecht: Françoys Boels, 1655).

11. A. Eekhof, *De Negerpredikant Jacobus Elisa Joannes Capitein 1717–1747* (The Hague: Martinus Nijhoff, 1917).

12. Paasman, *Reinhart*, p. 103.

13. *The Holy Bible*, Genesis 9:22–27. Davis, *Slavery and Human Progress*, p. 43.

14. Van der Linde, *Heren, Slaven, Breeders*, p. 80.

15. Paasman, *Reinhart*, pp. 98–101. J. Picardt, *Korte beschryvinge van eenige vergetene en verborgene antiquiteten der provintien en landen gelegen tusschen de Noord-Zee, de Yssel, Emse en Lippe.[. . .]* (Amsterdam: Gerrit van Goedesbergh, 1660). H. de Groot, *Van 't regt des oorlogs en vredes, behelzende het regt der nature en der volderen, mitsgaders het voornaamste van 't openbaare borgerlijke regt. Van nieuws vertaalt* (Amsterdam: François van der Plaats, 1705), p. 705.

16. J. Hondius, *Swart register van duysent sonden, als een staeltje/diende to ontdeckinge/ende opweckinge/van den vervallen yver en godtvruchtigheydt der hedendaeghsche genaemde ledematen in de gereformeerde christelijcke gemeynten van Nederlandt* (Amsterdam: Gerardus Borstius, 1679).

17. Davis, *Slavery and Human Progress*, p. 134. William Cohen, *The French Encounter with Africans*, p. 85.

18. The Dutch Reformed Church was sometimes described interchangeably as *Hervormde* and *Gereformeerde* before the nineteenth-century formal organization of various groups using the one term or the other to denote variant interpretations of orthodoxy.

19. Th. van den End, "Zending vanuit Nederland," in *De Heiden moest eraan geloven: geschiedenis van zending, missie en ontwikkelings-samenwerking* (Utrecht: Stichting Het Catharijneconvent, 1983), pp. 7–9.

20. *Zendings Prentenkaart* (Leiden: P. W. M. Trap), Atlas van Stolk Collection.

21. Van den End, "Zending . . . ," p. 10.

22. Van den End, "Zending . . . ," p. 17.

23. J. M. Hogema, "De missiebeweging van Katholiek Nederland," in *De Heiden moest eraan geloven*, p. 19.

24. A. J. J. M. van den Eerenbeemt, *De Missie-actie in Nederland (+/− 1600–1940)* (Nijmegen: J. J. Berkhout, 1945).

25. Hogema, "De missiebeweging," p. 24. Jan Roes, *Het Groote missieuur, 1915–1940: op zoek naar de missiemotivatie van de Nederlandse Katholieken* (Bilthoven: Ambo, 1974).

26. Debrunner, *Presence and Prestige*, p. 302.

27. *Handelingen van de Maatschappij ter Bevordering van het Godsdienstig On-derwijs onder de Inlandsche Bevolking in de Kolonie Suriname* ('s Gravenhage, 1831–1877).
28. Van den End, "Zending . . . ," p. 11.
29. Eerdmans, "De cultuur en de zending," *De Macedoniër* 7 (1889): 79–86.
30. Van der Linde, *Heren, Slaven, Broeders*, p. 103.
31. Van der Linde, *Het visioen van Herrnhut en het apostolaat der Moravische Broeders in Suriname 1735–1863* (Paramaribo, C. Kersten & Co., 1956), pp. 95–101. A. G. Spangenberg, *Unterricht für die Brüder und Schwestern welche unter den Heiden am Evangelio dienen* (Barby, 1784). O. Uttendörfer, *Die wichtigsten Missionsgrundsätze Zinzendorfs* (Herrnhut, 1913).
32. Van der Linde, *Heren, Slaven, Broeders*, p. 94; Venatius Willeke, "Kirche und Negersklaven in Brasilien 1550–1888," *Neue Zeitschrift für Mission-swissenschaft* 32 (1976), p. 17.
33. Cornelis Ch. Goslinga, *The Dutch in the Caribbean and on the Wild Coast 1580–1680*, p. 350.
34. Eekhof, *De Negerpredikant Jacobus Elisa Joannes Capitein*. R. P. Zijp, "Predikanten in Guinea, 1600–1800," in *De Heiden moest eraan geloven*, pp. 30–37.
35. Debrunner, *Presence and Prestige*, pp. 82–85. Zijp, "Predikanten in Guinea," pp. 33–37.
36. Richard Price, *Alabi's World* (Baltimore: The Johns Hopkins University Press, 1990).
37. H. F. de Ziel, ed., *Johannes King: Life at Maripaston* (The Hague: Martinus Nijhoff, 1973).
38. Gert Oostindie, "Kondreman in Bakrakondre," in Gert Oostindie and Emy Maduro, *In het Land van de Overheerser*, Deel II, *Antilleanen en Surinamers in Nederland, 1634/1667–1954* (Dordrecht: Foris Publications, 1986), pp. 42–44.
39. *Neerlands Hooft-en Wortel-Sonde, het Versuym van de Bekeering der Hei-denen*, and *Nuttige en Noodige Bekeeringe der Heidenen* (Leeuwarden: Pieter Koumans, 1756).
40. Van der Linde, *Jan Kals*, pp. 48–69.
41. *Berigten uit de Heiden-Wereld* 2 (1851): 18–19.
42. *Berigten uit de Heiden-Wereld* 2 (1840): 30–31.

Chapter Six: The Black Presence in the Dutch World

1. John William Blake, *Europeans in West Africa, 1450–1560* (London: Hakluyt Society, 1942), pp. 207–08. J. Denucé, *Afrika in de XVI^de eeuw en de handel van Antwerpen* (Antwerp: De Sikkel, 1937), pp. 35–36. S. E. Preedy, *Negers in de Nederlanden 1500–1863* (Nijmegen: MASUSA, 1984), p. 12.
2. Pierre Goemaere, "Anvers et ses esclaves noirs," *Revue mensuelle* (June 1963): 29.
3. J. A. Goris, "Uit de Geschiedenis der vorming van het Antwerpsch Stadsrecht: Slavernij te Antwerpen in de XVI^de eeuw," *Bijdragen tot de Geschie-*

denis 15 (October 1923): 541–44. Goemaere, "Anvers et ses esclaves noirs," pp. 30–31. To the number of relevant documents now located by these scholars at the Stadsarchief of Antwerp might be added others related to sixteenth-century acts in Cerificatieboeken 6, 15, and 18.

4. Denucé, *Afrika in de XVI^de eeuw en de handel van Antwerpen*, p. 32. N. Huyghebaert, "De eerste zwarten te Sint-Andries," *Biekorf*, Westvlaams Archief voor Geschiedenis, Archeologie, Taal- en Volkskunde (1981): 175.

5. Pieter Emmer, "The History of the Dutch Slave Trade, A Bibliographical Survey," *Journal of Economic History* 32 (June–December 1972): 728.

6. Gert Oostindie, "Kondreman in Bakrakondre," in Gert Oostindie and Emy Maduro, *In het Land van de Overheerser, Deel II, Antilleanen en Surinamers in Nederland, 1634/1667–1954* (Dordrecht: Foris Publications, 1986), pp. 6–19, 140–49.

7. R. Buve, "Surinaamse slaven en vrije negers in Amsterdam gedurende de achttiende eeuw," *Bijdragen tot de Taal-, Land- en Volkenkunde* 119 (1963): 8–16.

8. P. J. van Winter, " 'West-Indië' in de Groninger samenleving," in *De Westindische Compagnie ter Kamer Stad en Lande* (The Hague: Martinus Nijhoff, 1978), pp. 212, 235, 243–44.

9. L. Kooÿmans, *Onder regenten; de elite in een Hollandse stad. Hoorn 1700–1780* (Amsterdam: De Bataafsche Leeuw, 1985), pp. 182–83.

10. Petronella J. C. Elema, "Louis Alons, een neger uit Curaçao," *Tijdschrift voor Genealogie, Naam- en Wapenkunde* 24 (January 1979): 32–36. This sketch also owes some detail to unpublished research by the Reverend L. Alons of Eelde.

11. Letter of Emeritus Reverend L. Alons dated 16 December 1982, from Eelde, to the Centraal Historisch Archief in Curaçao. Telephone interview with Alons, 3 July 1986, in Eelde.

12. U. M. Lichtveld and J. Voorhoeve, *Suriname: Spiegel der vaderlandse kooplieden* (The Hague: Martinus Nijhoff, 1980), pp. 99–120.

13. A penetrating treatment of this process for the Saramaccaners is Richard Price, *First Time: The Historical Vision of an Afro-American People* (Baltimore and London: The Johns Hopkins University Press, 1983).

14. Lichtveld and Voorhoeve, *Suriname*, p. 77.

15. Lichtveld and Voorhoeve, *Suriname*, pp. 121–129. Silvia W. de Groot, *From Isolation Towards Integration* (The Hague: Martinus Nijhoff, 1977), pp. 11–23. See also *Vredesonderhandelingen tussen het gouvernement en de Tempati-negers aan de Aucarivier, 1758–1760*. Z.Z.G. nr. 921, Rijksarchief, Utrecht.

16. John G. Stedman, *Narrative of a Five-Years' Expedition Against the Revolted Negroes of Surinam, in Guiana, on the Wild Coast of South America* (London: Johnson, 1796). See also Richard and Sally Price, eds., expanded version of Stedman, John Gabriel, *Narrative of a Five Years Expedition Against the Revolted Negroes in Surinam* (Baltimore: Johns Hopkins University Press, 1988).

17. De Groot, *From Isolation Towards Integration*, p. 8.

18. De Groot, *From Isolation Towards Integration*, pp. 106–07.

19. J. C. M. Warnsinck, "De laatste tocht van Van Wassenaer van Obdam voorjaar 1665," in *Van vlootvoogden en zeeslagen* (Amsterdam: Van Kampen, 1940; originally published in *Marineblad*, 1932), pp. 242–90.

20. Related photos may be found in the records of the Rijksinstituut voor oorlogsdocumentatie (Indische Afdeling) in Amsterdam. See also R. van Yperen, *De Nederlandse militaire muziek* (Bussum: C. A. J. van Dishoeck, 1966), illust. 26.

21. Silvia W. de Groot, "Rebellie der Zwarte Jagers: De nasleep van de Bonni-oorlogen 1788–1809," *De Gids* (December 1970): 291–93, 300; and "Het Korps Zwarte Jagers in Suriname Collaboratie en opstand II," *OSO* 8 (May 1989): 6–20. See also a drawing in the Atlas van Stolk Collection, "Koloniale Guides van Suriname," Cat. no. 5581(20).

22. Silvia W. de Groot, "Rebellie der Zwarte Jagers," pp. 298–300.

23. Smith's original name was De Smet, changed by his father during the Napoleonic period for political purposes. Although in the British service, Smith also had been knighted by the Dutch king with the *Militaire Willemsorde*, the highest military decoration. B. de Gaay Fortman, "De oorsprong van de werving van negers voor het Indische leger," *De Indische Gids* 51 (1929): 562–63.

24. "De oorsprong van de werving van negers voor het Indische leger," pp. 569–74.

25. Bram Oosterwijk, *Koning van de koopvaart: Anthony van Hoboken (1756–1850)* (Rotterdam: Stichting Historisch Publicatis Rotrodamum, 1983), p. 208.

26. Rene Baesjou, *An Asante Embassy on the Gold Coast* (Leiden: Afrika Studie Centrum, 1979), pp. 24.

27. P. C. Emmer, "Engeland, Nederland, Afrika en de slavenhandel in de negentiende eeuw," *Economisch Sociaal-Historisch Jaarboek* 36 (1973): 146–215 and 37 (1974): 44–144.

28. Oosterwijk, *Koning van de koopvaart*, p. 209. J. M. van Dam, "Grepen uit de krijgsgeschiedenis van het K.N.I.L. De Afrikanen in ons Leger," *Orgaan der Nederlandsch-Indische Officiersvereeniging* 20 (December 1915): 576–80.

29. Oosterwijk, *Koning van de koopvaart*, p. 209. Rob Hezemans, "De Nederlandse rekrutering aan de kust van Guinee, besteemd voor 'Java' " (unpublished paper, courtesy of the author). See also J. S. G. Gramberg, *Schetsen van Afrika's Westkust* (Amsterdam: Weijtingh en Brave, 1861); and A. van Dantzig, "The Dutch military recruitment agency in Kumasi," *Ghana Notes and Queries* 8 (1966): 21–24.

30. S. Kalff, "Inlanders en Afrikanen in het O.I. Leger," *Indisch Militair Tijdschrift* 59 (1928): 779–82.

31. *Encyclopedie van Nederlandisch-Indië*, Part 1 (1917), p. 547.

32. M. P. Bossenbroek, *Van Holland naar Indië: Het transport van koloniale troepen voor het Oost-Indische leger 1815–1909* (Amsterdam: De Batafsche Leeuw, 1986), pp. 106–09.

33. *Verzameling der Algemeene Orders en van eenige der meest belangrijke besluiten en instructiën uitgevaardigd aan de Koninklijke Nederlandische Landmagt dienstdoende in Oost-Indië* (Breda: Broese & Co., 1855), p. 46.

34. Oosterwijk, *Koning van de koopvaart*, p. 204–210.

35. Baesjou, *An Asante Embassy on the Gold Coast*, pp. 23–26. Van Dam, "Grepen uit de krijgsgeschiedenis van het K.N.I.L. De Afrikanen in ons Leger," p. 577. Oosterwijk, *Koning van de koopvaart*, pp. 209, 212.

36. Daniel Cordus, "Blanda Itam in Nederland," *Ghana Nieuwsbrief* 14 (March 1985): 19.

37. "Een voorstel in het belang der Indo-Afrikanen," *Indisch Militair Tijdschrift* 7–12 (1891): 481–83. *Verzameling der Algemeene Orders*, p. 111. *Pligten en Regten van den Indischen Militair in het bijzonder van den infanterist* (Batavia: Ogilvie & Co., 1882), pp. 192–94.

38. Interview with *Blanda Itam* descendants Gert and Anna van Riessen, Daniel Cordus, and Freddy Klink, 14 April 1986, Maastricht. For paintings which provide a picture of Dutch East Indies society in general in the mid-nineteenth century see Van Pers, *Oost-Indische typen*. Van Dam, "Grepen uit de krijgsgeschiedenis van het K.N.I.L. De Afrikanen in ons Leger," p. 577. Martin van der Kuil and Peter Hermes, "Blanda Items," *Ghana Nieuwsbrief* 10 (Summer 1984): 15–18. One authority says the Africans were first oriented in the Netherlands and there acquired their Dutch names. D. A. Visker, *Indische Familienamen: Een genealogische inleiding tot de kennis van de Europese geslachten uit het vroegere Nederlands-Indië tevens een alfabetische index van het Indisch Familie Archief t 's-Gravenhage* (The Hague: Moesson, 1983).

39. W. A. van Rees, *Herinneringen uit de loopbaan van een Indisch officier* (The Hague: Visser, 1863–1865).

40. X, "Het behoud van het Afrikaansche element bij het Indische leger," *Indisch Militair Tijdschrift* 1–6 (1881): 377.

41. "Het behoud van het Afrikaansche element . . . ," p. 386.

42. S. de la Parra, "De werving van Amerikaansche negers voor het Indische Leger," *Indisch Militair Tijdschrift* 7–12 (1881): 1–7.

43. "Westindische negers als soldaten," *De Indische Gids* 14 (1892): 282.

44. *Indisch Militair Tijdschrift* (January–June 1878): 438–39.

45. *Overveluwsche Weekblad*, 18 June 1898. Visker, *Indische Familienamen*, p. 37.

46. "Het nieuwe corps Afrikanen in het O.-I. Leger," *De Indische Tolk van het Nieuws van den Dag*, Wednesday 20 May 1891. Fasin, "Aanvulling en inhoud van het Europeesche element in het Ned.-Ind. leger," *De Indische Tolk van het Nieuws van den Dag*, Wednesday 8 June and Tuesday 14 June 1892.

47. "Het Afrikaansch Recruten Korps," *Indisch Militair Tijdschrift*, Part 1, 1892. Van Dam, "Grepen uit de krijgsschiedenis van het K.N.I.L. De Afrikanen in ons Leger," p. 577.

48. Oosterwijk, *Koning van de koopvaart*, p. 214. Henri Baudet, "Un sang qui ne saurait mentir," in J. Vansina, C. H. Perrot, et al., *Etudes africaines* (Paris: Ecole de Hautes Etudes en Sciences Sociales, 1982), p. 153.

49. H. J. de Graaf, "De blanda Item's"; Rob Hezemans, "De Nederlandse rekrutering aan de kust van Guinee."

50. Interview with *Blanda Itam* descendants Gert and Anna van Riessen, Daniel Cordus, and Freddy Klink, 14 April 1986, Maastricht.

51. Hans Olink, "Surinamers in Nederlands-Indië," *De Tijd*, 18 August 1989, in *Het Bestaan*, pp. 34–37. Ineke van Kessel, "De vergeten geschiedenis van de zwarte Hollanders," *Onze Wereld* 7 (July 1985): 34–37. Cordus, "Blanda Item in Nederland," pp. 19–21; also interview of 14 April 1986.

52. Capitein, *Staatkundig-Godgeleerd Onderzoekschrift over De Slaverny*, p. 52, emphasis in the original.

53. *Uitgewrogte predikatien, de trouwherrige vermaaninge van den apostel der heydenen Paulus, aan zynen zoon Timotheus, uit 2 Timotheus II. vers 8. te Muiderberg, den 20. Mey 1742. alsmede de voornaamste goederen van de opperste wysheit, uit Spreuken VIII. vers 18. in twee predikatien, in 's Gravenhage, den 27. Mey 1742. en T' Ouderkerk aan den Amstel, den 6 Juny 1742. gedaan door Jacobus Elisa Joannes Capitein, Africaansche Moor, Beroepen Predikant op D' Elmina aan het Kasteel St. George* (Leiden and Amsterdam: Philippus Bonk and Gerrit de Groot, 1742).

54. This is part of the introductory section to *Uitgewrogte predikatien.*

55. Debrunner, *Presence and Prestige*, pp. 106–08. Burchard Brentjes, *Anton Wilhelm Amo: der schwarze Philosoph in Halle* (Leipzig: Koehler & Amelang, 1976).

56. Richard Price, "Kwasimukamba's Gambit," *Bijdragen tot de Taal-, Land- en Volkenkunde* 135 (1979): 151–69. Lichtveld and Voorhoeve, *Suriname*, pp. 180–86.

57. Price, "Kwasimukamba's Gambit," pp. 163–69.

58. Lichtveld and Voorhoeve, *Suriname*, p. 181.

59. G., "Aquasie Boachi," *De Ingenieur* 29 (1904). H. Linse, "Aquasie Boachi," *Eigen Haard* (November 1900). Peter van den Akker, "Aquasi Boachi," *Ghana Nieuwsbrief* 20 (April 1986): 5–9.

60. Van den Akker, "Aquasi Boachi," pp. 10–11.

61. *Encyclopedie van Nederlandsch-Indië*, p. v (The Hague: Martinus Nijhoff, 1927), s.v. Boachi (Aquasi).

62. Fred. Oudschans Dentz, "Eenige bladzijden uit het leven van Dr. George Cornelis Berch Gravenhorst." *Nederlandsch Tijdschrift voor Geneeskunde* 86 (6 June 1942): 1430–36. C. P. Rier, *De Levensgeschiedenis van Dr. Adolf Frederik Gravenberch, Stedelijk Heelmeester, 1855–1906* (Paramaribo: C. P. Rier, 1908). I am indebted to Laura Aerts-Weertman for first bringing the story of Gravenberch to my attention, and to John P. Rier for providing me copies of his grandfather's biography on Gravenberch.

63. Rier, *De Levensgeschiedenis*, preface.

64. C. P. Rier, *Na veertig jaren* (Paramaribo: C. P. Rier, 1904), quote taken from excerpt translated by Hilda van Neck-Yoder, 1983; text located in the Moorland-Spingarn Research Center, Howard University, Washington, D.C.

65. C. P. Rier, "Over den landbouw," a lecture delivered July 1, 1914, quoted from Hilda van Neck-Yoder translation, 1983; Moorland Spingarn Research Center, Howard University, Washington, D.C.

66. Raphael Sommes, *Service Afloat or the Remarkable Career of the Confederate Cruisers Sumter and Alabama* (Baltimore: The Baltimore Publishing Co., 1887), p. 200.

67. Theodore Kornweibel, *No Crystal Stair: Black Life and the Messenger, 1917–1928* (Westport, Conn.: Greenwood Press, 1975).

68. Theodore Draper, *American Communism and Soviet Russia* (New York: Octagon Books, 1960), pp. 324–26.

69. Allison Blakely, *Russia and the Negro* (Washington, D.C.: Howard University Press, 1986), pp. 84–85. Harry Haywood, *Black Bolshevik* (Chicago: Liberator Press, 1978), pp. 256–68.

70. Otto E. Huiswood, "World Aspects of the Negro Question," *The Communist* (February 1930): 132–33. Haywood, *Black Bolshevik*, pp. 321–25.

71. Huiswood, "World Aspects of the Negro Question," p. 138.

72. Blakely, *Russia and the Negro*, p. 92.

73. Gert Oostindie, "Kondreman in Bakrakondre," in Oostindie and Maduro, *In het land van de overheerser*, pp. 63–64, 77–85. I am indebted to Bert Altena for sharing unpublished, collected materials on Huiswood.

74. A. de Kom, *Wij slaven uit Suriname* (Amsterdam: Contact, 1934), p. 1.

75. Oostindie, "Kondreman in Bakrakondre," p. 67.

76. De Kom, *Wij slaven uit Suriname*, p. 3.

77. Oostindie, "Kondreman in Bakrakondre," p. 70.

78. Herman Vuijsje, " '*Met discriminatie moeten we net zo omgaan als met onze agressiviteit en seksualiteit*'—*R.A.J. van Lier, . . . over zijn Surinaamse achtergrond en zijn studie . . .* " NRC Handelsblad, 23 January 1986, p. 3.

79. Vuijsje, " '*Met discriminatie moeten we net zo omgaan.*"

80. Vuijsje, " '*Met discriminatie moeten we net zo omgaan.*"

81. G. P. H. Zimmermann, "De Surinaamsche inboorlingen op de tentoonstelling," *Eigen Haard Geillustreerd Volkstijdschrift* (1883): 401–05, 413–14.

82. Oostindie and Maduro, *In het land van de overheerser*, pp. 45–54, 165–73.

83. Teun A. van Dijk, *Communicating Racism: Ethnic Prejudice in Thought and Talk* (Newbury Park, Cal.: Sage, 1987), pp. 46–47.

84. Vuijsje, " '*Met discriminatie moeten we net zo omgaan.*"

Chapter Seven: Converging Images in a Changing World

1. This point is made very forcefully by Albert Boime in a review of volume four of *The Image of the Black in Western Art*. Albert Boime, "Invisible in the Foreground," *The New York Times Book Review*, 2 April 1989, p. 14. It is also the topic of Boime's *The Art of Exclusion: Representing Blacks in the Nineteenth Century* (Washington: Smithsonian Institution Press, 1990).

2. Allister Sparks, *The Mind of South Africa* (New York: Alfred A. Knopf, 1990), pp. 23–44. Winthrop R. Wright, *Café con leche: Race, Class, and National Image in Venezuela* (Austin: University of Texas Press, 1990).

3. George M. Fredrickson, *The Black Image in the White Mind* (New York: Harper & Row, 1971), pp. 39–40. David Brion Davis, *Slavery and Human Progress* (New York: Oxford University Press, 1984), p. 38.

318
Notes to Pages 283–290

4. Simon Schama, *The Embarrassment of Riches: An Interpretation of Dutch Culture in the Golden Age* (New York: Alfred A. Knopf, 1987), pp. 174, 267.

5. Herman Vuijsje, "Prof. dr. W. F. Wertheim," *NRC Handelsblad*, 13 February 1986.

6. Arend Lijphart, *The Politics of Accommodation* (Berkeley: University of California Press, 1968) p. 22.

7. Lijphart, *The Politics of Accommodation*, pp. 1–22, 35–57. William Z. Shetter, *The Netherlands in Perspective*, pp. 178–87.

8. Schama, *Embarrassment of Riches*, p. 595.

9. There are, for example, documents from the time of the German occupation showing racist remarks by the Amsterdam Chief of Police about black Surinamers. See Gert Oostindie, "Kondreman in Bakrakondre," in Oostindie and Maduro, *In het Land van de Overheerser*, Deel II, *Antilleanen en Surinamers in Nederland, 1634/1667–1954* (Dordrecht: Foris Publications, 1986), p. 91.

10. Rosemary Brana-Shute has found in a recent study that kinship also played a very prominent role in determining manumission of slaves in Suriname. Rosemary Brana-Shute, "The Manumission of Slaves in Suriname, 1760–1828" (Ph.D. Dissertation, University of Florida, 1985).

11. Vuijsje, "Prof. dr. W. F. Wertheim."

12. Stanley B. Greenberg, *Race and State in Capitalist Development: Comparative Perspectives* (New Haven: Yale University Press, 1980), p. 15.

13. Robert Rydell, *All the World's a Fair: Visions of Empire at American International Expositions, 1876–1916* (Chicago: University of Chicago Press, 1984). A. F. Paula, *From Objective to Subjective Social Barriers* (Curaçao, 1967) p. 9. Greenberg, *Race and State*, pp. 58–59. William Julius Wilson, *The Declining Significance of Race: Blacks and Changing American Institutions* (Chicago: University of Chicago Press, 1980), pp. 1–15.

14. This process, as universal now as the music itself, is most advanced in the United States. See George Nelson, *The Death of Rhythm & Blues* (New York: Pantheon, 1988).

15. Greenberg, *Race and State*, p. 25. Chris Mullard, "Race, Class and Ideology: Some Formal Notes" (a paper published by Race Relations Policy and Practice Unit, University of London Institute of Education, 1985).

16. Martin Bernal, *Black Athena, The Fabrication of Ancient Greece, 1785–1985* (New Brunswick: Rutgers University Press, 1987), pp. 1–73.

INDEX

Index

ALLISON BLAKELY is Professor of European History and Comparative History at Howard University. He is the author of *Russia and the Negro: Blacks in Russian History and Thought,* winner of an American Book Award.